Spectral Mansions

The Making of a Dublin Tenement, 1800–1914

TIMOTHY MURTAGH

FOUR COURTS PRESS

Set in 10 on 14 Baskerville for
Four Courts Press Ltd
7 Malpas Street, Dublin 8, Ireland
www.fourcourtspress.ie
and in North America for
Four Courts Press
c/o IPG, 814 N Franklin St, Chicago, IL 60610

© Timothy Murtagh and Four Courts Press 2023

A catalogue record for this title is available
from the British Library.

ISBN 978-1-84682-867-6

All rights reserved. No part of this publication may be reproduced, stored in or introduced into a retrieval system, or transmitted, in any form or by any means (electronic, mechanical, photocopying, recording, or otherwise), without the prior written permission of both the copyright owner and publisher of this book.

This project was commissioned by Dublin City Council Heritage Office
and received funding from the Heritage Council in 2018.

Book design and typesetting by Anú Design, Tara
Printed in Poland by L & C Printing Group, Krakow

Contents

Foreword by David Dickson … vii

Acknowledgments … ix

Introduction: townhouses to tenements … 1

1. Dublin after the Union, 1800–41 … 29
2. Famine and decline, 1845–90 … 53
3. Life and death in a tenement, 1800–1910 … 95
4. The beginnings of reform, 1900–14 … 133
5. Henrietta Street and the Irish Revolution, 1914–23 … 165

Epilogue: Dublin of the future? … 193

List of abbreviations … 226

List of illustrations … 227

Notes … 235

Bibliography … 253

Index … 263

Foreword

Three centuries ago, the north side of Dublin city was undergoing enormous change. The principal city markets were now here, as were many of its wealthiest merchants, and the military were filling the enormous new barracks complex. To add to this, a city property developer, the first Luke Gardiner, marked out a generously proportioned new street in the 1720s, a cul-de-sac on rising ground overlooking the markets district. It was to be the site for a string of huge private houses to be built for upper-class families who wished to make their mark in the Irish capital. And he lived long enough to bring his plan fully to life, although it took nearly thirty years before the two great brick terraces of 'Henrietta Street' were completed.

The street has indeed many claims to fame – as the earliest example of 'Georgian' street planning, with interiors rivalling any of the great Dublin houses elsewhere in the city; as winter home of the richest and most powerful families resident in eighteenth-century Ireland; and as prime exemplar of the decline and fall of a once-glamorous aristocratic world. But Tim Murtagh takes the story of the street far beyond that world and beyond the first century of the street's inhabitants. He reveals how in the following two centuries it developed very different claims to fame. As demand for very large private houses – entertainment boxes for those endowed with long rent-rolls – declined sharply after the closure of the Irish parliament in 1801, Henrietta Street became the hub of the legal profession, the most dynamic sector in a changing economy. Located in the shadow of the new King's Inns, the street seemed destined to become the centre of legal education in Ireland and where barristers' chambers would colonize every mansion. And other organs of the state took space along the street, including the Encumbered Estates Court, set up in the wake of the Great Famine, and the Dublin militia. They came and then they went, the street's restricted public space and awkward access weakening its attractions. But it was the growing poverty of the wider district – south and particularly west of Henrietta Street – that ended its role as a salubrious neighbourhood dominated by lawyers and officialdom.

Tim Murtagh brings to life the dramatic third act of the street's history, beginning in the nineteenth century as it became a zone of tenements, where houses were partitioned and sub-partitioned, great rooms let and sub-let, to literally dozens of 'roomkeepers'. The street's new residents were part of the vast casual workforce of the city, many never far from absolute poverty, while its public spaces came alive as never before with children. But it is only when we reach the beginning of the twentieth century, when Murtagh is able to use the 1901 and 1911 census records, that we get a full sense of this new Henrietta Street world, its volatility and deprivation: in 1901 only 1 per cent of the street's population was aged over 65, well below the city average, and even more telling is the comparison of Henrietta Street's population in 1901 and 1911: only 16 of the 152 families present there in 1901 were still on the street ten years later.

But as the Gardiners became a distant memory there had been several individuals who invested heavily in the street and who, Murtagh suggests, might have created a very different future if their enthusiasms had been followed up and sustained by others (including their heirs): Tristram Kennedy, Thomas Vance, even the much-maligned Joseph Meade, all had a vision for a renewed street. But it was not to be. Only the Daughters of Charity, setting up in the street late in the nineteenth century, persisted, and they certainly made a lasting impact on the wider community around them.

Henrietta Street, although never the worst of tenement zone, became the symbol of the infamous Dublin housing problem – the woefully inadequate supply of cheap clean housing for the labouring population of the city. The wheel only began to turn in the 1930s, and the end of the tenements was very slow in coming, as oral histories of the street confirm. It is only now as a very different Henrietta Street approaches the start of its fourth century that we have an opportunity to take stock and reflect on this extraordinary evolution, and to learn again that nothing was ever what it seems at first sight.

David Dickson
Professor Emeritus, Trinity College Dublin

Acknowledgments

Thanks to Dublin City Council and in particular to Owen Keegan, Chief Executive, Richard Shakespeare, Assistant Chief Executive, Paul Clegg, former Executive Manager, Máire Igoe, Acting Executive Manager, John O'Hara, City Planner, Deirdre Scully, Deputy City Planner, and Paraic Fallon, Senior Planner. I would like to thank Arthur Seefahrt, the Graduate Heritage Officer in the Heritage, Archaeology and Conservation Section of the Planning and Property Development Department. I wish to also acknowledge the generous grant awarded to this publication from the Heritage Council's County Heritage Plan Grant Scheme. Thanks are also due to Four Courts Press, and in particular Martin Fanning and Sam Tranum who have been extremely helpful and endlessly patient in guiding this project. Needless to say, I owe a huge debt to Charles Duggan, the Heritage Officer for Dublin City Council. In addition to being one of the driving forces behind the creation of the museum in Henrietta Street, Charles has been a tireless supporter of my research and writing. I am grateful for his insights, as well as the historical material he has been able to provide thanks to his passionate devotion to preserving the story of Henrietta Street. The daunting prospect of assembling the current selection of images has only been possible because of Charles' expertise and tireless efforts. I count myself lucky to have had such a great collaborator on this project and he deserves much of the credit for this book's completion.

Spectral mansions was developed out of research that was commissioned as part of the conservation and development of the museum at No. 14 Henrietta Street. This initial research was funded by Dublin City Council, with additional support from a Centenaries Capital Grant from the Department of Culture, Heritage and the Gaeltacht and the Heritage Council. Following the opening of the museum in 2018, I have also had the pleasure to work with the new custodians of the building, the team at Dublin City Council Culture Company. I would like to thank the CEO Iseult Byrne and the team at 14 Henrietta Street and the several guides of the museum for their dedication to telling the story of Dublin's tenements.

A very special thanks is due to Professor David Dickson, my former doctoral supervisor who has been kind enough to provide a foreword to this book, as well as offering advice and guidance throughout its writing. I am also grateful for the help and constructive criticism of Dr Ciarán Wallace and Professor Ciaran O'Neill, both of whom have helped enhance and refine my research, having read early iterations of this book. I am similarly grateful for the friendship and assistance of Ellen Rowley, Susan Galavan, and Brian Hanley, all of whom offered vital insights regarding the story of Henrietta Street. I would like to thank several other scholars who were kind enough to share their knowledge: Melanie Hayes, Padraig Yeates, Séamus Ó Maitiú and James Curry. Donal Fallon was also extremely generous with his time and research, for which I am very grateful. I have also benefitted from my conversations with Catriona Crowe, Joseph Brady, Peter Hession, Tommy Graham, Fergus Whelan, and John Gibney. Needless to say, any and all errors contained within this book are mine and mine alone.

This book is obviously indebted to the help of the staff of the libraries and archives used in the course of its research, particularly in regard to the use of images. I wish to thank the staff of the National Library of Ireland, especially the Prints and Drawings Department, the staff of the National Photographic Archive in Temple Bar, the staff and archivists at the Dublin City Library and Archive in Pearse Street, the archivists and librarians in the Manuscript and Early Printed Books Departments at Trinity College Dublin, the staff of the UCD Library and Archives, the staff at the Glasnevin Trust especially Conor Dodd. I would particularly like to thank the Royal Society of Antiquaries of Ireland, who have been extremely generous in permitting the use of the very important images of John Cooke's 'Darkest Dublin' photographs. Similarly, I would like to express thanks to William Laffan and Churchill Press for allowing the use of Hugh Douglas Hamilton's 'Cries of Dublin' sketches. I am also grateful to the staff at the National Library of Ireland, the Irish Architectural Archive, the Guinness Archive, the Bureau of Military History, the National Museum of Ireland, Kilmainham Gaol (Office of Public Works), the archival staff at the Valuations Office Ireland, Brian Kirby at the Irish Capuchin Provincial Archives, the staff at the Grangegorman Development Agency, and the RTÉ photographic archives. I wish to thank Dr Brian Ward, School of Architecture TU Dublin, for his guidance and Philip Marron who produced the exquisite architectural drawings of 14 Henrietta Street for this book. In addition to these repositories, much raw material and information was offered by private individuals and families with ties to Henrietta Street: Aileen Woods, Siobhan Morrell and Paul Appleby were all generous in sharing their research and knowledge of their families, while I have also benefitted from the insights of Ian Lumely, Pat Wigglesworth, and Michael Casey.

I am, of course, very grateful for the encouragement and support of my family: my sister Ellie, my aunt Deirdre, and my parents, who both imparted to me the value of empathy (as well as rigor) in historical scholarship. However, my greatest debt is to my amazing partner Sarah, for her love and support during the writing of this book, for which I am forever grateful.

'He picked his way deftly through all that minute vermin-like life and under the shadow of the gaunt spectral mansions in which the old nobility of Dublin had roistered.'

James Joyce, 'A little cloud', *Dubliners* (London, 1914).

Figure 1 The door of No. 14 Henrietta Street.

Introduction:
town houses to tenements

To walk down Henrietta Street is to walk down one of the finest streets in Dublin. Despite being a relatively short street, it projects an imposing sense of grandeur. Its buildings are astonishing not only in their size but also in the beauty of their design. When these houses were built in the eighteenth century, they were some of the largest and most ornate homes in Dublin, belonging to some of the most powerful members of the Irish ruling class. Yet the facades of these impressive houses mask a very different story, one not of aristocratic excess but of poverty and hardship. Henrietta Street began its existence as an elite enclave, an urban oasis for the privileged few. By the beginning of the twentieth century almost every house on the street was a tenement, and the wealthy had long since abandoned it as an address. In 1911, the nineteen buildings on the street contained over 900 people, with several buildings containing 100 inhabitants under a single roof. James Joyce, undoubtedly the greatest

Figure 2 'A tenement nocturne', reproduced in *The Capuchin Annual* (1940).

chronicler of Dublin during these years, pointed to Henrietta Street as an emblem of the city's larger decline. In one of his short stories, Joyce described a character walking down Henrietta Street, passing by a

> horde of grimy children [that] populated the street. They stood or ran in the roadway, or crawled up the steps before the gaping doors, or squatted like mice upon the thresholds ... He picked his way deftly through all that

> minute vermin-like life and under the shadow of the gaunt spectral mansions in which the old nobility of Dublin had roistered.[1]

Joyce's description of the houses in Henrietta Street as 'spectral mansions' conveyed how, at the start of the twentieth century, the ghostly presence of Dublin's past still overshadowed its present. Dublin seemed like a city whose best days were behind it: a deposed capital that was a ghost of its former self. Indeed, the theme of Dublin being literally haunted by its past has been used by several artists and writers. For instance, one satirical cartoon from the 1940s (*opposite*) depicted the twentieth-century residents of a Dublin tenement being visited by the ghosts of a building's eighteenth-century occupants.

Similarly, No. 14 Henrietta Street is a building that seems to summon up spectres of the past. Following the preservation and reopening of the house as a museum in 2018, the poet Paula Meehan was commissioned to write a series of poems inspired by No. 14. Appropriately enough, a major theme of these poems is that of a building haunted by its history. In one poem, Meehan imagines the ghosts of various people who inhabited No. 14 mingling together, once all the staff and tourists have left:

> Some nights when the moon is full the ghosts come out to dance:
> they reel and they jig and they jitter across the boards.
> They clasp each other's spectral hands throughout the ages,
> Republican shimmies with Ascendancy lady,
> Militia Captain toe to toe with Scullery Maid.

The poem captures the variety of different people who have inhabited the building over its nearly three centuries of existence.[2] This book hopes to convey something of this range of experience, both that of the 'Militia Captain' and the 'Scullery Maid'. However, like the museum at No. 14, this book will also use the story of the building to explore the wider history of Dublin housing and urban experience. While Henrietta Street may have been created in the 1700s, the focus of this book is what happened to the street (and the city) after 1800, investigating the nature of Dublin's housing crisis in the late nineteenth and early twentieth centuries. It was a crisis whose scale shocked observers at the time and since. At the turn of the twentieth century, a quarter of Dublin's population (72,000 people) lived in single-room tenements, large numbers of which were deemed unfit for human habitation.[3] How did this happen? How did a city once described as the second city of the British Empire become a city of slums? How did a location like Henrietta Street go from a street of mansions to one of tenements? It is a story of adaptation, not only of buildings but of people. It is a story of decline but also of resilience.

While this book examines the deep structural changes that effected Dublin's economy and society, it is fundamentally about people and the very human stories of those who found themselves living in places like Henrietta Street. It hopes to reveal something about the larger story of Dublin's working classes and those who inhabited the city's tenements. The story of Dublin's tenements is often described as beginning in 1800. In this year, the Act of Union abolished the Irish parliament, merging Ireland into the new United Kingdom. Dublin's loss of status as a 'capital' city coincided with a prolonged period of economic stagnation. This is frequently presented as the natural consequence of Dublin losing the free-spending Irish aristocracy, those who had made the city their home in the eighteenth century, but who now began to migrate to London. While there is some truth to this story, it has the effect of telescoping the history of the entire nineteenth century into two contrasting images: an eighteenth-century 'golden age' and a nineteenth-century 'dark age'. The reality is more complex. In order to understand Dublin's decline, it is worth having a look at the 'golden age' that created Henrietta Street: the age of Georgian Dublin.

Georgian Dublin: myth and reality

Technically, the term 'Georgian' refers to the years between 1714 and 1830, the reign of four successive English kings named George. But 'Georgian' Dublin is more than just a matter of chronology. Rather, it is a romanticized image of the city's past, a lost age of elegance, a bygone era of taste and refinement. As one Irish aristocrat would reminisce, Dublin in the eighteenth century was 'perhaps, one of the most agreeable places of residence in Europe. There were no conveniences belonging to a capital, in those days, which it did not possess. Society in the upper classes was as brilliant and polished as that of Paris in its best days'.[4] While the eighteenth century may not necessarily have been a golden age, it was still a crucial time for Dublin's development. This was the period during which the city centre, with its narrow winding lanes and alleys, was replaced by an arrangement of wide and elegant streets. During this hundred years, the city's population tripled in size. By 1800, Dublin's 180,000 inhabitants meant it was the second biggest city in the English-speaking world, after London. Not only was it the second city of the British Empire, it was at one point the ninth-largest city in Europe. Within Ireland, Dublin was easily the largest city, its nearest rival, Cork, only a third of the size. Dublin economically dominated the rest of the island. It was the busiest Irish port, as well as being the financial and banking hub for the country. This dominance was the result of the remarkable range of functions that were concentrated in the one city. Dublin was the seat of the vice-regal court, it was Ireland's legal and administrative centre and a university city. It was a garrison town, containing one of the largest barracks in Europe. It was also the seat of the Irish parliament. By the end of the century, Dublin was beginning to live up to this status in both physical size and appearance. The limits of the city now extended out towards the new canals, with the North and South Circular roads acting as informal boundaries. Within this expanded area, a new city centre had emerged, with a series of impressive new buildings: the Irish Parliament House (1729), the colossal front gate of

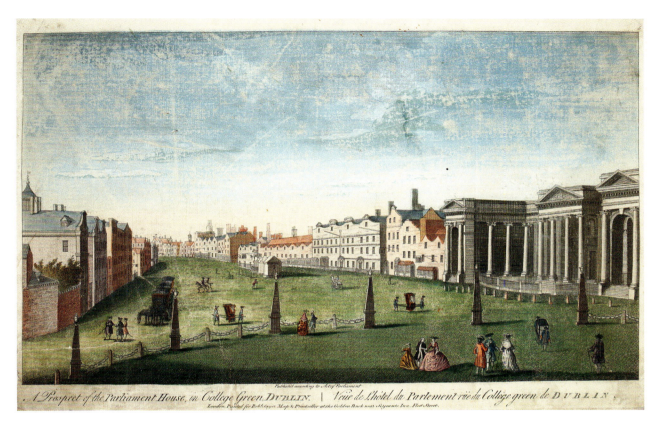

Figure 3 Joseph Tudor, *Prospect of the Parliament House in College Green*, from *Views of Dublin*, 1753.

Trinity College (1759), the Royal Exchange (1779, now the city hall), the new Custom House (1791), and the Four Courts (1796).

However, more impressive and important than all of these buildings was the Parliament House in College Green, built in the 1730s. The Irish parliament building represented more than just impressive architecture; it was also a loud statement of self-confidence by a ruling elite who were reaching the pinnacle of their power. The eighteenth century was a period of unchallenged Protestant dominance in Ireland, with Catholics totally excluded from power through a series of measures known as the 'penal laws'. These laws barred Irish Catholics from public office and most of the professions, stripped them of all political rights and representation, as well as restricting Catholic education and the open practice of their faith. As a result, political power was exclusively in the hands of a Protestant landed elite, often referred to as the 'Anglo-Irish Ascendancy'. Georgian Dublin was the playground of this Ascendancy, and the parliament the outlet for their political aspirations. History has not been kind to the memory of this privileged class, who are now remembered more for the lavish lifestyle they maintained, than for any political ideal they pursued. In 1810, a writer well acquainted with the city argued that the Ascendancy's politics 'did not much benefit the city of Dublin, but its money did ... frugality was not among its faults'.[5]

INTRODUCTION 5

The business of parliament attracted more than MPs or Lords, it brought an entire social world into the city. Irish politics was very much a spectator sport; the observers' gallery of the Irish House of Commons could hold several hundred people, with many regularly watching debates as a form of entertainment. In the weeks before a session of parliament opened, the roads into Dublin would be clogged with the carriages of the wealthy. For Ireland's landed gentry, living in their country estates, Dublin was an antidote to boredom and isolation, with a growing number of the upper class spending at least part of their year (and a sizeable part of their income) in the city. These were the 'winter gentry', the prosperous upper classes who came to the city for sessions of parliament during the winter months. The sitting of parliament coincided with an entire calendar of social events – musical concerts and drama, charitable fundraisers and vice-regal balls. Dublin provided a range of musical venues and theatres, coffee houses and assembly rooms, not to mention the often-lavish events hosted in private homes. In Dublin's private clubs, an exclusive set of gamblers had a well-earned reputation for 'high play' and debauchery. For those entering the upper-class marriage market, the city's fashionable promenades were often the start of a successful courtship. For those with a taste for luxury goods, the city was also home to the country's finest shops and retailers. The city was the cultural epicentre of the entire island, it attracted all those who aspired to be part of fashionable 'polite' society, while disseminating the newest trends to the provinces. Dublin was a hub for luxury

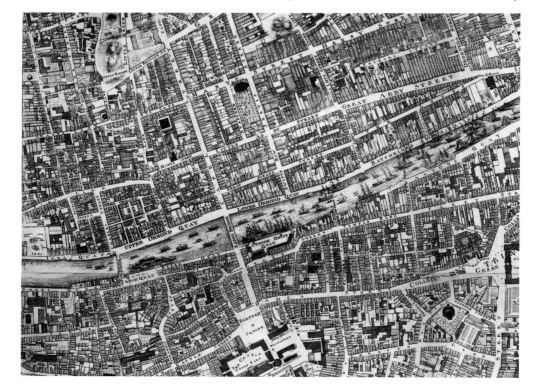

Figure 4 John Rocque, *An exact survey of the city and suburbs of Dublin*, 1756, (detail), showing something of the scale and density of the city by mid-century.

Figure 5 *The Doors of Dublin*, Aer Lingus postcard showing colourful 'Georgian' doors.

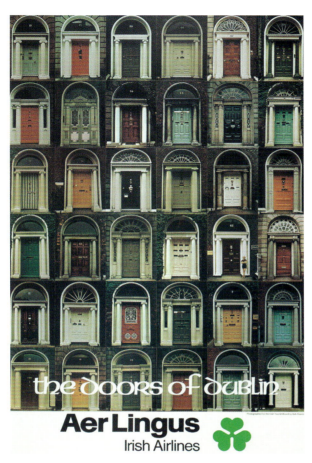

goods and services, acting as the 'warehouse' and distribution centre of the country. It thus developed a substantial manufacturing base, drawing huge numbers of craftsmen and shopkeepers to the city. Dublin's growth and commerce could increasingly be seen in the physical environment, as reflected in contemporary maps.

All these factors gave Dublin the flavour of a capital city, with many describing it as London in miniature. Yet Dublin was an unusual metropolis. Unlike many other European capitals, Dublin was not home to a resident monarch or court, and despite the impressive public buildings within the city's centre, it was the new districts of *residential* buildings that increasingly gave Dublin its character. Eighteenth-century Dublin was dominated by property developers, who happily catered to the demand of the landed elite who desired a foothold in the city. On both sides of the river Liffey, entire neighbourhoods of upper-class residences sprang up, consisting of rows of spacious town houses. These town houses were usually brick-built, three or four storeys tall, often over a basement and characterized by simple but elegant exteriors. Certain features of these town houses have become iconic parts of 'Georgian Dublin', such as the ornate fanlights and colourfully painted doors.

As a result of the explosion in the building of these town houses, the shape of the city was increasingly determined not by the state, but by ambitious entrepreneurs. These were the major developers who purchased large stretches of land which were then divided and laid out into elegant streets and squares. The names of these men are still immortalized in local street names: Molesworth, Dawson, Fitzwilliam, Jervis. However, the most important figure in the construction of Georgian Dublin was Luke Gardiner.

Little is known about Gardiner's origins, although it seems he came from a humble background; he was reputedly the son of a coachman and grew up in the Coombe. As an adult he established a prosperous dynasty thanks to his financial and political skills, although helped by an advantageous marriage and backed by several influential patrons. Gardiner carved out a successful career as a civil servant, eventually becoming deputy vice-treasurer and paymaster general of Ireland, as well as being an influential MP. He was esteemed by some of the leading politicians of the day as a 'thorough man of business and a great weight in this country'.[6] A clever and discrete man, Gardiner used his position to set himself up as a private banker, soon acquiring vast wealth, which he channelled into an impressive Dublin property portfolio. Early on in his career, Gardiner purchased land on the south quays, before acquiring the old St Mary's Abbey estate, lands which stretched across a large chunk of the north of the city. Having acquired these lands, Gardiner became the largest landowner on the north bank of the Liffey. He also became the single-greatest influence on the development of Dublin, imposing a strategic pattern on the city's eventual spread eastwards. Gardiner's main contribution was that he encouraged the building of large neighbourhoods of exclusive residences where a high quality of design and a degree of uniformity were ensured by means of leases specifying building conditions. His first great experiment in creating a fashionable enclave was in Henrietta Street, with Gardiner purchasing the parcel of land in 1721.

Figure 6 John Brooks after Charles Jervas, *Luke Gardiner, MP* (d.1755).

There had been exclusive housing developments before, such as in Molesworth Street on the south side, but Henrietta Street was something new. Gardiner chose to lay the street out on a green-field site, on the rising ground at the top of Bolton Street, providing splendid views across the city. The street was named after a vice-regal duchess, with the area's exclusivity further enhanced by its sheer scale. The building plots in Henrietta Street were twice the size of those in nearby streets, with rents set at a level that only the wealthiest could afford. Construction of the first houses began in the early 1720s, with Gardiner building his own house at the highest point of the street. Gardiner's home was the perfect showcase for his newly acquired wealth. Not only was the house designed by one of the leading architects of the day, its interior decoration and furnishings also proclaimed Gardiner's taste and worldliness. Indeed, the street as a whole was an extension of Gardiner's ambition and desire for social recognition.[7]

Figure 7 John Rocque, *An exact survey of the city and suburbs of Dublin*, 1756, detail showing Henrietta Street and environs.

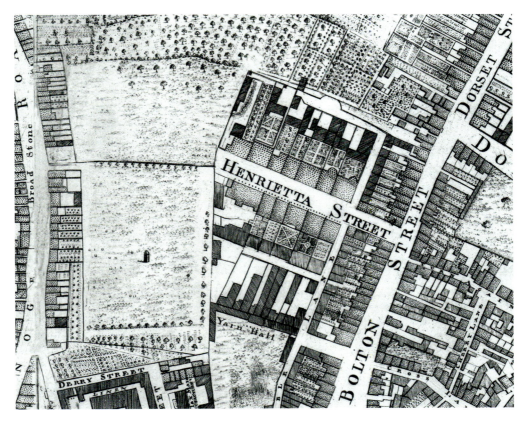

Figure 8 *His Grace Doctor Hugh Boulter, lord archbishop of Armagh, primate*, John Brooks after Francis Bindon, 1742.

Tellingly, Gardiner's home was not the first to be constructed. From the very beginning he had been careful to secure the street's fashionable status by securing a prestigious 'anchor tenant': Hugh Boulter, the archbishop of Armagh. Boulter was convinced to take several of the plots opposite Gardiner's home, erecting a single palatial mansion which was to become the official city residence for the archbishop. While the house itself no longer exists (it was replaced by the King's Inns Library in 1824), Boulter nonetheless left a lasting mark on Henrietta Street, as it became popularly known as 'Primate's Hill' in his honour.

It would take another thirty years for the rest of the street to be completed, with Gardiner's protégé Nathaniel Clements constructing Nos. 4 to 8 on the north side of the street during the 1740s. By the time of Gardiner's death in 1755, the street was a startlingly elegant alignment of massive town houses. The houses ranged in scale from five bays to three, with their frontages ranging from 35 feet across to over 60 at their largest, their plain brick facades belying their vast interiors. Some of the houses were the product of speculative building, receiving a standardized treatment. However, several of the more 'bespoke' houses (such as Nos. 9, 10, 11 and 12) set new standards of architectural and decorative splendour.[8] In turn, these homes attracted some of the leading figures of Irish society. As Melanie Hayes has illustrated, during the first thirty years of the street's existence, it was home to no less than six titled residents, two military generals, three archbishops, and two speakers of the Irish House of Commons.[9] The building at No. 14 Henrietta Street attracted an impressive stream of early inhabitants. Its first resident was General Richard Molesworth, the commander-in-chief of his majesty's forces in Ireland. Following his departure in 1758, the house was then occupied by John Bowes, who had recently been appointed lord chancellor of Ireland. It seems that, while Archbishop Boulter may have been Henrietta Street's first anchor tenant, it never became a sleepy, ecclesiastical conclave. Instead, it became the playground for the Irish political class. Indeed, at times it seemed like Ireland was being governed from Henrietta Street, rather than from Dublin Castle or College Green. This reputation started with Archbishop Boulter himself, who was a political as well as religious figure, serving as a lord justice (one of the three men who governed the country during an absence of the lord lieutenant). However, it was one of Boulter's successors as primate, George Stone, who established Henrietta Street as *the* political address in Dublin.

Figure 9 Allan Ramsay, *George Stone, archbishop of Armagh* (1708–64).

Stone was an Englishman who had first came to Dublin as the chaplain of a lord lieutenant in 1731, quickly rising up the Church of Ireland hierarchy. Stone was also a presence in the Irish parliament, becoming a skilful power-broker on behalf of the English interest in Ireland. One of Stone's skills was his ability to make political allies over the dinner table, providing lavish hospitality at his home in Henrietta Street. Stone was described as living in 'Polish magnificence' in the primate's mansion, while it was reported that at his dinner parties 'the rake took the place of the archbishop'.

Figure 10 Stephen Slaughter, *Henry Boyle, 1st earl of Shannon*.

Stone was far from alone in this, his neighbour Nathaniel Clements was also said to live in 'Parisian luxury', with a similar reputation for a boozy style of entertaining.¹⁰ There are several accounts of heavy drinking sessions at Clements' house resulting in controversial and disrespectful toasts being given by inebriated guests. Irish politicians were a hard-drinking group. One English visitor to Dublin noted that an Irish gentleman was not considered a real drinker unless he could drink a gallon of wine 'cooly', claiming that 'the Irish drink the most of any of his majesty's subjects with the least injury'. In Georgian Dublin, eating and drinking were a key part of parliamentary activity: 'It is hardly an exaggeration to say that wine was the medium through which the King's Government was carried on'.¹¹

Irish politics was certainly an unusual business. In theory the king set policy via his appointed lord lieutenant, but in practice most viceroys were absentees. Instead, government subcontracted most parliamentary business to an elite group of political managers known as the 'undertakers' (since they 'undertook' to pursue the king's business). In return for managing parliamentary business on behalf of the executive in Dublin Castle, these undertakers would control a large share of government patronage, dispensing plum jobs and pensions to their supporters. Henrietta Street was already home to one of the greatest of these 'undertakers': Henry Boyle, the speaker of the House of Commons and the chancellor of the Irish exchequer. However, his success encouraged him to take an independent stance, increasingly antagonizing his British masters. Boyle was soon opposed by a new lord lieutenant, the duke of Dorset, who wanted to establish a more direct control of the Irish parliament. In his fight against Boyle, the lord lieutenant allied himself to Archbishop Stone, who had his own personal reasons for opposing Boyle. These tensions came to a head in an event known as the 'Money Bill dispute' (1753–6).

While on the surface this was a dispute over surplus tax revenue, in reality it was a power struggle between different factions over who would be the main dispenser of government patronage – the head 'undertaker'. Boyle had thought he could reassert his power by reminding government how much they needed his support. He used his influence to veto a 'Money Bill', a bill required to fund the government. In response, Boyle and his allies were dismissed from office. Archbishop Stone then tried to

INTRODUCTION II

replace the Boyle faction with his own supporters and cronies. What followed was an aggressive public campaign, in which Boyle represented the conflict as being between a 'patriotic' Irish faction (himself) and a corrupt wing of the Castle administration (Stone and his allies). This use of nationalistic rhetoric was blatant cynicism on Boyle's part. Following negotiations behind closed doors, Boyle was bought off, soon being reinstated and given a peerage (he was made the earl of Shannon). The Money Bill dispute was a contest over position and status, not principles or ideology. Indeed, it could be described as little more than a feud between neighbours. Archbishop Stone and Henry Boyle lived nearly next-door to each other on Henrietta Street, while several other residents were also key figures in the dispute: the earl of Bessborough, Thomas Carter, Nathaniel Clements, and even Luke Gardiner himself. The fact that so many of the protagonists lived in the same street revealed much about the insular, and sometimes petty, nature of Irish politics in these years. The central role of Henrietta Street in these political controversies nonetheless confirmed that Luke Gardiner's plan had succeeded.[12]

Servants and staff

The houses in Henrietta Street were obviously well-suited to entertaining, a fact helped by their imposing size, with their grand reception rooms and parlours. Yet these homes only functioned thanks to the labour of domestic servants, most of whom lived under the same roof as their employers. The cooking, cleaning and maintenance necessary to run a town house was made possible by a staff of perhaps ten to fifteen domestics.[13] The very layout of these homes was designed to keep them hidden from view. Servants' quarters were usually in the attic rooms or garret, with more senior staff (such as the butler or housekeeper) located in the basement. Meanwhile, a series of back or service stairs allowed for unseen movement of staff between different parts of the house.[14] The hours and conditions for domestic servants could be hard and

Figure 11 John Opie, *Mary Wollstonecraft*, 1797.

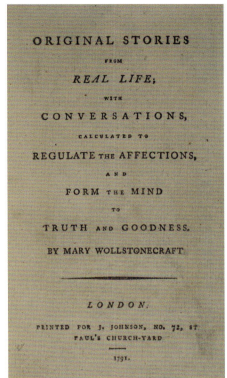

Figure 12 (left) Mary Wollstonecraft, *Original stories from real life*, 1788.
Figure 13 (right) Margaret King, *Lady Mount Cashell in profile*, 1801.

discipline often strict. Yet compared to many other lines of work, the wages were relatively good. Some staff were also afforded better conditions and privileges, such as those charged with looking after a family's children. In certain cases, the influence of a teacher or governess could be crucial. A good example is that of the family of Sir Robert King, the 2nd earl of Kingston, who lived in No. 15 Henrietta Street. The earl was a notorious womanizer who engaged in numerous extra-marital affairs. Yet, ironically, in 1786 the earl would employ the pioneering feminist Mary Wollstonecraft to be his children's governess.

Wollstonecraft found the three young women in her charge to be ill-disciplined and starved for attention, describing them as 'wild'. She provided the girls with a progressive curriculum and was well liked by her young students, but her popularity with the children caused tensions with Lady Kingsborough. Caroline blamed Wollstonecraft for alienating the affections of her daughters and in the summer of 1787, Mary was let go. Yet her experience in Henrietta Street would influence Wollstonecraft's writing, such as her *Original stories from real life*, which featured an enlightened governess who cures two spoilt girls of laziness and unkindness, very obviously drawing from her experience of the King children. Even more revealing was her landmark *A vindication of the rights of woman* in 1792, which included a scathing description of a 'fine lady' Wollstonecraft had once worked for that is clearly Lady

INTRODUCTION   13

Kingsborough. Wollstonecraft certainly influenced one of her former students in Dublin: Lady Kingsborough would describe Wollstonecraft as 'the extraordinary woman to whose superior penetration & affectionate mildness of manner I trace the development of whatever virtues I possess'. Margaret would pursue an unconventional life, running away from an unhappy marriage and moving to Italy. Margaret was a radical in her politics, making the acquaintance of revolutionaries such as Thomas Paine and Robert Emmet. She would later befriend Wollstonecraft's widower, William Godwin, a radical novelist and early anarchist philosopher. After her move to Italy, Margaret pursued a literary career, as well as studying medicine in the universities of Jena and Pisa.[15]

The city moves east

From the beginning Henrietta Street was only part of a more ambitious building programme envisioned by Luke Gardiner. From mid-century, however, the growth of the Gardiner Estate was towards the east, as Henrietta Street was followed by building in Dominick Street, Rutland Square, and most conspicuously after 1749 in Sackville Mall, a 150-foot-wide tree-lined avenue that would eventually become O'Connell Street.

Figure 14 Joseph Tudor, *Sackville Street and Gardiner's Mall*, (c.1750).

The building of this elite residential and shopping district, adjacent to the newly laid out gardens and lying-in hospital in Rutland Square, helped to shift the focus of the city eastwards.[16] Following Gardiner's death in 1755, his descendants continued his ambitions, setting out areas like Gardiner Street and Mountjoy Square in the eastern portion of the city. This was accompanied by a similar expansion of elite residences in the south-eastern quarter. The Fitzwilliam Estate grew rapidly after 1750 with the layout of Merrion Square, expanding ever further south and east to Pembroke Street and Fitzwilliam Square. To realize the full potential of these developments, both north and south of the Liffey, they needed to be joined by a new bridge. The obvious site for this bridge would be to connect the now-extended Sackville Street across the river to the complex of buildings around College Green. However, this would require relocating the old Customs House further downstream where it could still be reached by tall-masted ships. The plan was initially resisted by vested interests who feared such a move would lower values in the older parts of the city, west of Dame Street. This conflict went on for several decades until the building of the new Customs House by the architect James Gandon commenced in the 1780s, allowing for the construction of the new Carlisle Bridge (now O'Connell Bridge) in 1795. The opponents of this eastward move were conciliated by the building of Gandon's other notable project, the new Four Courts. Nonetheless, the eastward expansion was now consolidated with Sackville Street becoming the city's main thoroughfare, and the new bridge linking the eastern Gardiner Estate to the fashionable quarter around College Green. As the century drew to a close, the new high-end residential areas were all in the east of the city, such as Mountjoy Square and Fitzwilliam Square. When Gardiner had chosen the site for Henrietta Street in the 1720s, it had been at the apex of the city's main axis, at the top of Capel Street. With the construction of Sackville Street and the larger shift towards the east, Henrietta Street was left stranded on the north-western periphery of the expanding city.[17]

One effect of this eastward shift was a slow but steady deterioration of the older neighbourhoods in the western part of the city. Moreover, the new streets and squares, with their adoption of classical motifs and styles, sharpened the visual disparity between the wealthier and more impoverished areas. For instance, just beyond Henrietta Street, the markets district of Smithfield and Ormond Quay presented a very different appearance from the new fashionable areas in the east, as did neighbourhoods across the river like the Coombe and Thomas Street. The result was an increasing contrast between the eastern and western halves of the city, a division that gives the lie to a lot of the myths about Georgian Dublin. It is telling that so many of the pictures we have of eighteenth-century Dublin are of either public buildings or else of homes in the eastern quarters, particularly the new squares of town houses. The most popular of these depictions are undoubtedly the series of prints produced by James Malton in the 1790s, a set of images that continue to shape how many view the city during this era.[18]

Figure 15 James Malton, *Charlemont House, Dublin*, 1793, depicting Rutland Square (now Parnell Square).

Images of Georgian Dublin

While such images are seductive, they are misleading. These are pictures overwhelmingly populated by elegant gentlemen and ladies, stepping out of their carriages or strolling through the well-paved streets. However, if you look carefully, you can see hints of the city's lower classes, its artisans, coachmen and beggars.

While Malton's prints may be the best-known visual source for Georgian Dublin, there are other images showing a very different city: for example, a series of drawings by Hugh Douglas Hamilton. Hamilton was born in Dublin in 1740, soon proving himself a talented artist and finding success painting portraits of the English and Irish upper classes. While his portraiture was enough to secure his artistic reputation, a lost volume of drawings by Hamilton, rediscovered in 2002, sheds light on another aspect of his work. This volume of sixty-six drawings depicts Dublin's street life, notably the 'cries' of its retailers. In the eighteenth century, depictions of the 'cries' of a city's street markets and sellers were a common subject, with sets of the 'cries' of London or Paris depicting the street sellers who advertised their wares with a shout or a rhyme. Drawn in 1760, Hamilton's Dublin cries are significant because of their comparative rarity.

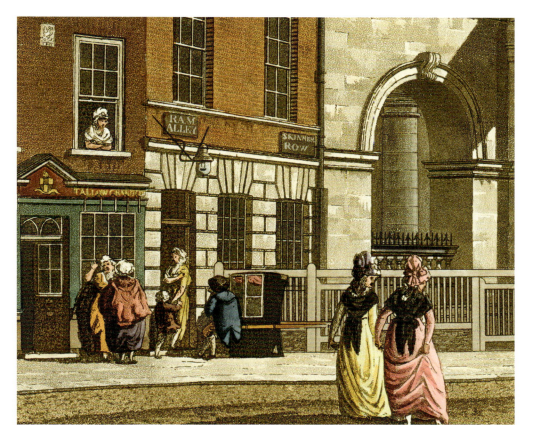

Figure 16 James Malton, *Tholsel, Dublin*, 1793, detail showing sedan chair-man talking to women.

Figure 17 James Malton, *View from Capel Street, looking over Essex Bridge*, 1793, detail showing beggar and tradesmen in distance.

(Clockwise from top left)
Figure 18 Hugh Douglas Hamilton, *A crippled beggar*, 1760.

Figure 19 Hugh Douglas Hamilton, *Rags and old clothes*, 1760.

Figure 20 Hugh Douglas Hamilton, *A rambling cobbler and his boy*, 1760.

Figure 21 Hugh Douglas Hamilton, *Rare news in the Evening Post*, 1760.

So many of our images of Georgian Dublin are derived from paintings and drawings of the elite, or sanitized depictions like those of Malton. Instead, Hamilton chronicled the city's working poor, producing images which, although not technically sophisticated, nonetheless provide a window into the world of Dublin's 'lower orders': a cobbler bent over his work in concentration, a girl talking to a boy selling stationary, a woman selling milk from the back of a cart, a chimney sweep walking alongside his apprentice. *The cries of Dublin* are a source of information on topics ranging from diet and clothing, to literacy and social class in the eighteenth-century city. In their depiction of the brutal realities of working life, these images remind us that the myth of Georgian Dublin often obscures a more complex reality.[19]

While the newly constructed areas of Georgian Dublin may have been visually impressive, it is important to remember how this architectural brilliance was paid for. The majority of the upper class of Dublin did not derive their wealth from commerce or trade but instead from land. From the mid-century on, soaring agricultural exports produced rural prosperity, the vast majority of which was funnelled into the pockets of those at the top. Eighteenth-century Ireland was a deeply unequal society, one in which landowners were guaranteed a large share of their tenants' earnings. As a result, the agricultural boom of the eighteenth century meant the gentry now had even more disposable income to spend on a Dublin town house, like those on the Gardiner or Fitzwilliam Estates. This infusion of new wealth not only reflected the inequalities of the countryside, but led to a sharpening of class divisions within Dublin. The perception that Dublin's 'slum problem' only really begins in the nineteenth century is a mistake. Georgian Dublin had its equivalents of the tenements, with pockets of shocking deprivation. Already in the 1720s and 1730s, hundreds of houses in the older parts of the city were decaying and overcrowded. Jonathan Swift's early satires had drawn attention to the dire conditions that the city's poor lived in. Swift's notorious *Modest proposal* highlighted the injustices of this 'beggarly city' which failed to provide either adequate food or shelter for the working poor, sarcastically suggesting that the poor could solve their troubles by selling their children to the rich as food. It was a grim but fitting metaphor for Irish class divisions.

Swift had been the dean of St Patrick's Cathedral and his knowledge of the local poor was derived from his acquaintance with the surrounding streets. In fact, we have an illustration of the more riotous aspects of Dublin thanks to a painting of this very neighbourhood. *The surroundings of St Patrick's Cathedral*, a painting by the amateur artist John Nixon, is undoubtedly an exaggerated vision of the city, in the same way that the cartoons of William Hogarth or Thomas Rowlandson exaggerated Georgian London.[20] But its depiction of carnivalesque license and anarchy likely captures something of the unruly nature of Dublin life. As one contemporary guide to the city described it, during a walk through Dublin, 'Our sight was constantly struck with objects disgraceful to human nature; with wretched strumpets, tricked out in tawdry apparel, or covered in tattered weeds; and where our ears were continually assaulted with vociferations that would startle deafness, and appal blasphemy'.[21] Such impressions stand in stark contrast to received notions about Dublin in an era of 'wide and convenient streets'.

At the time Swift was writing in the first half of the century, the real contrast was still between the city and an even more impoverished countryside. By the later decades, however, commentators were increasingly struck by shocking disparities

Figure 22 John Nixon, *The surroundings of St Patrick's Cathedral, Dublin* (c.1790).

within the city itself. In 1796, a local pamphleteer described Dublin as the 'gorgeous mask of Ireland's distress', an example of 'pomp and pageantry alongside abject poverty'. Again, the most conspicuous contrast was that between east and west: 'the East part of the capital, indeed, displays some grandeur in palaces, public buildings, and works, which instead of disguising rather make mere glaring, the huge poverty, the gigantic misery, that fills this great city'.[22] In the same year, one French visitor to Dublin stated that 'although the part of the city where the well-to-do people live is perhaps as beautiful as anywhere similar in Europe, nothing anywhere can compare with the dirt and misery of the quarters where the lower classes vegetate'.[23]

Dublin's 'polite' society was not bothered by this deterioration of the old city because they were no longer part of it. Previously, aristocrats and master-tradesmen had shared addresses like Smithfield or Francis Street. Now these areas were being deserted by those with money. Instead of a mix of high- and low-status housing, there were now two separate 'Dublins': one for the rich and one for the poor. The full impact of this segregation was not felt at first, thanks to favourable economic conditions for Dublin workers. The rapid growth of the city had coincided with a boom in the construction sector and in manufacturing, particularly of luxury goods. While there was still poverty, the middle decades of the century were (broadly-speaking) prosperous times for the city's working classes. However, by the later decades, the living standards for many began to slip, due to several factors. First, a growing number of rural migrants were being drawn into the city, undercutting wages and exacerbating overcrowding in deprived areas. Second, new technologies in manufacturing, combined with the decline of the guild system, meant that the earning power of skilled artisans was increasingly under threat. The result was a rise in urban poverty and the deterioration of the older working-class areas of the city, bringing overcrowding and environmental degradation.[24] In 1798, one survey described how in the city's poorer districts 'the streets are generally narrow; the houses crowded together; the rears or back yards of very small extent, and some without accommodation of any kind ... This crowded population, wherever it obtains, is almost universally accompanied by a very serious evil – a degree of filth and stench inconceivable, except by such as have visited those scenes of wretchedness'.[25]

The later eighteenth century

As the eighteenth century came to a close, these conditions seemed far removed from the elite world of Henrietta Street. In the final decades of the century, the street was still a highly desirable place to live, home to some of the city's most prominent figures. Despite the expansion of the Gardiner Estate to the east, Luke Gardiner II (the grandson of the first Luke Gardiner) still made his home on the street, having recently been ennobled as Viscount Mountjoy. The street was still home to some familiar names, most notably Richard Boyle, the 2nd earl of Shannon. The younger Boyle lived extravagantly, leasing two houses on the street (Nos. 11 and 12), merging them into a single grand residence, where he reportedly threw lavish parties. The street was still a political hub, with both Boyle and his neighbour at No. 15, Edward King, being active in Cork's politics. Several Irish MPs made their homes on the

Figure 23 (left) Joshua Reynolds, *Richard Boyle, 2nd earl of Shannon* (1759).
Figure 24 (right) Joshua Reynolds, *Luke Gardiner, 1st Viscount Mountjoy* (1773).

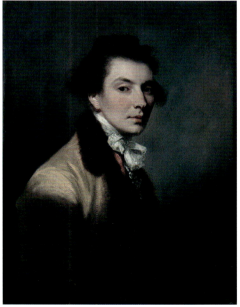

STREET ELEVATION 1756

street, such as John O'Neill and Owen Wynne. Between the years 1768 and 1794, the MP Sir Lucius O'Brien made his home at No. 14, injecting the new reform politics of Ireland's 'Patriot' party into this longstanding political haunt.

However, while the street was still home to MPs and peers, it was no longer the focus of political power it had been in the 1750s. The 2nd earl of Shannon was not the powerful 'undertaker' his father had been, nor could men like O'Neill and King exert the level of influence that earlier residents had done. This had less to do with Henrietta Street's status than it did with the changed nature of Irish politics. By the 1780s, the age of the great 'undertakers' was over. It had ended partly because of the controversies of the 1750s, which Henrietta Street residents had done so much to create. From the perspective of the British government, the Money Bill affair had highlighted the fickleness of the existing system of parliamentary management in Ireland. Previously, the British cabinet was happy to trust a local 'undertaker' to smooth the way for English policy within the Irish parliament. After 1760, however, a new solution was beginning to emerge: that of a resident lord lieutenant who would take a direct role in conducting policy by the means of a 'Castle party', a grouping of Irish MPs who were directly loyal to the administration in the Castle, and not to one

Figure 25 Street elevation of Nos. 13–15 Henrietta Street, c.1756.

of the local 'undertakers'. No one man would be allowed to accumulate the level of power that Henry Boyle had once held.[26]

There had been other developments, as well. The 1750s had seen a growing sense of grievance about British management of Irish politics, with the Boyle faction opposing interference from London, seeing it as an affront to Irish national pride. While Boyle had used these sentiments for cynical purposes, he had let a genie out of the bottle. Over the next several decades, a new 'Patriot' opposition emerged in the Irish parliament. These Patriots included some of the most talented speakers of the age: Edmund Sexton Perry, Henry Flood, and, of course, Henry Grattan. These men persistently criticized the British government, a government that seemed to be tightening the imperial bonds throughout its territories, in Ireland no less than in North America. Indeed, the impact of the American Revolution upon Ireland was striking. The war between Britain and the American colonists led many to question the nature of British governance in Ireland. It also provided the Irish Patriots with the leverage to demand concessions from London. In 1782, just as the American War was reaching a conclusion, a series of measures granted the Irish parliament a new level of autonomy, freeing it from the legal restrictions that had allowed Dublin Castle to tightly manage Irish affairs. This new legislative independence allowed the parliament to pursue its own agenda. The resulting era of 'Grattan's Parliament' was more ideologically driven and polarized than the age of the undertakers.

Figure 26 Francis Wheatley, *The Irish House of Commons*, 1780.

Yet, these developments pale in comparison to the real legacy of the 1750s: the growth of 'popular' politics. Both sides in the Money Bill dispute had invoked crowds and protests. Political agitators used public entertainments such as bonfires and the dispensing of alcohol to draw crowds. Boyle and the 'Patriot' side found support among the city's tradesmen, particularly those in the clothing industry: weavers and tailors, many of whom had been badly hit by a recent economic downturn. Government officials described Dublin's streets as being under the control of these crowds, some of whom were singing so-called 'brimstone ballads', offensive songs mocking politicians like Archbishop Stone.[27] The Dublin 'mob' was an increasingly literate one, with close to 200 pamphlets having been produced about the Money Bill dispute during the years 1753–5, many aimed at a popular readership. Moreover, the city's crowds were also willing to directly intervene in national politics, in ways that the elite could not control. When Boyle and his cronies reconciled with the government in 1756, there was widespread revulsion, with the city's workers staging a mock trial and execution using an effigy of Boyle. Several years later, in 1759, an even more startling example of 'street politics' took place when a riot broke out in College Green. This had been prompted by a rumour that a union between Ireland and England was to be introduced. The riot eventually turned into an invasion of the parliament building by the crowd, who mockingly placed an old woman in the speaker's chair, declaring that 'many an old woman had sat there before'. The Dublin mob was now a force to contend with.

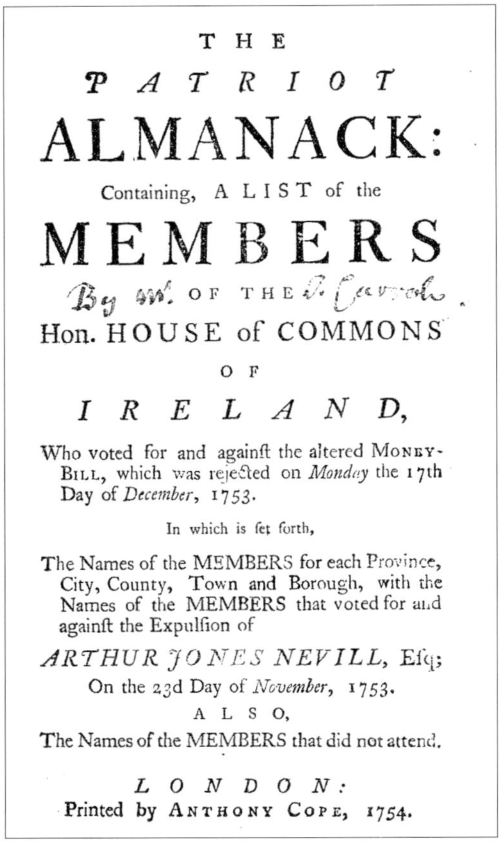
THE

PATRIOT

ALMANACK:

Containing, A LIST of the

MEMBERS

OF THE

Hon. HOUSE of COMMONS

OF

IRELAND,

Who voted for and againſt the altered MONEY-BILL, which was rejected on *Monday* the 17th Day of *December*, 1753.

In which is ſet forth,

The Names of the MEMBERS for each Province, City, County, Town and Borough, with the Names of the MEMBERS that voted for and againſt the Expulſion of

ARTHUR JONES NEVILL, Eſq;

On the 23d Day of *November*, 1753.

ALSO,

The Names of the MEMBERS that did not attend.

LONDON:

Printed by ANTHONY COPE, 1754.

Figure 27 *The Patriot Almanack* (London, 1754), an example of one of the many pamphlets provoked by the Money Bill dispute.

Whether it was by Patriot MPs or the Dublin crowd, calls for political reform grew louder in the final decades of the eighteenth century. The American War had a particularly dramatic effect in this regard, as the withdrawl of British troops to fight in America raised the possibility of the British army enlisting Irish Catholics, something that was prohibited by the penal laws. The 'Catholic Issue', as it came to be known, would become the central issue of Irish politics, as a new generation of assertive Catholic leaders sought civil and political rights. The issue of Catholic rights had a particular resonance in Dublin. At the beginning of the eighteenth century, Catholics had constituted perhaps less than 30 per cent of the city's population. By the later half of the century, more than half the population of Dublin was Catholic. Increasingly, Dublin was the centre of not only the Irish Protestant 'nation', but also a disenfranchised Catholic 'nation' in wait.[28] The question of Catholic relief and political rights became even more pressing after 1789, with the downfall of the French monarchy. The debates provoked by the French Revolution raised questions about Ireland's own 'ancien régime', with Protestant reformers and MPs forced to rethink their attitudes towards Irish Catholics.

Inspired by the dramatic events in Paris, a new group appeared in Ireland – the Society of United Irishmen. The Society had been founded by a small group of Belfast reformers in October 1791, with a Dublin branch opening the following month in the Eagle Tavern on Eustace Street. The membership of the group had initially been middle and upper class, consisting mainly of lawyers and doctors, with a smattering of gentry. However, as the 1790s progressed, government repression targeted the Society, imprisoning some of its leaders and resulting in a radicalization of the remaining membership. Following their official suppression, the United Irishmen reinvented themselves as a mass movement, appealing to workers and peasant farmers. They were now dedicated to the overthrow of British power in Ireland, in favour of an independent republic. In the hope of achieving this aim, they allied

Figure 28 *The United Irish Patriots of 1798.*

Figure 29 James Gillray, *United Irishmen upon duty*, 1798. Gillray's depiction of the United Irishmen as maurading savages was in keeping with many of the crass stereotypes of its day, but also expresses the deep-seated fear of domestic revolution among the British elite.

themselves with the government of Revolutionary France. The French would attempt a naval expedition to Ireland in late 1796, although it failed to land. Nonetheless, the prospect of foreign invasion and domestic subversion provoked further government repression. In turn, the United Irishmen began to plan for a revolution unaided by the French. The culmination of their planning occurred in the summer of 1798, when multiple insurrections against the government broke out throughout Ulster and south Leinster, in an event known as the 1798 Rebellion. After several months of sporadic and at times brutal fighting, the Rebellion was crushed by government forces, but at a heavy cost. In the span of only a few months, at least 10,000 people had been killed in battle, with some estimates as much as double that figure. It represents one of the most concentrated episodes of violence in Irish history.

Obviously, the 1798 Rebellion had deeply frightened and unnerved Dublin's elite. While the Rebellion took place almost entirely in the countryside, Dublin nonetheless lived under a cloud of fear. During the summer of 1798, the city was on lock-down. Dubliners slowly began to see grisly evidence of the fighting in Leinster, with the corpses of captured rebels hanged from lampposts and a mass grave dug to bury rebels, what would become known as 'Croppies Acre'. There were real fears of an insurrection being led by Dublin's workers, a group who were known to have been radicalized in recent years. Just as in Paris, the poverty of Dublin had produced its revolutionary discontents, as the United Irishmen's membership had grown to 10,000 in the city. There had been an attempted rising in the city in May 1798, but the government had been able to contain it thanks to the help of informers. Nonetheless, rumours continued to circulate of various plots aimed at the city's upper classes: reports of shadowy meetings in the backstreet taverns, clandestine signals being passed to rebels in the surrounding mountains, and rumours that servants were conspiring to poison their masters.[29]

The wealthy inhabitants of Henrietta Street were likely gripped by these fears. However, it would be the fighting outside the city that claimed the lives of two of the street's residents. Luke Gardiner II had travelled to Wexford to command a regiment of militia. On 5 June, during the crucial Battle of New Ross, Gardiner was ambushed and piked to death. Only days later, Gardiner's next-door neighbour in Henrietta Street, John O'Neill (Viscount O'Neill), was wounded by rebels during an attack on Antrim town, later succumbing to his wounds. The deaths of O'Neill and Gardiner shocked observers. They were members of the establishment, certainly, but both men had also been liberals who supported the granting of civil and political rights to Catholics. However, it was reported that O'Neill had been killed by one of his own tenants, while others remarked on the irony that the reformist Gardiner was killed by (it was assumed Catholic) men 'whose cause he was the first great advocate for'.[30] These killings did more than just shock, they undermined the faith of the Anglo-Irish elite in themselves. The death of a figure like Luke Gardiner in 1798, a man who had done so much to create the Georgian city, greatly affected upper-class Dubliners. The 'Gorgeous Mask' had started to slip.

The 1798 rebellion marks a turning point for Dublin in another sense. After receiving news of the rebellion, the response of British Prime Minister William Pitt was to ask 'cannot crushing the rebellion be followed by an act appointing commissioners to treat for a Union?'[31] For Pitt, 1798 had demonstrated that the Irish governing class was incapable of doing just that: *governing*. In 1799, with the Rebellion only recently suppressed, the first attempt at a union was introduced in the Irish parliament. This initial attempt failed, but the government was not dissuaded. Over the next year (1799–1800), an intense debate concerning a union occurred, with the city's rich and powerful divided on the question. There would be accusations (some warranted) that the Union was passed thanks to the bribery of Irish MPs. Yet the question of what constituted 'bribery' in the eighteenth century is a tricky one. Moreover, there were many within the Irish elite who supported the measure out of conviction. Many of Dublin's main property developers, including the majority of the Wide Streets Commissioners, voted in favour. While Luke Gardiner's death means we cannot know his opinion on the matter, it seems his former neighbours in Henrietta Street were divided. The 2nd earl of Shannon and his son (living at what is today Nos. 11 and 12) both supported the Union, while Owen Wynne (at No. 3) and the young Lord Kingsborough (at No. 15) both opposed it. As the eighteenth century drew to a close, the political future of Ireland seemed uncertain. The following century was to be a confusing and turbulent period for Dublin and its citizens.

Figure 30 'College Green before the Union' – a cartoon depicting Dublin before the Union, published by J.J. Stockdale (London, 1812).

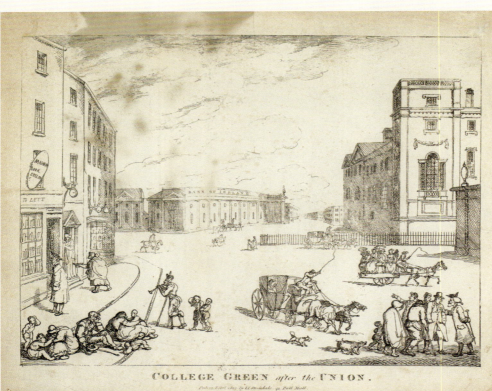

Figure 31 'College Green after the Union' – a cartoon depicting Dublin after the Union, published by J.J. Stockdale (London, 1812).

1

Dublin after the Union, 1800–41

The debate over the Act of Union convulsed Dublin. While the Act obviously had huge consequences for Ireland as a whole, it was in Dublin that opposition to the Union was loudest. The city was home to the parliament that would be abolished by a union, with all the damage that would ensue for the different groups whose livelihood depended on the parliament's activities and presence. In 1799, the city's lawyers, merchants, guilds and property developers had all declared their opposition to the measure, arguing that the presence of a parliament was bound up with Dublin's prosperity and prestige as the second city of the empire. Without the Irish parliament, they argued, the city would lapse into a sleepy backwater.[1] One cartoon, published during the debates, elaborated these fears particularly vividly. Titled *Union Street or ease and plenty*, the image is a prediction of what College Green would be like after the Union, with the Irish parliament buildings and Trinity College in the middle distance, and the premises of the elite Daly's Club in the foreground. The cartoon depicts College Green as overgrown, with pigs and dogs grazing in the streets. Daly's Club has been converted into a warehouse and cheap tavern, with plants growing from its parapets. The colonades of the parliament buildings have become a home to cows, while Trinity College is now a barracks, its front gate dominated by red-coated soldiers. Grass grows in the street, while vegetation creeps along the top of several buildings as the city seems to be returning to nature.

The idea that Dublin would be ruined by the loss of parliament had also been assiduously promoted by the numerous anti-Union pamphlets that were published during the Union debates. The *Freeman's Journal* reported how 'pamphlet writing is such a rage at present, that persons of all classes are scribbling upon the Union. It is the common question now in the street, "Are you writing a pamphlet against the Union?"'[2] These pamphlets made several arguments against the Union, but the most frequent was that the loss of the Irish parliament would lead to an exodus of Dublin's wealthy inhabitants. Not only would MPs and lords relocate to London, but the city would lose the colourful social world that the parliament helped sustain. Some anti-Union writers attempted to quantify the amount of money the city would lose with the departure of the 'winter gentry'. One writer asserted that the majority of Irish MPs kept a house in Dublin, which combined with peers and bishops meant the city contained 327 'active spenders', pumping over half a million pounds a year into the city economy. Later estimates would put the loss of money to the city as high as several million.[3] As another writer pointed out, these 'active spenders' helped sustain not only the construction industry, but a whole array of luxury trades – 'coach-makers, cabinet makers, woollen drapers, haberdashers … who live by the consumption of people of fortune'. In short, the Union would mean that 'Dublin must be a desert'.[4]

Yet, despite these warnings, the Union passed smoothly through parliament. On 1 January 1801, when the Act of Union formerly took effect, many expected distrubances in Dublin. On that day, Ireland offically became a part of the United Kingdom, while in the yard of Dublin Castle the new 'Union Jack' flag was hoisted for the first time. Groups of people crowded into the Castle yard. Yet, surprisingly, they seemed to have been drawn by curiosity rather than any desire to protest. Officials repeatedly commented on the tranquility with which the Union had been received in Dublin. The lord lieutenant, General Cornwallis, shrewdly observed that even if the Union was unpopular it was unlikely to motivate Dublin's poor. In his opinion the 'lower orders … hate both the British Government and their Irish rulers, but the latter I believe with more acrimony'.[5] Many of the city's inhabitants were by now severely disillusioned about the 'patriotic' credentials of the Irish parliament, while the recent rebellion and its subsequent repression had made many apathetic and weary. There was to be no riot over the Union Jack in Dublin in 1801. Yet, little more than a decade after the passing of the Union, one London publisher would release a set of images that argued the city had been adversely affected by the Union. The first image shows

Figure 32 Thomas Kelly (attributed), *Union Street, or ease and plenty* (Dublin, 1800).

Dublin before 1801, its streets full of carriages and elegant pedestrians, with busy shops and a procession of figures marching towards the parliament. The city is then shown after the Union, depicted as desolate with its streets empty except for beggars and a few stray coachmen. The parliament has been converted into a bank, and Trinity College's gates are empty and barren. It is a similar image to the earlier *Union Street* cartoon, portraying the city as economically depressed and near-vacant.

How accurate were such cartoons? One interesting source of information is the acccounts of visitors. In 1815, one traveller still claimed that Dublin was 'one of the finest cities I have ever visited, except London, to which however, in some respects, it is superior'. A decade later the novelist Walter Scott wrote that 'Dublin is splendid beyond my utmost expectations … They tell me the city is desolate [since the Union] of which I can see no appearance, but the deprivation caused by the retreat of the most noble and opulent inhabitants must be felt in a manner a stranger cannot conceive'.

Certainly, locals saw things differently. In 1818, the novelist C.R. Maturin, a native Dubliner, described his city in gothic terms: 'Its beauty continues … but it is the frightful lifeless beauty of a corpse; and the magnificent architecture of its public buildings seems like the skeleton of some gigantic frame, which the inhabiting spirit has deserted … the bones of the Behemeth'.[6] Who was right? There is evidence that a depature of the city's wealthy did indeed occur. In 1800, it was estimated that more than 200 MPs had their residence in the city. In 1823 only 6 MPs kept Dublin homes.[7] The loss of the parliamentary elite had changed the atmosphere of Dublin life, as one traveller observed 'the general character of the inhabitants, which was once gay and dissipated has now become more serious and religious … club-houses and gaming-tables are nearly deserted'. Others similarly commented on the serious mood and the absence of any local 'bucks' or dandies, indicating that the pace of life in Dublin seemed to slow down.[8]

One of the main predictions of anti-unionists had been that it would cause a Dublin property crash. There had indeed been a downturn in Dublin's construction sector, with a lowered demand for town houses in the immediate post-Union years. However, this lull was followed by a modest recovery after 1807. On the Fitzwilliam Estate, construction picked up on the area between Merrion Square and the Grand Canal, while on the north side the unfinished plots on Mountjoy Square were being laid out, with Gardiner Street continuing to be built up till 1820. However, there were indications that the type of house in demand was changing, with a preference for smaller homes. The average width of plots was generally shrinking, and the preference

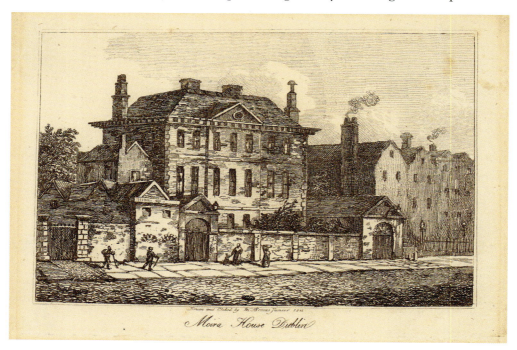

Figure 33 William Brocas, *Moira House, Dublin*, 1811. Once home to the aristocratic salon of Lord and Lady Moira, the house was purchased in 1826 by the Association for the Suppression of Mendicancy.

Figure 34 James Holmes, *Charles Gardiner, 1st Earl Blessington*, 1812.

was now for smaller, highly finished homes. The buildings in Henrietta Street ranged from three to five bays wide and had cavernous interiors. As such, they were no longer desirable or practical for many house buyers. It was telling that the larger city mansions were being repurposed as offices and public buildings. By 1830, Powerscourt House had become a Stamp Office, Aldborough House was a school, and Leinster House had become the headquarters of the Royal Dublin Society. Even Moira House, once the luxurious home of the earl of Moira, had become the Mendicity Institution, a body tasked with providing aid to Dublin's street beggars.[9]

Meanwhile, many of the larger town houses were being converted into hotels. By 1821 both the Shelbourne and Morrison hotels had become established as resorts of the gentry, with a city almanac listing 39 hotels, mainly concentrated around Sackville Street and Dawson Street, with beds available for 2 or 3*s.* a night.[10] As one account in 1822 described: 'the number of hotels in Dublin is prodigious. All the members of parliament, going and returning, pass a few days in Dublin: it was formerly a great capital, the seat of legislation, it is now a great place of passage'.[11] As a 'place of passage' there was a reduced demand for premium houses. The proliferation of hotels indicated the new, more mobile lifestyle of a section of the Irish elite, as cheaper transport made trips to the city both shorter and more frequent, and hence a town house less desirable.

There were also some other challenges to areas like the Gardiner Estate. Following the death of Luke Gardiner II in 1798, the estate came under the management of Charles John Gardiner, the 1st earl of Blessington (1782–1829). Blessington was only 16 when he inherited the estate and, in the words of one historian, 'He was feckless, extravagant, susceptible to the charms of the wrong sort of women, and too rich for his own good'.[12] After a chequered marital history, Blessington and his second wife left to live on the Continent in 1822, where they would spend the rest of that decade. In addition to their 'racy' social circle (they counted Lord Byron among their friends and allegedly engaged in an open relationship with a French count), the couple also accumulated serious debts due to a lavish lifestyle.[13]

Blessington's absence and instability led to the neglect of his Dublin property. Much of the Gardiner Estate's potential was squandered, with important projects stagnating. A good example was the plans for a 'Royal Circus', just beyond Dorset Street. Originally the brainchild of Luke Gardiner II, the plan was for a huge oval-shaped design, with two facing crescents of houses (not unlike the Royal Crescent in Bath). Had the Royal Circus been built it would have linked the different corners of the estate, with roads radiating from the Circus integrating the district. It was never constructed, although it would still appear on maps until the 1830s.

Meanwhile, existing parts of the estate were changing in ways that damaged its social status. The new bridge connecting Sackville Street to College Green had been a victory for the Gardiners in the 1790s. But the new bridge also transformed Sackville Street from a quiet residential district into a bustling thoroughfare. The result was a flight of the wealthier residents. By 1810, a travelogue dismissively described Sackville Street as including 'peers, pastry cooks and perfumers, bishops, butchers and brokers in old furniture, together with hotels … and a tolerable sprinkling of gin and whiskey shops'.[14] One of the results of Sackville Street's social decline was that it became an informal boundary, cutting the Gardiner Estate in two: the newer 'up-and-coming' residences to the east, and the older developments along Dorset Street/Bolton Street, such as Henrietta Street.

Which is not to say that Henrietta Street could no longer dazzle. In the decades after the Union, it was still home to some wealthy residents, if not quite as grand as in previous times. As mentioned, the earl of Blessington, the heir to the Gardiner Estate, maintained a home on the street, although he spent most of his time on the Continent. The street also was home to a fellow of Trinity College, the younger brother of Lord Donoughmore and several rich widows. One of these widows, Lady Harriet Daly, was reported to have owned an exceptional art collection, including a self-portrait by Remembrant, works by Federico Barocci, Guido Reni 'and others of equal merit', as well as 'two fine Bassans, Rubens, Tenier, &c'.[15] However, by far the most impressive figure on the street was Captain George Bryan (1770–1843), who had taken over one of the houses that the earl of Shannon had occupied.[16] Bryan is an intriguing figure. In his politics, he was active in the campaign for Catholic emancipation, being a correspondent of Daniel O'Connell and vigorous in his political advocacy. He was sometime described as Ireland's richest commoner, having inherited large estates from both sides of his family.[17] Bryan reportedly spent lavishly, keeping a coach-and-four that rivalled that of the lord lieutenant, and he allegedly paid to keep a mistress in a house near one of Dublin's fashionable squares with servants and a carriage of her own.[18] Bryan was an extravagant entertainer. One report from 1826, describing that year's festive season, reported on a ball given by Captain and Mrs Bryan

> at their mansion in Henrietta Street … The rooms were splendidly lighted with gas and wax lights – the rooms, stairs, &c were decorated with shrubs, flowers and laurels, tastefully disposed … .The company continued to arrive from ten to eleven, and an elegant and abundant supper laid out in lower apartments was announced at one. Champagne flowed briskly – dancing was resumed at two, and the gay party did not disperse till the morning light.[19]

Another indication of Bryan's lifestyle while at Henrietta Street can be gleaned from an account book which survives for his household which indicates the scope of their social entertainment: 'To de Villiers for champagne & liquors £15-3-0', an enormous sum to spend on alcohol.[20]

Yet despite the lifestyle of Captain Bryan, Henrietta Street was still not as glamorous or exclusive as it had been in the eighteenth century. In the years immediately after the Union, a local magazine had claimed that 'Henrietta Street, once the proud residence of the O'Neills, the Shannons, the Ponsonbys, the Kingsboroughs, the Mountjoys and the primates and chiefs of our religious establishments, is now a heavy melancholy group of monuments of our recent prosperity, it is literally covered with grass' (once again the image of grass growing in the streets was a powerful one).[21] While this was a massive exaggeration, by 1820 none of the street's residents were MPs or representative peers in the British parliament. In the cases of the former homes of Lismore and Shannon, buildings had been subdivided (or rather re-divided to the original layout), indicating a less ostentatious lifestyle.

Post-Union economy

If the residents of Henrietta Street were still enjoying at least moderate prosperity, what about the rest of the city? One of the predictions made by opponents of the Union was that the loss of the 'winter gentry' would mean less money being spent on Dublin-made luxury goods. Meanwhile the terms of the Union itself involved the removal of tariffs protecting Irish industry from British competition. The nineteenth century certainly did, it is true, witness a deterioration in Dublin's economy. While it is easy to blame this on the Union, the story is more complicated. For instance, the first decade or so after the Union was actually a period of mild prosperity. Following a subsistence crisis in 1800–1, the years up to 1815 were good times for city merchants and manufacturers, as an agricultural boom in the countryside also led to an influx of money into the capital. Brewing, distilling and light textiles all did well in these years. However, this came to an end in 1815 with the close of the Napoleonic Wars, as the bubble burst in Irish agricultural prices. With landlords and strong farmers unable to collect the high rents they had been accustomed to, the wealthy began to reduce their consumption of Dublin goods and to avoid visiting the city itself. Instead, they went to the Continent where living was cheaper, or else remained on their rural estates to 'retire to the bacon and poultry about their country house'.[22]

A later inquiry would claim that it was not the Union, but the end of the wars in 1815 that did the real damage to Dublin's economy 'in consequence of the absence of the nobility and gentry who went to the Continent'.[23] The end of the wars also coincided with severe weather patterns due to volcanic eruptions, as 1816 was the 'year without a summer'. The result was a subsistence crisis that only exacerbated urban unemployment, with more than 10,000 people seeking relief in city fever hospitals or

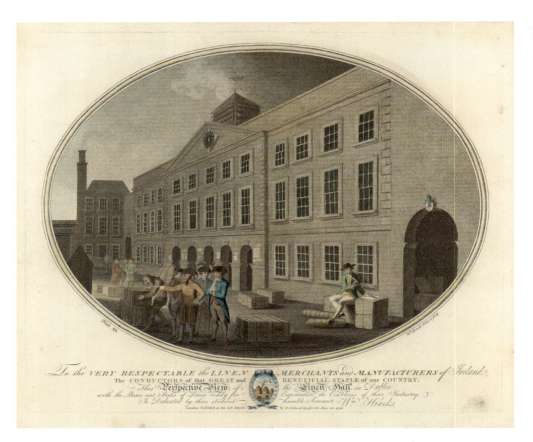

Figure 35 William Hincks, *A view of the Linenhall in Dublin*, 1791.

the House of Industry. There would be little recovery for Dublin's economy after 1817, however, as a series of further crises hit the city hard. There was a run on Irish banks in 1820, which further depressed business confidence. Yet even worse was to come. In 1825, the final remaining tariffs on British imports were removed under the terms of the Union. This occurred just at the moment of a depression for British manufacturers who responded by 'dumping' their goods onto Irish markets at heavily discounted prices. This was a disaster for Dublin, heavily damaging the city's textile industries. Manufacturing textiles like silk and wool had once provided jobs to tens of thousands in Dublin. By the 1830s these jobs were drying up.[24]

In certain industries it was a case of competition from other Irish cities. For instance, by the 1820s Dublin was decisively losing its share of the Irish linen trade to firms in Ulster. In the eighteenth century, Dublin's Linenhall had been a bustling centre for that trade. Located around the corner from Henrietta Street, this complex of buildings contained several courtyards and a series of storehouses linked by galleries and piazzas, as well as a coffee room and a boardroom for the trustees of the city's Linen Board. Dublin's linen workers had always relied on Ulster for their raw material, and again the evidence is in the local street names: Lurgan Street, Coleraine

Street, Lisburn Street. In the nineteenth century, however, Ulster manufacturers were bypassing Dublin and taking over the processing, sale and export of linen goods.[25] The Linenhall, which had employed so many local weavers, had ceased to function as an active market in 1828, largely due to competition from Belfast.[26]

The 1820s were also the period when steam-powered shipping meant that transport costs dropped quickly, further integrating Ireland into the British industrial economy. Dublin's economic problems were due to wider trends that the city was far from alone in experiencing. Dublin was fundamentally a high-cost location specializing in luxury manufactures. Its workshops had been struggling against British competition for several decades before the Union. The process of industrialization worked against Dublin retaining its workshop industries. On the whole the Industrial Revolution did not favour the older commercial and capital cities like Dublin – it was to be the age of newer towns like Birmingham, Manchester and, significantly, Belfast. This shifted the terms of trade in ways that hurt Dublin manufacturers. Increasingly Dublin was a conduit for agricultural Ireland, with its own workshops losing out. The industries that did prosper during the nineteenth century tended to be those linked with the food and drink trade. None of these employed numbers large enough to compensate for the decline of Dublin's traditional industries. As a result, working-class Dubliners were increasingly reliant on low skill and casual labour.[27]

St Michan's Parish

These shifts in Dublin's economic and social structures could be easily observed in the neighbourhoods that bordered Henrietta Street. The street had always been situated in a socially diverse area; it was technically part of St Michan's Parish. The parish extended northwards from the river, extending to the west as far as Smithfield, and to the east nearly as far as Capel Street. It ran along the spine of Church Street to encompass not only the King's Inns, but the Linenhall and the workhouse as well. The parish represented a large chunk of the north-west of the city, and contained a range of very different neighbourhoods. Along the quays the Four Courts attracted solicitors and attorneys, with Ormond Quay a busy commercial thoroughfare. Stretching northward behind these quays lay an area characterized by small traders, workshops and marketplaces.

St Michan's contained one of the densest concentrations of food and animal markets in the city: vegetables, eggs, meat, straw, horses, fish, cattle – all of these could be purchased in nearby markets like Smithfield's Cattle and Hay Markets, as well as Ormond Market. Linked to the presence of these markets were the numerous slaughterhouses that dotted the area, with butchers, chandlers and the leather manufacturers all plying their trade. The area's very street names reflected the importance of the markets: Duck Lane, Fisher's Lane, Bull Lane, Beef Row.

In the eighteenth century, St Michan's had been home to several thriving artisan communities, with various small manufacturers providing good employment, such

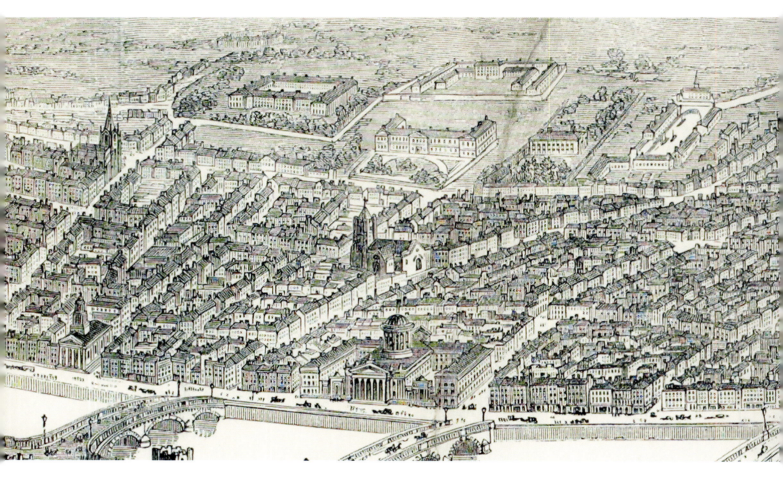

Figure 36 'Panorama of the City of Dublin', published in *The Illustrated London News*, June 1846. Detail showing north-west of the city, including the parish of St Michan's.

as those firms involved in glove-making or silk weaving. In the years after 1815, these local industries stagnated and in 1818 a report claimed that nearly half the parish's 22,000 inhabitants required some sort of poor relief, and that a large number of those were skilled artisans unable to find work.[28] By 1845, there were few manufacturing jobs left in St Michan's. The good jobs were in Jameson's, the three breweries and three foundries that still remained, but even in these businesses work tended to be casual and low paid.

The parish's economy continued to be dominated by the food and drink trades, thanks to the presence of the various markets. This was important, as these trades attracted many of the men and women from the countryside who were coming to Dublin in increasing numbers due to a series of rural crises.[29] Many of those who came in search of work found themselves in the north-west of the city, approached by the northern and western roads, or perhaps by the Royal Canal. Many found accommodation in one of the growing number of 'lodging houses' in the neighbourhood of St Michan's. It was said that the markets district attracted 'a vast number of paupers, some seeking

Figure 37 Ordnance Survey map of Dublin, 1847. Detail showing part of St Michan's Parish, including the Fish Market, Bull Lane and Boot Lane. As the names indicate, the parish was characterized by food markets and small clothing manufacturing.

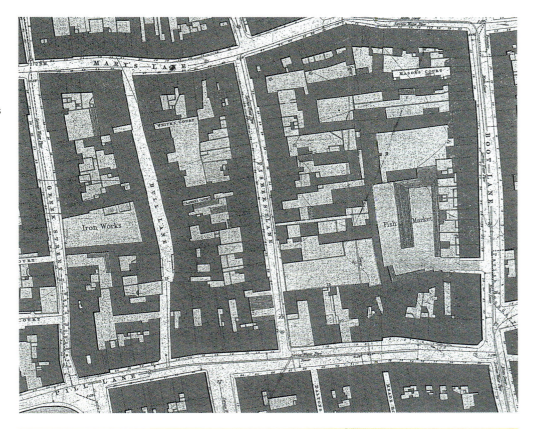

Figure 38 Jameson's Bow Street distillery; illustration from *The whiskey distilleries of the United Kingdom* (1887).

to live by employment therein, and others by very objectionable means'.[30] Even more came to Dublin in search of charity or official relief, and it was repeatedly observed that

> in times of great distress or severity when only such aid is resorted to, the poor from various parts of the country flock to the city [Dublin], in hopes of obtaining a share of these contributions which, under better regulations, should be exclusively appropriated to the local poor.[31]

Dublin contained the largest number of these poor relief institutions, whether it was the House of Industry, the several fever hospitals, or the various charitable infirmaries and religious missions.

Workhouses, railways and lawyers

The issue of poor relief, and the institutions that dispensed such aid, was crucial to the history of Henrietta Street. To the west of the street lay the neighbourhood of Grangegorman, an area that was home to a dense concentration of institutions that catered to the sick and the poor. Since 1791, the House of Industry had been located

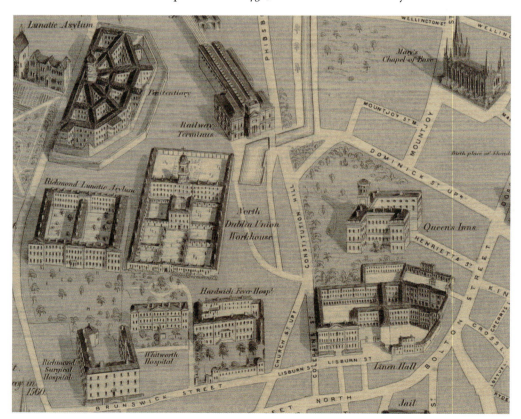

Figure 39 Daniel Heffernan, *Dublin in 1861*, map, 1861. Detail showing the complex of institutions at Grangegorman, including penitentiaries, asylums and hospitals; as well as the nearby railway terminus.

Figure 40 George Petrie, *The King's Inns and Royal Canal Harbour*, 1821.

Figure 41 Henry Adlard, *Terminus of the Midland Great Western Railway* (c.1850).

DUBLIN AFTER THE UNION, 1800–41

Figure 42 William Brocas, *Dublin's King's Inns*, mid-nineteenth century.

here, with several other institutions springing up nearby in the first two decades of the Union: the Hardwicke Fever Hospital (1803), the Bedford Asylum for Children (1806), the Richmond Surgical Hospital (1811), the Richmond Asylum (1811–15), and the Whitworth Chronic Hospital (1818). The founding of the Richmond General Penitentiary in 1820, which included a female penitentiary, produced one of the most intimidating set of buildings in the entire complex. This grim prison was based on the ideas of Jeremy Bentham, with a radial layout in which a small numbers of staff kept the entire prison under perpetual surveillance, with prisoners placed in solitary confinement upon their arrival.[32] In essence, the nineteenth century witnessed not only an immiseration of Dublin's working classes, but also an 'institutionalization' of misery in the shape of new, repressive institutions. It was no longer sufficient to simply pity the poor or move them along, there was now an impulse to classify, confine, discipline and punish.[33] Thousands of the poor flocked to these institutions out of desparation, seeking aid wherever they could find it.

In addition to Grangegorman, Henrietta Street was also in close proximity to an emerging transport hub, with the Royal Canal Harbour at Constitution Hill linking the nearby markets district to the countryside. After 1842, the area grew even busier with the construction of the massive terminus of the Midland Great Western Railway, designed in an imposing Egyptian style by the architect John Skipton Mulvaney.

While all these areas (St Michan's, Broadstone, Grangegorman) had an effect on Henrietta Street, the single greatest influence was its proximity to a hub of the Irish

Figure 43 Photo of the gate between Henrietta Street and King's Inns.

legal profession, the new buildings of the King's Inns. Ground was broken on the site in August 1800 after the old site of the King's Inns (where the current Four Courts are located) had become dilapidated. The Benchers of the King's Inns, its governing body, bought two plots at the top of Henrietta Street named Plover's Fields and the Primate's Gardens.

The King's Inns was James Gandon's last public project in Dublin, although it was eventually completed by others, such as his assistant Henry Aaron Baker and, much later, Francis Johnston (the man who designed the General Post Office). Despite Gandon's impressive reputation, his plans had not been popular with Luke Gardiner II. Gardiner objected to the orientation of the layout, with the King's Inns having its back to the street. Writing in 1798, Gardiner angrily stated that 'I have already seen two plans and elevations, the one by Mr Gandon, which I entirely disapprove of, as I think it would rather be a deformity than an improvement'. Gardiner complained that Gandon's building was located 'without any attention whatsoever' to the street.[34]

In the years immediately after 1800, the site was already a hub of activity for the legal profession, with temporary buildings erected on the site in early 1798. The complex was completed in 1817, but it seems that the Benchers had financially overstretched themselves, having committed to disadvantageous leases on the property. As a result, they agreed to allow the government to convert the library range of the new site into a registry of deeds, in return for financial concessions. With government taking over part of the new building, the Society of the King's Inns needed a new site for their library. For this purpose they purchased the former primate's residence in Henrietta

Street in 1823. While the plan was originally to merely convert the building, retaining the façade, structural problems resulted in the house being demolished and the current premises being built by Frederick Darley. Supposedly completed by 1828, it was only ready for readers in 1832.[35] Even before the library had been built, the primate's residence had been used as the offices of the 'Prerogative Court' – a type of ecclesiastical court with jurisdiction over divorce proceedings and the probate of certain wills.[36] The presence of the prerogative court led to several lawyers who worked in the court coming to live on Henrietta Street. The opening of the King's Inns Library in the 1830s attracted several more lawyers to the street, creating an informal collegial network. By 1834 almost every building in Henrietta Street was listed as containing a member of some branch of the legal profession: 9 proctors, 4 attorneys, 1 barrister and a judge.[37]

There had been even more ambitious plans to make the area the centre of Irish legal education. At this time, the King's Inns did not provide any formal legal education, and as a result Ireland's trainee attorneys were obliged to attend the Inns of Court in London. However, once they returned to Ireland their careers differed from their English counterparts. Unlike in England, Irish legal students rarely enrolled in 'Chambers'. The practice of 'keeping Chambers' was where several barristers shared rooms, usually under a form of partnership which specialized in certain fields of law (land law, criminal law, etc.). For students, a term in these chambers could be a useful opportunity to learn vital aspects of a barrister's job. In contrast, in Ireland, young barristers were (and still are) left to take their chances 'deviling', hitching along to an individual barrister for a period before being left to their own devices. Which is not to say that there were not attempts to introduce such a system of chambers to Ireland. In fact, the issue of building legal 'chambers' near the King's Inns had repeatedly arisen over the years. One of the reasons why the King's Inns had been constructed facing out onto Constitution Hill was that it was assumed that just such a series of chambers would later be built on the site. In 1804, James Gandon supplied several different estimates for the building of such chambers, while a series of drawings for these hypothetical chambers was done by the architect Francis Johnston in 1813. The issue of chambers arose again in 1825, with the architect Frederick Darley drawing sketches of a new street, leading from the grounds of the King's Inn to new chambers.[38]

Nonetheless, these various proposals came to nothing. In addition to a lack of funds, there was a disagreement within the Law Society over whether it was best to locate potential chambers near the King's Inns or at the Four Courts. As a result, 'official' chambers were never built. Nonetheless, an informal system of chambers sprung up in various parts of the city, with barristers sharing rooms under specialized partnerships. However, one man had a plan to change this situation by transforming Henrietta Street into a series of formal chambers. This was Tristram Kennedy (1805-85), a lawyer, land agent and politician. The son of an Anglican clergyman from Donegal, Kennedy had received his legal training in both London and Dublin, being

Figure 44 (opposite) Drawing of King's Inns with proposed additional buildings and map of planned circle of 'chambers' in front of existing structure. While never constructed, these plans demonstrate the ambitions of some in the legal community to transform the King's Inns into a much larger complex.

Figure 45 Blessington House, illustration from *Dublin Penny Journal*, 13 February 1836.

called to the Irish bar in 1834. As he began to practice law in the 1830s, there was a growing movement for the reform of legal education in both Britain and Ireland. Kennedy was part of this optimistic wave of reform and in 1839 he launched a new school, the Dublin Law Institute. Its aim was to provide 'a preparatory system of legal education; to elevate the standard of knowledge in both branches of the legal profession; to cultivate diligence; to encourage the study of law as a science'.[39] Kennedy had recruited rising and talented barristers as lecturers for the Institute. Even more impressively, for the Institute's premises he had purchased Blessington House, the former home of Luke Gardiner at No. 10 Henrietta Street.

Tristram Kennedy had acquired the house in 1837, converting it and renaming it as 'Queen's Inns Chambers' after the launch of the Law Institute two years later. In 1840, Kennedy threw a lavish party in No. 10 to celebrate the marriage of Queen Victoria to Prince Albert, with one newspaper describing the event:

> the building was tastefully illuminated and the several transparencies with which it was decorated were much admired for their elegance. The large centre figure of the queen, surrounded by the allegorical emblems of the arts and sciences, was beautiful in the extreme, and the judicious application of the gas-light tended much to heighten the effect.[40]

Figure 46 Portrait of Tristram Kennedy.

The following year Kennedy purchased the house next door, linking Nos. 9 and 10 together into what he called 'Queen's Inns Chambers Upper'. The distinction of 'Upper' was because Kennedy soon purchased No. 3 Henrietta Street, at the very end of the same terrace, which he dubbed 'Queen's Inns Chambers Lower'. The Dublin Law Institute was short lived, with Kennedy winding it down in 1845, largely due to the hostility of the King's Inns and certain prominent members of the Irish legal world. Shortly after this, Kennedy was to end his own legal career, instead focusing on politics, being elected as an MP for Louth in 1852. Yet despite his withdrawal from the legal profession, Kennedy continued to purchase houses on Henrietta Street for the purpose of leasing them as legal chambers. Over the next several decades, Kennedy acquired one entire terrace, from Nos. 3 to 10, as well as Nos. 11 and 13 on the opposite side of the street. These were all referred to, informally, as the Queen's Inns Chambers and in 1884 the street was described by the *Irish Times* as having the 'air of a legal university'.[41] After the 1860s, Tristram Kennedy moved to England, splitting his time between Somerset and London. However, he continued to be active in Irish legal and political circles. Notably, he continued to argue in favour of Henrietta Street as a legal enclave. He attempted to persuade the Benchers of the King's Inns to purchase the remaining property on the street that was not already in use as chambers. He further suggested erecting a gateway at the bottom of the hill to encompass the street as an enclosed legal quarter akin to the Temple in London, a suggestion that was not followed up. Instead, Kennedy's death in 1885 would result in the sale of his many properties and would drastically change the profile of the street.[42]

A middle-class city?

By the 1840s, Henrietta Street had seen some stark changes: Luke Gardiner's house was now legal chambers, the old Archbishop's mansion was now the King's Inns library. The eighteenth-century Protestant elite had been replaced by the legal profession. Dublin had once been a city dominated by the aristocracy, now it was a city defined by its middle classes. For instance, College Green, the symbolic heart of the city, was no longer dominated by a parliament, but had grown into a central business district,

Figure 47 Sidebotham, *A view of the Four Courts*, c.1810.

with stockbrokers, insurance agents and banks. While finance was important, among the 'middling' classes it was professionals who set the tone. In 1810 a visitor to Dublin wrote how 'a physician here is almost at the pinnacle of greatness: there are few resident nobility or gentry since the Union and the professors of law and medicine may be said to form the aristocracy of the place'.[43] The *Irish Times* later described Dublin society as 'essentially a professional aristocracy. Doctors, lawyers and clergymen and their families form its staple ingredients. The Four Courts supplies the aristocracy which has deserted Dublin'.[44] This was reflected in the huge growth in the numbers training in law and medicine in the city, with numbers peaking in 1830.[45]

Yet the rise of the middle classes could not mask the serious social problems that were affecting the city. As early as 1822, a parliamentary inquiry reported

> Dublin's advance as a place of commerce, and as the seat of the courts of law, has counteracted in some respects the decline of its wealth and resources; but the increasing poverty of its inhabitants is still most melancholy and rapid … many of the most valuable houses and streets of the city of Dublin … have fallen into decay, and are now inhabited either by the most abject poor, or at least by the humblest traders.

Insurance evaluations confirm that large chunks of the city were decreasing in value.[46] The transformation of previously well-off neighbourhoods into 'slums' was the single

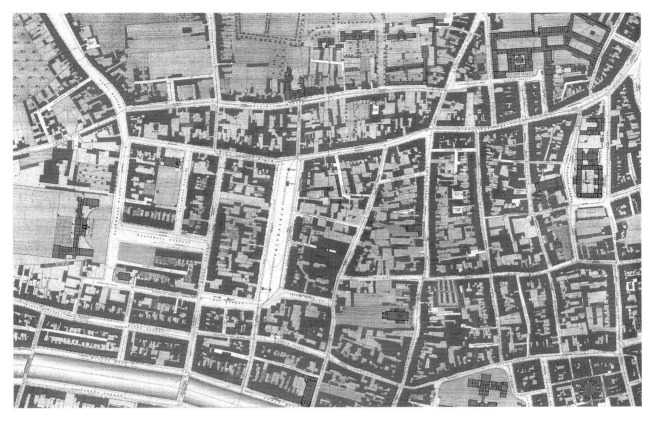

Figure 48 Ordnance Survey map of Dublin, 1847, showing the north-west of the city.

biggest development during these years. As the historian Maurice Craig remarked 'after the Union Dublin could not afford such a vast acreage of "good" property; the "good" tenants simply were not there to live in it all: and even the truly incredible numbers of lawyers who moved into the "good" streets on the north side were unable to hold it up forever'.[47] While Henrietta Street benefitted from the presence of lawyers, only metres away, the neighbouring streets and alleys were going into a serious decline.

Behind the 'good' streets like Henrietta Street or the area around the Four Courts, there was a labyrinth of narrow lanes and alleys that were very far from 'good'. In the parish of St Michan's, the numerous slaughterhouses and markets, combined with a lack of running water or drainage, produced horrific conditions. At the beginning of the century, St Michan's had *not* been one of the most deprived areas in the city. By mid-century, however, things had begun to change, as this parish, which had been described as being 'once one of the most respectable in Dublin', was now quickly falling into decay.[48] Parish records from the 1830s reveal a growing number of houses being listed as 'down', indicating they were ruined but not unoccupied. The records expose clusters of appalling poverty in now-forgotten back courts like Rice's Yard or Smith's Court.[49] In 1833, an investigation revealed that 24,000 people in the parish were living in 1612 houses, three-quarters of which were 'in such a state of filth as, in itself, would be sufficient to generate disease'. A later report described how 'the courts and backplaces are … quite unfit for the residence of human beings … pipewater, lime washing, dust bin, privy – these are things almost unknown. The stench and disgusting filth of these places are inconceivable'.[50] The lord mayor went as far as to call the parish the 'most pestilent part of the city', a verdict that had been confirmed by the high proportion of casualties in the recent 1832 cholera epidemic, with 1,600 dead in St Michan's out of a city-wide total of 6,000.[51]

The poverty in the areas surrounding Henrietta Street was well known thanks to the work of one man – Thomas Willis. In 1845, Willis published a pamphlet entitled *Facts connected with the social and sanitary condition of the working classes in the city of Dublin*. It was an astonishing analysis of the poverty and hardship in St Michan's Parish, using both the information provided by the recent 1841 census as well as Willis' own first-hand investigation. The pamphlet gave a vivid description of the living conditions of the poor, as well as providing statistical evidence about the depth of the public health crisis in the city. Willis hoped that by exposing the conditions in one of Dublin's poorest parishes, it would, hopefully, encourage reform. While there had been earlier attempts to focus attention on Dublin's slums, these efforts to clean up the poorer neighbourhoods tended only to happen during times of epidemics such as typhus or cholera, and these were temporary efforts, abandoned once a crisis was over. Thomas Willis now argued that this was not good enough, something much bigger and long term was needed to help the city's poor.

What made Willis' study so powerful was his genuine empathy for the poor and his willingness to go door-to-door, even into the most squalid backstreet tenements, in order to chronicle the plight of those in need. Willis described over-crowded conditions and squalor that was to become all too common over the next decades:

> In some rooms in these situations it is not an infrequent occurrence to see above a dozen human beings crowded into a space not fifteen feet square. Within this space the food of these wretched beings, such as it is, must be prepared; within this space they must eat and drink; men, women and children must strip, dress, sleep. In cases of illness the calls of nature must be relieved, and when death releases one of the inmates the corpse must of necessity remain for days within the room.[52]

Willis' description of St Michan's came from close first-hand experience, having lived and worked in the area his entire life. Willis was a local apothecary (a type of pharmacist who also offered general medical advice), having been based in North King Street and then Upper Ormond Quay. He took a close interest in the lives of his customers and neighbours, and in 1842 he had been elected to the board of guardians of the North Dublin Union, bringing him to even greater contact with the sick and destitute. Willis was convinced that the problems of disease could not be solved by

Figure 49 (left) Thomas Willis, *Facts connected with the social and sanitary condition of the working classes in the city of Dublin*, 1845.
Figure 50 (right) Photograph portrait of Thomas Willis.

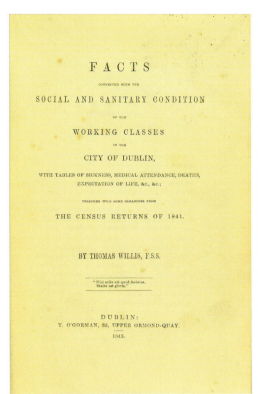

medicine alone, but by improved sanitation and a healthier environment for the working class. What was needed was improved access to running water, better sewage disposal and refuse collection. While these things would cost money, Willis was clever in appealing to a middle-class readership by arguing that such infrastructure works would actually save the taxpayer money. He pointed out that the cost of improving water and sanitation would be less than the cost of maintaining large workhouses, as fewer people would have to resort to the workhouse in times of disease and epidemic. Willis argued that institutions like the workhouse were 'destructive to the best feelings of the human heart … There must be something rotten in the state of society when such remedies alone exist for disease and destitution'. Willis would long campaign for social reform and the betterment of conditions for Dublin's poor. Despite worsening health problems (including the onset of blindness in his later years), he continued to be active in a range of charities, being closely involved with the work of the Society of St Vincent de Paul before his death in 1881. Yet Willis remains best known for his landmark 1845 pamphlet, a work that was published only months before the onset of a famine that would have grave consequences for the parish and for the city.

Figure 51 James Mahony, *Dublin from the spire of Saint George's Church, Hardwicke Place*, 1854.

2

Famine and decline, 1845–90

Among the collections of the National Gallery of Ireland is a watercolour by the artist James Mahony. Painted in 1854, it is a view of Dublin, looking out from the spire of Saint George's Church, in Hardwicke Place. The spire's height allowed Mahony to look south over the city, providing a panorama. In the foreground, on the left, is Mountjoy Square, its gardens colourfully depicted. In the right-hand corner are the Rotunda Gardens; and to the left of them is Sackville Street, leading down to the river. In the middle distance, the southside of the city spreads across to the Dublin mountains. It is a beautiful and fascinating painting, portraying a city that looks like it is thriving; its chimneys smoking, its quays packed with ships. Yet this had been painted in the immediate aftermath of a famine that had killed over a million people. In fact, despite his undoubted skill as a painter, Mahony is perhaps better known for his famine sketches, showing emaciated figures in Skibbereen and Clonakilty. While there had been crop failures before, the Great Famine which occurred between 1845 and 1851 was something else entirely. The Famine is arguably *the* defining event in modern Irish history. In only five years, somewhere in the region of 1.1 million Irish people died, with another 1.2 million emigrating out of desperation.

The Famine was most deeply felt in the western seaboard counties, with the most common images of famine being those associated with the remote countryside. There is a perception that Dublin was little affected by the crisis, an idea that Mahony's painting might seem to confirm. It is true, that the poor in Dublin had certain advantages over their rural counterparts: their diet was not quite as reliant on potatoes, they had access to food imported via the port, and they also had access to a well-developed network of medical and charitable institutions in the city. However, it is wrong to think the city was unaffected by starvation. In 1846, an American woman named Asenath Nicholson described her arrival in Ireland. While she had heard reports of the famine that had recently swept across the country, she was shocked to find signs of starvation even in Dublin. She recounted meeting a Dublin man 'emaciated to the last degree; he was tall, his eyes prominent, his skin shrivelled … In my childhood I had been frightened with the stories of ghosts, and had seen actual skeletons; but imagination had come short of the sight of this man'.[1]

With the onset of the Famine, Dublin's poor were under increased strain, with reports of many resorting to pawnshops, as well as an increased number of beggars. There was also a rapid deterioration of the urban environment, with the streets muddied and strewn with waste, a result of the large numbers coming into the city. The Famine resulted in the large towns and cities of Ireland actually increasing in size, as the starving fled to them in search of short-term relief or the opportunity to emigrate.[2] Dublin's population grew during the Famine, increasing by 25,000, a growth of 11 per cent, between 1841 and 1851. Tellingly, the areas whose populations had grown the most were the docklands. The reason was the vast numbers passing through the port, some of whom were sent back by British authorities, with this 'reflux' settling near the docks. The other area whose population increased rapidly was the area near Grangegorman, due to the location of the North Dublin Union Workhouse. One of the reasons so many migrants came to Dublin was the concentration of health, aid and administrative functions within the city. After London, Dublin was the key decision-making centre, containing the office of the Lord Lieutenant, the Poor Law Commission, the Board of Works and the Central Board of Health. In addition to its two huge workhouses, there were several charitable hospitals, infirmaries and asylums, all of which would fill beyond capacity in these years.

These institutions attracted those suffering in the countryside, and by late 1847 the capacity of Dublin's two workhouses had been increased to 4,000 inmates, while overcrowding at the south city fever hospital resulted in temporary fever 'sheds' being opened at Kilmainham and Glasnevin. The North Dublin Union recorded how

Figure 52 John Leech, 'A court for King Cholera', *Punch* magazine, 1852.

'numbers of persons are crowding through the streets, in Fever, from want of room in the hospitals, and that unless immediate accommodation is provided for them there will be a fearful spread of fever'. By the next year, as many as 60,000 people in the city were in receipt of outdoor relief. The number of deaths due to famine in Dublin city has been estimated as being close to 5 per cent of its 1841 population. Death rates were highest among children who entered the workhouses alone, as well as among those who had made their way to the city from the southern and western counties. Those who fled to Dublin were often malnourished and sick. and as a result exacerbated a health crisis, as typhus, dysentery and fever ran rampant. An epidemic of cholera swept through the city in 1849, brutally revealing the vulnerability of the poor.[3] While depictions of the Famine in an urban setting are comparatively rare, we do have a vivid image from an English publication, *Punch* magazine, depicting the unsanitary urban conditions that functioned as a 'court for King Cholera'.

Just as in earlier famines, entry points to the city for rural migrants were badly hit by disease. In St Michan's in the north-west, a chilling indication of how the Famine affected the poor was in the noticeable drop in the number of baptisms in the parish in 1847–8, as infant mortality spiked. The contrast had never been starker between the prosperous areas of the city, insulated from the Famine, and the poverty-stricken slums. The wealthy of Dublin seemed largely indifferent to the plight of their fellow citizen. As the *Freeman's Journal* noted we find that the citizens of Dublin have a more intimate knowledge of the want, and misery, and suffering of the cottier population of Skibereen, of Mayo, and of Clare, than they have of the more appalling destitution of the hundreds of human beings who are huddled together in the lodging houses of Dublin.[4]

In 1851, as the country slowly began to recover from the worst of the Famine, a new census revealed how Dublin had been affected. In addition to having added some 25,000 new inhabitants, the city had changed in other ways. Close to 40 per cent of its residents were not Dublin-born. Strikingly, the new census revealed a shrinking of the middle class. In 1841, two-thirds of Dubliners derived their income from 'vested means, professions or the direction of labour'. In 1851, this group had more than halved, to only 30 per cent. Clearly the urban bourgeoisie had been badly hit by the economic collapse the Famine had precipitated. Many had used their remaining resources to emigrate, whether to Britain, America or beyond.[5] However, in Henrietta Street it was clear that one part of the middle class, the lawyers, were actually finding plenty of work due to the Famine. Henrietta Street was to become the home of an important new institution: the Encumbered Estates Court.

The Encumbered Estates Court

To understand what the Encumbered Estates Court was, we need to quickly examine the nature of landownership in Ireland before the Famine. In the nineteenth century, a frequent criticism of Irish landlords was that they did not invest in their estates, failing to introduce improvements or new agricultural techniques that required capital. There was a reason for this. Irish landlords may have been pitiless in extracting rents and evicting overdue tenants, but, ironically, they too were often pursued by merciless creditors. Having frequently indulged in lavish lifestyles that their rental incomes could not afford, many landlords were heavily in debt even before the Famine. Many landlords had inherited their estates as part of a trust or 'entail' which prevented the sale or division of estates, sometimes placing various financial obligations on the inheritor. Combined with the various obligations of extended family and farm, many landed estates had been mortgaged multiple times. With multiple mortgages and liens against these properties, debts frequently accumulated far beyond the value of the land used as collateral. These claims by creditors to the indebted landlord's estate were known as 'encumbrances'. As estates were often the subject of multiple 'encumbrances' from several creditors, there were, therefore, multiple parties who had a claim to the property. The result was that the land could be described as having a 'defective title', as the 'title' or deeds to the land could not be legally transferred to a new buyer until all the encumbrances were first taken care of. As such, many potential buyers were hesitant to purchase these estates, as they feared long and costly court proceedings.

Figure 53 'Heroism of an Irish landlord: the Irish tax-gatherer', *The Illustrated London News*, 1845.

This was an issue even before the Famine, representing an obstacle to the injection of capital into the countryside from new owners. However, following the repeated failures of the potato crop after 1845, the effect of lost rents, heavy poor rates and (in some cases) significant expenditures on charity, these indebted landowners were in an even tighter spot. Foreclosure notices rained down upon Irish landlords unable to discharge the claims of their various creditors, yet simultaneously unable to sell due to a market frozen by fears over 'defective titles'. As a result, two Encumbered Estates Act were passed in 1848 and 1849, which were designed to facilitate the sale of these lands. These Acts established the Encumbered Estates Court, a venue through which the state took ownership of properties and sold them on, without any drawn-out proceedings and accompanied by a new parliamentary title which ensured there was no further threat of contested ownership.[6]

The new Encumbered Estates Court was composed of three commissioners, who first met in 1849, acquiring premises at No. 14 Henrietta Street. The house was soon altered, with the coach house at the back of the building being adapted into a courtroom, a place where the commissioners would sit together twice a week and where public sales of estates would be held. This backyard courtroom was fairly basic, later described as a 'large, chilly-looking room, without a ceiling between the roof and the floor, furnished with some rows of seats for the public, a small table covered with green cloth for the bar and the attorneys, and an elevated bench unadorned even with the royal arms, for the commissioners'. While sales days and formal appeals took place in this courtroom, within the main building each commissioner tackled their individual caseloads. Each of the commissioners had sets of private and public chambers, located on the first and second floors of No. 14. Indeed, every floor of the house was put to use, with the basement and attic occupied by a housekeeper and several servants. The ground floor was as the public office of the chief commissioner, with one of the side rooms acting as a private chamber for the commissioner and his clerk. So great were the commissioners' demands for space that they also took over No. 4 Henrietta Street, across the road. This building was not used for public sales but instead was used as a registry and records office, with No. 4's basement made 'fire-proof for the safe custody of title deeds, &c'.[7]

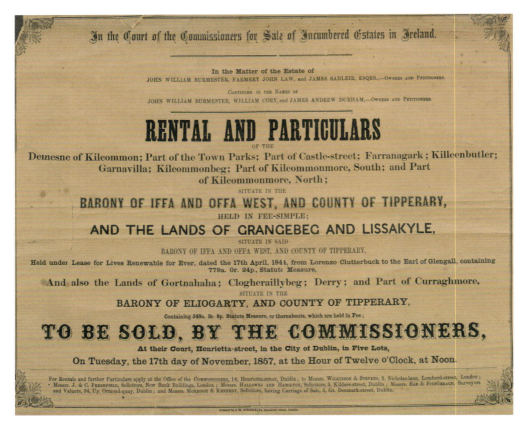

Figure 54
Advertisement for sale of lands in Tipperary by Incumbered Estates Court, 1857. The auction would have taken place in No. 14 Henrietta Street.

By all account the court was busy: 'the quantity of work which flowed in upon the court, especially in the years 1851–4 was in excess of all anticipations … Little account was made of the usual office hours, or even of customary periods of vacation. The only anxiety was to clear off the heavy work in the offices as rapidly and efficiently as possible'.[8] There is a vivid account of the activities of the court, written in 1858 and describing the court at No. 14 as a no-frills, no-nonsense place: 'everything about it has the same naked unpretending air. The visitor will observe little of that tranquillity and silence which usually reign in courts of law'. However, the author claimed that it was during the auctions of estates that 'the action of the court may best be observed … There is, in all probability, little trace of the law to be seen. Barristers there are none. On a day like this, *their* occupation is gone. Attorneys indeed are present in abundance, but their whole duty is to bid for those who either are absent on other business, or whose timidity will not allow them'. The account paints a picture of a busy sales day akin to a country auction: 'all are busy with the printed rentals which contain the description of the different lots … some making calculations to see how far they may bid'. These auctions were also an occasion in which lawyers and land agents swapped gossip, particularly about rural disturbances: 'one idler tells another how an agent was shot here a year ago; how a process-server was beaten almost to death there; and how the population of *Ballyblank* generally have from time immemorial been a very rough set to deal with'.[9]

Despite the rough-and-ready nature of the court, commentators had high hopes that it could rectify many of rural Ireland's problems. It was believed that the court was paving the way for a new landowning class that was better positioned to invest in the countryside, 'mercantile men ... with capital and energy'. These new landlords, it was hoped, would displace 'the old race of proprietors ... so long as the old lords of the soil remained, there could be but small hope for the progress of Ireland'. Obviously, the older generation of landlords felt differently. The communist Frederick Engels described how Irish landlords 'live in fear of the Encumbered Estates Court'.[10] The legislation that established the Estates Court also allowed for the sale of estates *without the consent of the owner*, provided the level of debt was great enough. This meant that the sale of an estate could be forced at a time of depressed land prices, something Irish landlords bitterly resented. One such landlord was Stephen Moore, the 3rd earl of Mountcashel. Lord Mountcashel was no stranger to Henrietta Street: his mother was Margaret King who had grown up in No. 15, next door to where the Estates Court now sat. The earl was outraged at the sale of some of his estate at what he felt was a low rate. He made his displeasure known, particularly in regards to one of the commissioners, a Mr Hargreaves, a rather short gentleman, whose office was located on the third floor of No. 14. During the court proceedings, Mountcashel yelled out that it was bad enough to have his estate confiscated, but to be 'sold up by a dwarf in a garret' was 'more than he could endure'.[11]

Despite the brisk business being done by the court in Henrietta Street, ultimately it proved to be an unsuitable location for the court. As early as 1850, *The Times* referred to several complaints having been made about 'the limited size of the court, as it is facetiously called'. In one case, a sale of an estate had to be adjourned and carried out elsewhere because of the restrictions of the premises.[12] The possibility of fitting up yet another house in Henrietta Street (in addition to Nos. 4 and 14) was found to be unsuitable, as the house would have to effectively be rebuilt and the street itself was not large enough to 'afford suitable accommodation for the number of vehicles constantly attending this office'.[13] Considering the great width of Henrietta Street, this indicates just how busy the court really was. There was also the issue of location. Despite the proximity to the King's Inns, Henrietta Street was not a convenient location for most lawyers, being at a distance from the headquarters of the legal profession in the Four Courts. Related to this, there was also the accusation that the location of the estate commissioners in Henrietta Street had led to a cliquish network of a few selected barristers working in the court. There were even charges that this had encouraged nepotism, with family relations of the commissioners being granted 'the great portion of the business', and that there was now a 'very strong feeling amongst the Bar that it would, as a matter of public policy, be very desirable that the Commissioners should be sitting at the Four Courts or the neighbourhood, so as to open the whole court to the profession'.[14] As a result of all of these factors, the decision was taken to move the Encumbered Estates Court in 1857. However, the following year, the Encumbered Estates Court was actually dissolved and replaced with a new body known as the Landed Estates Court, which dealt with much the same sort of cases. This new Estates Court would be based in newly constructed premises at the Four Courts in 1860. This left No. 14 vacant until the arrival of the Dublin Militia in 1863 (discussed below).

Social change, 1860–80

Even before the Encumbered Estates Court had been created, several major estates had been dissolved, including the Gardiner Estate. In the eighteenth century, the first Luke Gardiner had acquired vast holdings in Dublin, but his nineteenth-century descendants had mismanaged the estate and racked up crippling debts. The Gardiner Estate was broken up and sold via a special act of parliament in 1846, which authorized the raising of up to £350,000 to satisfy the demands of the estate's various creditors, as well as clearing any annuities due to the various claimants in a complex and drawn-out legal dispute concerning the earl of Blessington's will. Chunks of the estate were sold off over several months in 1846, as was recorded in newspaper adverts. Yet this sale does not seem to initially have affected Henrietta Street, with the sale of most freehold sites of houses only occurring much later.[15] But if the street remained (largely) in the same hands for the time being, the rest of the north inner-city was not so lucky. From the 1860s, a startling and rapid deterioration began across many of the properties the Gardiners had once owned. A census in 1861 revealed the worsening of the tenement situation in the city, with tenements now constituting two-fifths of the total number of houses in the city. This situation further deteriorated during the subsequent decade, with the number of tenements in the city peaking in 1871.[16] These decades saw not only a growth in the number of tenements, but a shift in their location. The 'slum geography' of Dublin began to change as older districts (like the Liberties) finally decayed beyond repair, with overcrowded lodging houses literally falling down and being left as vacant lots. At the same time, large sections of the south-west of the city were being bought up and redeveloped by successful businesses like Powers and Guinness, which led to a decrease in the amount of cheap housing available. With the supply of cheap rooms falling, Dublin's poor sought accommodation in new parts of the city, moving into previously elite districts. On the north side of the city, the spread of tenements started in the west, before covering most of the old Gardiner Estate. In 1865, the *Irish Times* observed that 'the removal of one old house may send into the streets, 6 or 8 families to look for shelter where they can.'[17] A parliamentary committee in 1880 heard how tenements had spread over the previous decade, as

> the dilapidations that have occurred in localities like the Coombe and the Liberties have created a desire on the part of certain persons to supply the

Figure 55 South view of Henrietta Street, c.1860. This was an advertisement for the General Engineering, Geological Survey and Valuation Office, located at No. 16.

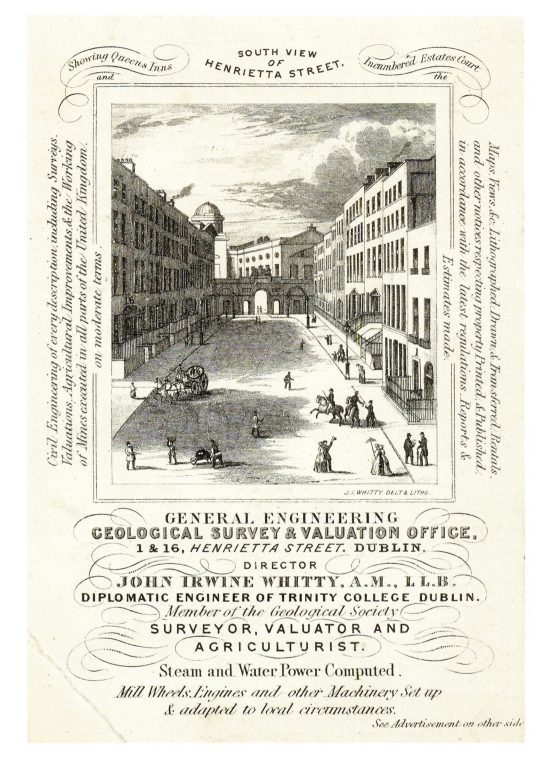

want by creation of tenement houses ... The increase of tenement houses in Dublin within the last eight or ten years must have been between 600 and 700.[18]

While tenements spread into places like Church Street and Beresford Street, nearby Henrietta Street remained a place of business rather than a residential area. Following the departure of the Encumbered Estates Court, Henrietta Street was dominated by the law profession, commercial offices and some government agencies. By the 1860s, the street contained the General Engineering, Geological Survey and Valuation Office, the Census Commissioners Office, the Scottish Equitable Life Assurance Office and the Agricultural Statistics Office.[19] An advertising card from this period shows a street that was well kept yet still bustling with activity.

However, the street was soon to be dramatically transformed by a new group of occupants: several regiments of the militia. These were reserve forces of the British military, very different from earlier forms of civilian militias which had fallen into disuse. Since 1852, the British army had raised and administered this new militia, which, although voluntary, was also a recruitment pool for the regular forces. Those who enlisted in the militia received an initial 56 days of training before returning to civilian life, committing to a further 28 days of additional training and deployment per annum. Recruits received full army pay during their training and a small retainer thereafter, making it attractive to casual labourers who needed the additional income. The militia were frequently used to man coastal fortifications, as well as being used more generally for home defence. In 1863, Henrietta Street became the home of two 'depots' or barracks for two militia regiments. The City of Dublin Regiment (an artillery corps) took possession of No. 12, while the County of Dublin Regiment (an infantry battalion) took over the house at No. 14.[20] Significantly, the Dublin County Militia would later be one of the units amalgamated into the new Royal Dublin Fusiliers in 1881. Due to the mobile and part-time nature of the militia, enlisted men frequently had 'followers', their families, who accompanied them to a regiment's accommodation. The militia stationed in Henrietta Street was no different, with several soldier's wives and children living with them there. As an example, we have a record of one member of the Dublin County Militia, John McAuliffe, who was a sergeant quartermaster, living in No. 14 with his wife Anne. Anne had several children while at No. 14, giving birth to daughters Susan and Elizabeth in 1865 and 1874, respectively.[21]

For the first ten years of the militia's presence on the street, there seems to have been few problems. However, in 1873 the Benchers of the King's Inns began a campaign to have the regiments removed, arguing that they disturbed the studies of young lawyers in nearby buildings. In a petition to the lord lieutenant, the Benchers argued that the militia's presence was inappropriate considering that most of the houses on the street were 'for the most part converted into law chambers or for the accommodation of members of the legal profression and law students'. They went on to complain

Figure 56 Portrait of John McAuliffe, sergeant quartermaster at No. 14 Henrietta Street, 1862–75.

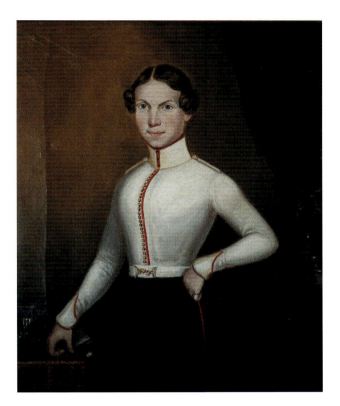

that 'since the staff of the Militia, with their numerous families, came to reside in the street. there had long been an absence of all order and quiet'. The reason for this was due to the street 'being made the resort of recruits and their followers … the street, being a cul-de-sac and consequently having little carriage traffic, is made a perpetual playground by the children of the Militia'. Two years later, one barrister complained that the street was the playground not only for the children of the Militia, 'but by numbers attracted from the district to participate with the Militia children in their uncontrolled games and sports'. An editorial in the *Irish Times* made a similar point about the location of the depots, writing that 'the din created by the children is enough to madden students and teachers – there goes on an eternal drumming and fife by incipient musicians'. In 1875, Charles Meldon, a barrister and MP, raised the issue in parliament, arguing that 'it was idle to suppose that legal education could be carried on there if these Militia barracks were to be continued'. He stated that under the current condition, members of the legal profession had to make their way through a street 'thronged with recruits and their followers'. Another writer observed that too frequently 'a quarrel sets the street in an uproar', perhaps hinting at the more riotous aspects of having enlisted men on the street.[22]

The initial petition by the King's Inns was unsuccessful, and in a parliamentary debate on the matter, the secretary of state for war commented that 'this so-called nuisance [in Henrietta Street] had existed for 12 years before any complaint was made about it'. However, the campaign for the removal of the militia continued, eventually resulting in the decision to remove the depots in 1876. The regiments were then moved south of the river, to accommodation in the Four Courts Marshalsea, a prison to the west of Bridgefoot Street. The premises in the Marshalsea was actually a three-storey-over basement, four-bay brick house, not unlike the style of houses in Henrietta Street. One correspondent to the *Irish Times* exclaimed that now the militia's staff 'will be much more comfortable there than they ever were in Henrietta Street, and will have the satisfaction of knowing they can annoy nobody'.[23] While the barristers and law students might have felt they had gotten rid of a nuisance, they could not envision the degree to which the street would deteriorate over the next few years.

The thirteen years in which the militia were based in Henrietta Street was a significant moment in its history. It was during this period that tenements were first listed on the street, in 1867. Significantly, the first buildings to be turned into tenements were Nos. 15 and 16, which were next to the militia depot at No. 14. Yet the removal of the militia did not stop the street's decline. After the depot was relocated, their former premises at Nos. 12 and 14 were left vacant for several years, leading to a physical deterioration of the buildings:

> the hall door [was] left standing wide open … There was not a whole pane of glass left in the windows of the first floor, and very few whole ones in any part of the front of the house … Inside all was rain and decay – the woodwork crumbling, the ceilings rotting, damp and desertion doing their work rapidly.[24]

It was the neglect of buildings like these that left the street vulnerable to speculative landlords willing to lease the houses out as tenements. The next two decades witnessed a rapid transformation of Henrietta Street into an address consisting almost entirely of tenements, with the real decline occurring during the 1880s. The earlier presence of the militia and the fact that several houses had been left vacant were obviously precipitating factors. But the death of Tristram Kennedy, the legal educator who had earlier bought up most of the street, was also a huge issue. After Kennedy's death in 1885, his property was sold off and was purchased by a man named Joseph Meade (discussed below), who re-let the houses as tenements. By 1888, Nos. 5, 6, 7, 12, 13, 14, 17 and 18 were all listed as tenements. Ten years later, in 1898, these were joined by Nos. 1, 2, 4, 15 and 16, meaning that almost all the street was let out as tenements (Nos. 4, 9, and 11 were still in use as offices, while No. 10 had been acquired by the Daughters of Charity).[25]

The street's transformation into tenements shocked those who could remember it in earlier times. The rapid decline of Henrietta Street was so dramatic because of its previous eighteenth-century heights. In this regard, its decline was symbolic of the city's transformation as a whole. In 1885, city councillors lamented that 'there is no other large city in Europe that has declined so rapidly of late as Dublin'.[26] This decline had hit the north side of the city the hardest. One of the most comprehensive studies of Dublin's tenements has gone as far as to state that 'the rapid loss of status which characterized the Gardiner estate … is perhaps the most spectacular element in the Dublin slum story'.[27] The transformation of these houses into tenements began in the 1880s, spreading from west to east. What occurred in Henrietta Street would occur a little later on in Gardiner Street and Mountjoy Square. By 1918, the spread of tenements in the north city was so noticeable that the city commissioned a survey that neatly demonstrates the extent of the problem.[28]

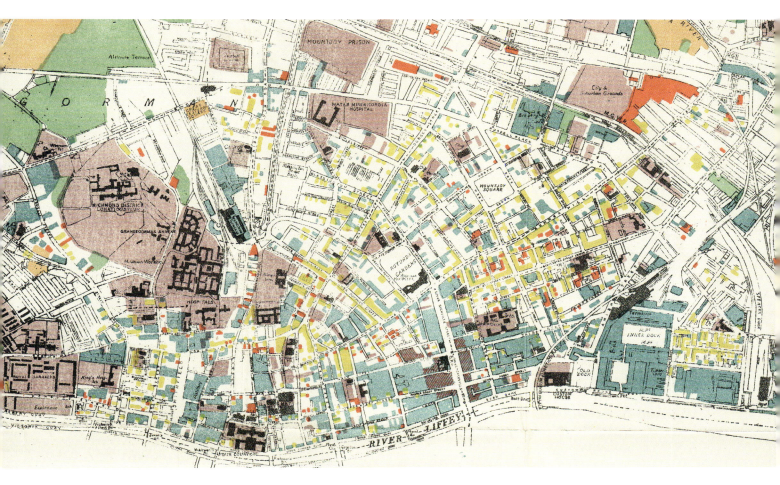

Figure 57 Land use map of Dublin north city, Dublin Corporation, 1918. Detail showing north inner-city.

If one examines the section of the map around Henrietta Street, the extent to which the street was at the heart of an entire tenement district by 1918 becomes clear. While the area around the King's Inns and the Linenhall Barracks were denoted as 'public institutions', the colours assigned to the rest of the area tell a different story. Henrietta Street was yellow (the colour assigned to tenements), as were large sections of the surrounding area, such as Church Street and Dominick Street. The red sections denote 'ruins & waste land', further indicating the extent to which the neighbourhood was physically dilapidated. If one looks at the map of the north side as a whole, the spread of tenements (the yellow) across the former Gardiner Estate is striking.

Economic change, 1850–1900

The above map illustrates the extent of Dublin's tenement problem by the early twentieth century, yet the city's social problems had been a long time in the making. As previously mentioned, there were worrying reports about the city's economic

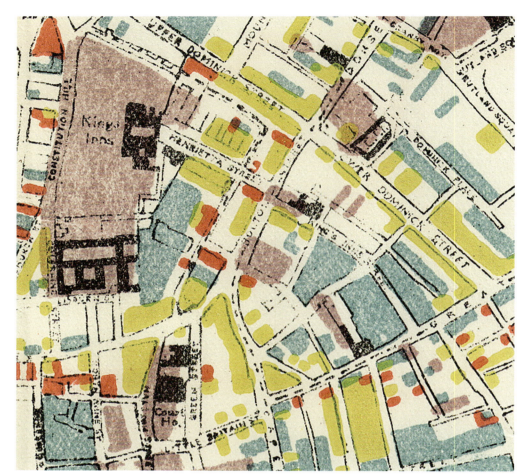

Figure 58 *Land use map of Dublin north city*, Dublin Corporation, 1918. Detail showing area surrounding Henrietta Street.

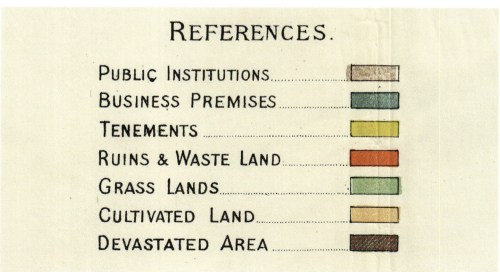

Figure 59 *Land use map of Dublin north city*, Dublin Corporation, 1918. Detail showing colour code for land use.

Figure 60 Robert French, Cattle market, Dublin, 1900. Located in the Prussia Street/ Aughrim Street area, in the early twentieth century this market was one of the busiest of its kind in Europe.

vulnerability as early as the 1820s, while by 1854 one official report chillingly declared that 'Dublin is in a position peculiar to itself, as compared with other towns of the empire. It is a metropolis for the poor, not for the rich'.[29]

Yet to some people, such statements would have been surprising. To a casual observer, Victorian Dublin had been a city that had seen some considerable economic successes. While it was true that local manufacturing had lost out to competition from Britain (the 'workshop of the world'), the closer integration of Dublin into the British economy had actually had some benefits too. Dublin had become the trading and distribution centre for Ireland's agricultural economy, with food and livestock processed and transported through the city en route to British markets. As a result, the food and drink industries increasingly dominated Dublin's economy. One of the legacies of the Famine had been a dramatic shift towards livestock farming, with the Irish countryside sending huge numbers of cattle and sheep to Dublin for processing and export. Physical evidence of this could be seen in the huge cattle market that was opened in the north-west of the city in 1863, providing work for herders, auction and sales clerks, as well as more business for the retail sector more generally in this area of the city.[30]

While the city's cattle market helped feed the British industrial economy, on the other side of the river, Ireland's largest brewer at St James' Gate helped quench its thirst. By the 1870s, Guinness had embarked on an expansion programme, with its more than 50-acre site providing employment to 2,000 men. It was at this moment, probably, the largest brewery in the world. The nearby Roe's distillery at Thomas Street, Power's distillery in John's Lane, and Jameson's in Bow Street produced impressive quantities of high-quality pot-still whiskey. Jacob's biscuits was another large firm, providing employment to over 2,000 people by the end of the century, with bakers like Boland's or Johnston, Mooney & O'Brien being examples of similarly impressive businesses.[31]

Much of the growth in the food and drink trades was due to the railways, which had improved the access of Dublin firms to rural suppliers. The railways themselves were also major employers. By 1881, one-eighth of Dublin's male workforce held transport-related jobs, with the railway boom providing employment to scores of engineers and maintenance technicians.[32] In addition to these industries, Dublin also remained the administrative and clerical centre of the island, benefitting from the highly centralized Irish state. Dublin was also the financial and commercial centre, providing banking services to the entire country. Some of the finest Victorian buildings in the city can be found in the area around Dame Street and College Green, evidence of this financial boom.

Yet, for all these success stories, Dublin was stagnating. In 1800, it had been the second-largest city in the British Isles; by 1881, it was the seventh. By the end of the century, it wasn't even the largest city in Ireland anymore (Belfast had just about overtaken it). This was a reflection of the city's underlying economic shortcomings. The successes of certain firms could not compensate for the decline of Dublin's older industries. The near disappearance of many traditional manufacturing jobs created huge social problems. Even though firms like Guinness and Jacob's had grown, the numbers they employed (relative to their market value) were small. The food and drinks trades were capital and not labour intensive. In 1871, a survey of Dublin's factories demonstrated that brewing, paper-making and printing together employed only about 4,000 people. As recently as 1824, the silk industry alone provided jobs to 6,000 in the city.[33] By the end of the century, the emphasis on transport and distribution meant there was an abnormally high level of casual workers, with consequent high levels of chronic under-employment. In 1911, almost a quarter of Dublin's male workforce described themselves as 'general labourer'.[34] In the same census, more than half of Dublin's men gave their occupation simply as 'other', most likely indicating that they were either in the carrying trades or in small-scale manufacturing. While it lacked a strong industrial base, Dublin continued to be a city of small workshops, producing goods like brushes, combs, coffins, mattresses and small furnishings. Nonetheless, Dublin's economy was characterized by low earnings, as well as high levels of unemployment.

Figure 61 Engraving of James' Gate Brewery, *The official illustrated guide to the Midland Great Western; (via London and North-Western), Great Southern & Western, and Dublin and Drogheda Railways, including descriptions of the most important manufactories in Dublin & in the towns on the lines* (London, 1866).

JAMES'S GATE BREWERY.

Occupation	Male workforce (%)	Female workforce (%)	Total workforce (%)
Labourer	24.0	0.3	11.5
Domestic	1.2	13.5	7.7
Textiles	4.1	7.5	5.9
Scholar	1.5	1.8	1.7
Grocer	2.7	0.5	1.6
Law & commerce	1.9	0.2	1.0
Maritime	1.2	0.7	0.9
Baker	1.4	0.3	0.8
Nurse	0.0	1.6	0.9
Military	1.5	0.1	0.7
Teacher	0.3	0.9	0.6
Alcohol industry	1.2	0.1	0.6
Butcher	1.2	0.0	0.6

Occupation	Male workforce (%)	Female workforce (%)	Total workforce (%)
Police	1.0	0.0	0.5
Apprentice	0.8	0.2	0.5
Healthcare	0.7	0.0	0.3
Other	50.8	18.5	33.8
Not stated	4.6	53.7	30.4
Total	100	100	100

Table 2.1: Occupations in Dublin city as proportion of workforce, taken from Census of Ireland: city of Dublin, 1911.

The new suburban townships

In 1900, an Irish MP named T.W. Russell observed that Dublin was 'essentially a city of poor people, and, to a large extent, of very poor people'. More to the point, Russell knew exactly why this was: 'a continuous stream of better-class people out of the city into the townships and suburbs … the homes of the better classes who had gone into the suburbs, had been occupied by a class lower', noting that homes previously lived in 'by mercantile and professional people … were now poor lodging houses, and in many cases tenements'.[35] And indeed, the spectacular growth of the suburbs was *the* key development during these years. In the earlier decades of the century, the tendency had been for the better-off to move from west to east within the city, flocking to the newer squares and streets downstream. Now the tendency was for the wealthy to live outside the city altogether, escaping the environmental and sanitary dangers of the city centre for a more idyllic suburbia.

The opening of the Dublin–Kingstown railway in 1834 was significant. It was not only the first railway in Ireland but was also the first suburban commuter railway in the world (earlier British lines had been commercial in nature). As a result, a series of new, independent townships outside of the city sprang up, which attracted the middle and upper classes who increasingly abandoned living in the city itself. The Dublin–Kingston line helped create what would become the townships of Dun Laoghaire, Blackrock, Dalkey and Killiney. After the Famine, this process of suburbanization intensified. Further new suburbs sprang up in places like Rathmines, Kilmainham, Clontarf, and Drumcondra. The part of the Pembroke Estate (formerly the Fitzwilliam Estate) that lay beyond the Grand Canal also established itself as an independent township, taking in an area that stretched from Eglin Road down through Sandymount to Ringsend. An 1840 Act had set the city's boundaries at the

DUBLIN AND KINGSTOWN RAILWAY,
From the Martello Tower Bridge at Seapoint, looking towards Kingstown.

Figure 62 Andrew Nicholl, *Dublin and Kingstown Railway, from the Martello Tower Bridge at Seapoint, looking towards Kingstown*, 1834.

canals, and as the century wore on the surrounding suburbs grew more assertive in their independence. By 1870, all of these townships were under the control of their own locally elected boards, which could levy taxes and enforce restriction on development.

In 1831, these suburbs contained around 30,000 people, against a Dublin city population of 230,000. Sixty years later, the suburbs had trebled in size to 90,000 people, while the city had grown only modestly.[36] Each township had its own character. The largest township, Rathmines, catered to professionals and the upper-middle class, with a board dominated by developers like Frederick Stokes. In Pembroke township, the earl of Pembroke owned nearly 80 per cent of the land and instituted a sort of benevolent paternalism, taking an active role in regulating building and sanitation. Not all suburbs were exclusively middle or upper class. Drumcondra mostly catered

to the clerical and artisan classes. Pembroke also included some working-class areas like Irishtown. In Kilmainham, which included Inchicore, the Great Southern & Western Railway provided substantial amounts of housing for its workers, which gave the district a working-class character. A map produced by the Boundary Commission in 1880 illustrates the manner in which the city was ringed by these independent townships.

Figure 63 Map of Dublin city and surrounding townships, Municipal Boundaries Commission, 1880.

Figure 64 Postcard of Rathmines, c.1900.

The tax incentives for fleeing to the suburbs could be considerable, as the city's municipal taxes and poor rates were significantly higher. To give an example, *Lower* Leeson Street, which was within the city, extended across the canal bridge to *Upper* Leeson Street, which was in Rathmines. In 1878, if you lived on the Rathmines' side of the bridge, your taxes were less than half of what they were on the city side.[37] Such an appealing taxation policy attracted wealthier Dubliners in their droves. Moreover, these townships could also prevent any of the working class from resettling within their boundaries by restricting the supply of affordable housing. Indeed, one of the reasons that the working class were obliged to live in tenements in the inner city was due to the policy of townships not to build working-class housing.[38] The independence of the townships from the Corporation's jurisdiction also allowed the suburbs to avoid contributing to city projects, as the Corporation's revenue was based on rates on property. Along with the slow increase in valuation of the city, the effect was to create a higher level of taxation on city property (a high 'poundage rate'), which discouraged new firms from building in the city.[39]

This exodus to the townships after 1840 was exacerbated by political developments. The long campaign for Catholic emancipation had come to fruition in 1829, and the granting of the franchise to Irish Catholics revolutionized municipal as well as national politics. For centuries, Dublin had been governed by the Corporation, an entirely Protestant body consisting of a small body of 'freemen' who elected candidates to all the key roles such as mayor and sheriff. By 1840, this system was no longer defensible and a Municipal Reform Act replaced this system with one based on a straightforward property qualification that gave Catholics a say in the city's government. In the subsequent 1841 election, two-thirds of the new Corporation Council were Catholic, while Daniel O'Connell himself was elected mayor, the first Catholic to hold the post since the seventeenth century.[40] O'Connell's election was indicitive of the growing influence and self-confidence of Dublin's Catholics, with a Catholic middle class that was willing to take a role in the city's government.

Figure 65 Daniel O'Connell in robes of lord mayor, late nineteenth-century etching.

Despite the return of a Catholic majority in the 1841 election, a loose power-sharing arrangement developed within the Corporation, in which the office of lord mayor would alternate between a Catholic/liberal candidate and a Protestant/conservative member. This arrangement endured for several decades, before finally coming to an end in the heightened political atmosphere of the 1880s, with Charles Stewart Parnell's agitation for Irish self-government. In the intervening decades, however, the composition of the Corporation had changed dramatically. At mid-century, the Corporation included members of the Chamber of Commerce, bank and railway directors, and chairmen of leading companies like Guinness and Jameson. By 1880, these prominent business leaders had been replaced with smaller businessmen, such as publicans and retailers. By 1890, approximately one third of Corporation members were in the grocery and drink trades. The social composition of the Corporation contrasted sharply with the makeup of the commissioners for Rathmines or Pembroke, which continued to be dominated by wealthier businessmen. Significantly, the contrast was not only one of social class, but of religion and political identity.[41] The narrative emerged of Dublin Corporation as a body dominated by Catholic nationalists, men who cared more about using the Corporation for political grandstanding on issues like the repeal of the Union, rather than sensible civic governance, thus justifying the flight of the wealthy to the new independent (and very Protestant) townships on the city's borders.[42] This obviously added a religious aspect to the division between city and suburbs. In 1871 Protestants were approximately 20 per cent of the city's population. On the other side of the canal in Rathmines, they constituted 52 per cent.

This vicious cycle of social segregation and suburbanization was at the forefront of an 1880 report on the question of the city's boundaries. The barrister representing the Corporation argued that although the suburbs fell outside the jurisdiction of Dublin, nonetheless 'they are part of the city. The gentlemen living in Pembroke and Rathmines Townships are large employers of labour, and their workmen live in the city'.[43] Understandably, Dublin Corporation wanted to extend the city boundaries to include this population of fleeing rate-payers. It was not an unusual proposal, as most British cities had found it necessary to extend their boundaries for similar reasons of middle-class flight; while Belfast enlarged its boundaries no less than four times during the nineteenth century. However, the political context of the late nineteenth century aided unionist townships in resisting annexation. In 1899, when the Corporation officially sought to annex the suburbs of Rathmines and Pembroke, their interests were defended by the leaders of Irish unionism, Edward Carson and Colonel Saunders. As a result, Rathmines and Pembroke would remain independent entities until 1930. Before this, however, with large numbers of wealthy inhabitants settling outside the Corporation's jurisdiction, the city's financial basis was effectively undermined, further exacerbating the contrast between the declining city centre and the affluent suburbs.[44]

The city left behind: how tenements spread

For those still living in the city centre, the second half of the century saw the spread of tenements, no longer being confined to back alleys or courts, but instead moving into the front streets and squares. By the 1900s, far from being hidden, 'as a rule the tenement houses face a thoroughfare of the city'.[45] In Dublin, there had almost always been 'tenements' in the sense of subdivided buildings used for cheap housing. What was now becoming common was something new: the conversion of Georgian town houses into slum housing, including some of the formerly most prominent addresses. Key to this shift were the stable buildings and gardens located in the lanes behind the main town houses. A housing inquiry in 1885 heard how 'the yards and gardens of a great number of houses have been built upon, and the back houses are very often rows of small cabins built in the gardens'.[46] The stable lanes (also called 'mews') behind these town houses had been built to serve the front-street houses and were particularly vulnerable to decline once the type of occupant in the main house changed. The same inquiry heard how 'different classes of persons now occupy the houses, and the people in the front houses no longer keep vehicles'.[47]

After 1879 there was a move by city authorities to close the worst back court and alley tenements, which pushed many of the residents into newer tenements on the main streets. The space behind Henrietta Street – Henrietta Place – was a good example of how tenements moved from back lanes to front streets. While tenements did not appear on Henrietta *Street* until the 1870s, they had been present at the rear, in

Figure 66 John Cooke, Stable Lane at rear of 20 South Cumberland Street, 1913.

Henrietta *Place,* nearly twenty years earlier. An image of Henrietta Place was captured in 1913, illustrating the type of back lane tenement that was frequently a precursor to the spread of tenements to a main street. In fact, Henrietta Place had once been the stable yard of No. 15 Henrietta Street, which can be seen in the background.[48]

The main town houses, those located on the front streets, had become vulnerable to 'tenementization' in the decades after the Famine. Ironically, the Encumbered Estates Court, which had been located in No. 14 Henrietta Street, had been key to this. In the Estates Court auctions, formerly 'handsome' houses were purchased at a discount, as indebted estates were sold off. With the breaking up of the Gardiner Estate, speculators now found plenty of opportunities to take over the leases of impressive Georgian buildings. Some of these speculators were wealthy men, including many who were essentially absentees, with their new properties administered by land agents or property managers. It was said that 'a very large number of the tenement houses of Dublin are owned by persons of the upper classes, many of these residing in the country, in England or abroad.'[49]

However, there were also many local investors, such as the sundry small 'businessmen' who found investments in tenements quite lucrative. These were the local 'house jobbers' that were being written about as early as the 1840s, men with long-term leases on an entire house who then subdivided and rented it out. These 'jobbers' were only too happy to lease their property out to 'middlemen' or agents who immediately sublet them to a number of families with minimum, if any, adaptation. Many of these 'middlemen' or 'house farmers' took only a short-term lease, often only leasing a single floor within the house. One account from the early twentieth century

Figure 67 John Cooke, Henrietta Place, 1913.

noted how 'those beautiful and dignified old houses, that had sheltered so many generations of opulent Dubliners, fell into the hands of a new and not-too-savoury class, a kind of urban gombeen man and every bit as bad as his rural cousin, known as a tenement or slum landlord'.[50]

There were two major consequences of this system. One was the astonishing profits these middlemen could accumulate. One witness to a housing inquiry described how one of these middlemen paid only £12 a year in rent, but was paid £40 to £50 a year by his tenants. It was reported that the tenements in Henrietta Street were sublet by middlemen at *three* times the amount that the landlord was actually paid. The second consequence was the several layers of ownership with as many as five or six different

Figure 68 'Attic occupied by a family of ten persons', *The Illustrated London News*, 1863. This image depicts a family in cramped conditions in a London tenement during the 1860s, but it also gives some idea of what conditions were like in the tenements of Victorian Dublin.

'middlemen'. The result was that it was usually unclear which one of these various 'landlords' or middlemen was responsible for maintenance or improvements on the building. As one witness described it,

> Dublin is peculiarly circumstanced with regard to the great number of the owners of houses, and I have stated the great difficulty, almost amounting to an impossibility, that there is of applying it [the bye-law] in Dublin where we have sometime six owners of one house. It might take about three year's proceedings to get a house re-constructed.[51]

An important aspect of this middleman system was that it involved people from a variety of social backgrounds as 'landlords'. In 1900, a local clergyman described how 'one of the greatest difficulties in connection with the question of the tenement houses was that arising from poor people trying to make a living out of their interests in such premises'.[52] In fact, one local building society, the Workingman's Benefit and Building Society, provided loans to working men, some of who it seems had already speculated in short-term leases in tenements. These were 'small' landlords, only a rung or two above their own tenants.[53] An analysis of Dublin Corporation records

Figure 69 Photograph of Dublin tenement, unknown location, 1913.

from the 1880s shows that, while a few tenement landlords were well off, many were of modest circumstance, a few even living in tenements themselves.[54]

As many landlords were of modest means, and the many layers of middlemen made it hard for the authorities to hold anyone accountable, repairs were rarely carried out. As a result, there was a swift decline in the physical integrity of the buildings, with 'walls honey-combed, their woodwork rotted, their roofs are masses of small and cracked slates, with innumerable patches upon them'.[55]

While negligent landlords and middlemen were certainly part of the problem, a significant issue was the buildings themselves. While Dublin was obviously not the only city with tenement housing, what a 'tenement' meant in Dublin was different from elsewhere. In other cities, tenements tended to be either purpose-built, or else were middle-class buildings that had later been subdivided. In Glasgow, speculative builders constructed tenement blocks which were high density but not poor quality (although many quickly became over-crowded). In Belfast, most of the houses that the working class lived in were purpose-built to at least some minimum standards, usually in the form of small, terraced houses. In densely populated cities like Berlin or New

York, tenements tended to be purpose-built multi-story blocks, as in Glasgow. While the conversion of aristocratic town houses into tenements was not unique to Dublin, it was more common there. That so much of Dublin's low-cost accommodation were homes built in the eighteenth century was significant. These buildings had been intended for a single family but now housed as many as 15 to 20 families. Once again, this was not unique to Dublin – the same type of tenements existed in many cities in Britain. But in Dublin these converted town houses constituted a much larger

Figure 70 (opposite) No. 46 Wolfe Tone Street, tenement, 1960 (Dublin City Library and Archives, Records of Dangerous Buildings Section). This image shows the rear of a tenement in Wolfe Tone Street (formerly Stafford Street), illustrating the physical decline of tenement buildings.

Figure 71 (right) John Cooke, photograph of the exterior of Grenville Street, 1913. Located just off Mountjoy Square, this image shows the tenement's windows mostly broken, indicating the degree of dereliction.

proportion of the working-class housing stock. As Dublin's chief medical officer noted, Dublin

> does not in the least resemble Belfast, Liverpool, Manchester, Glasgow and most other British cities. The latter consist in the chief part of new buildings, but they differ from Dublin in the important point that their working population live in houses built specifically for them, and adapted to their wants, whilst the Dublin artisans and labourers live chiefly in the decayed houses of former generations of people of superior rank.[56]

Dublin's poor were crowding into buildings that were, in some cases, already 150 years old. As observers repeatedly noted, these buildings (despite their grand origins), 'built at a time when sanitary science was not even thought of, are, in many instances, utterly unfit for human habitation'.[57] The physical layout of these buildings meant that adding features like running water or indoor toilets could be costly, while even simple refuse collection was difficult: 'There is no direct means of removing the refuse from the several floors, the common stair soon therefore becomes fouled; while the height of the houses – seldom less than three, and generally four storeys high – in no slight degree operates against cleanliness'.[58] Comparisons were occasionally drawn between Dublin and some Italian cities, where the working classes had also moved into formerly elite homes. However, the crucial difference was that in Italy these buildings were 'well calculated to resist not only the ravages of time, but the neglect or assaults of careless and riotous tenants … The great majority of Dublin eighteenth-century houses were, however, constructed of slight brick walls, slender wooden beams, and thin planks'.[59] While this may be too critical of Dublin's Georgian architecture, it was correct in pointing out the physical deterioration of the houses into which the city's poor were moving.

The worst of the worst? The owners of Henrietta Street's tenements

Exactly who owned the tenements in Henrietta Street? And what can that tell us about the conditions there? According to city directories, the first buildings on the street to be officially listed as tenements were Nos. 15 and 16, in 1867. While these were the only buildings listed as tenements for the next ten years, other buildings on the Street (Nos. 4, 12, and 14) were soon listed as vacant. In 1877, after several years of lying vacant, No. 14 Henrietta Street was sold and re-purposed as tenements. The man who purchased the property, Thomas Vance, was no mere property speculator or simple opportunist. Vance was one of the city's leading merchants, with his main business being the clothing trade, operating under the name of Vance and Beers. At the time of his death in 1889, he was also a director of the Gresham Hotel Company, a director of the Henry Street Warehouse Company, and on the board of the Dublin United Tramways Company.[60] Vance was also active in local politics, representing the Rotunda Ward on Dublin Corporation, while also being a member of the Poor Law Board of Guardians that managed the workhouse. Vance's brother John was a Unionist MP for Dublin for more than a decade, while Vance himself was one of the first commissioners for the township of Blackrock, having laid the foundation stone of the Blackrock town hall.[61] Vance had been wealthy enough to purchase Blackrock House, a palatial Georgian home that had once been the summer residence for the Irish lord lieutenant, and the nearby harbour bears Vance's name to this day. Upon his death in 1889, Vance left an estate worth £32,880, a very considerable sum for the time.[62]

The foundation upon which Vance had built this fortune was his construction business. Significantly, his firm had been responsible for building a series of 'model

Figure 72 *Exterior of the model lodging houses for families, Chapel Lane, Bridge St., Dublin, 1854.*

lodging houses' in the city, aimed at providing good-quality accommodation for the working classes. During the early 1850s, with much of the country still in shock from the Great Famine, there were serious fears about another cholera epidemic breaking out in Dublin, and this had led Vance to form a society for the construction of model lodging houses, its stated aim being 'to promote the health, cleanliness, comfort and morality of the labouring classes'. Vance began by constructing several lodging houses for single men in Capel Street in 1852, subsequently constructing 'model dwellings' for families at Lower Bridge Street the following year.

These model lodgings were intended to provide good quality accommodation at a reasonable price, with rooms for families available at a rent of between 3 and 5s. a week, with lodgings for single men at rents as low as 2 shillings. Vance provided these blocks with 'bath rooms, laundry, and drying rooms, with every sanitary accommodation'. This was the type of working-class accommodation that was sorely needed in the city and there was a consistent demand for the rooms in Vance's projects. The model lodgings proved so popular that Vance was induced to construct another such project at Bishop Street and Kevin Street in 1866, again aimed at families. By 1868, Vance's dwellings housed over 450 men and women.[63]

Figure 73 An aerial view of Vance's buildings in the twentieth century, opposite the Jacob's Biscuit Factory, Bishop Street (1934).

Therefore, at the time Vance had purchased No. 14 Henrietta Street in 1877, he already had experience in the construction and conversion of houses for working-class occupancy. In 1880, it was reported how Vance had taken 'an old house in Henrietta Street, and turned it into a better class dwelling-house, but that is a matter that only few men will do'.[64] There is some evidence that when Vance first converted No. 14 into tenements, his aim was to make these 'model' tenement rooms, that is rooms with some level of comfort and sanitation. For instance, within a year of purchasing the house, Vance was advertising apartments in the building described 'as recently papered, painted and fitted up with every modern sanitary improvement'. This included gas and toilets on multiple landings (as opposed to a toilet in the yard), with one located between the ground and basement levels at the rear of the house, and another between the first and second floors. There was also an oven for each tenant, and the provision of clean Vartry water, again provided on each landing.[65] In a city where most tenements still relied on 'dry privies' instead of toilets and where most tenants shared a single tap in the backyard, the conditions Vance was offering were better than most. This also seems to have been reflected in the higher-than-average rents for tenement rooms. Several adverts from the 1880s confirm that 3s. a week was the minimum one would pay for a single room, with the rent for a three-room apartment in Henrietta Street going as high as 6 shillings by 1900. This was roughly the same as was being charged in buildings run by groups like the Iveagh Trust or the Dublin Artisans' Dwellings Company, bodies that were criticized for mainly catering to skilled and better-paid workers.[66] In No. 14 there is evidence that, at least initially, the rooms there attracted those better off than the average worker. For example, in 1881, one of the building's tenants advertised that they were selling

Figure 74 Exteriors of Nos. 3–9 Henrietta Street, Records of the Irish Georgian Society, 1911.

their piano, and that they were willing to take £14 10s. for it. If this tenant had been one of Dublin's many desperately poor labourers, it is hard to believe that they would be in possession of such an expensive luxury item.[67] By 1900, it was estimated that the majority of Dublin's tenement families paid less than 3s. 6d. a week in rent. In No. 14, a large apartment cost considerably more than this (at least 4s. 3d. a week), with several apartments as high as 5 or 6s. a week.[68]

While Thomas Vance was the owner of No. 14, he was not the most important landlord in Henrietta Street. That title belonged to a man named Joseph Meade. Much like Vance, Meade had a background in construction. His father, Michael Meade, had been one of Dublin's most successful Catholic builders, establishing a business that was to grow further under his son. The Meade Company sawmills in Great Brunswick Street (now Pearse Street) was a city landmark. The Meade family business was responsible for some of the city's most significant Victorian buildings, such as the Catholic churches at Monkstown (1864–6), Donnybrook (1863–6), as well as the new Gaiety Theatre (1871). Even more noteworthy, Meade & Son were responsible for some impressive tracts of upper-class housing in suburban townships like Kingstown and Pembroke, as well as being a notable developer of property in Ballsbridge. Joseph Meade would himself come to live in an imposing mansion in Ailesbury Road. At one point, Meade was described as 'one of [the] largest employers in Dublin' and 'a merchant prince'.[69] Having inherited substantial property from his father, Joseph Meade was to further expand his real estate portfolio. At the time of his death in 1900, Meade owned over 122 properties, spread between the city centre and the suburbs. He was also politically active, being a Parnellite nationalist who was a member of Dublin Corporation. He was made an alderman in 1886, was later appointed high sheriff, and served two terms as lord mayor in 1891 and 1892. By the end of his life, Meade was also the owner of the majority of the houses in Henrietta Street, including the entire northern terrace, from Nos. 3 to 10.

Figure 75 Photograph of Joseph Meade, author of *Dublin main drainage scheme: souvenir handbook*, 1906.

Meade's first purchase on Henrietta Street took place in 1887, when he purchased No. 12 from a man named Thomas Crosthwaite and its neighbour No. 13 from the executors of Tristram Kennedy, the legal reformer who had died in 1885. No. 13 had recently been used as barrister's chambers and No. 12 had been vacant for eleven years after the departure of the Dublin Militia, with its hall door left open, its windows broken, and its interiors left to rot. It seems that Meade then carried out a 'large amount of remodelling work' on these properties, not leasing them out until four years later in 1891.[70] Meade was clearly happy with his investment in Henrietta Street, as in 1892 he purchased the remainder of Tristram Kennedy's property on the street, including Nos. 3 to 10. Consequently, by 1900 Meade was the main landlord of Henrietta Street, with most of his properties leased out as tenements.[71] During a later inquiry into the city's housing conditions, Meade was described as ruthlessly stripping out the staircases and mantelpieces of the houses for scrap and then subdividing them into decrepit tenements. It was said that he had bought the buildings so cheap that he was able to recoup the purchase price from the scrap value of the mantelpieces.[72]

However, the story of Meade's purchase and alteration of these homes is more complex than simply plundering them. First of all, by the time Meade took possession of these houses, many of them had either been left vacant or were already being leased out as tenements.[73] Moreover, many of the homes had been heavily altered over the previous century, including by Tristram Kennedy who had subdivided the buildings for use as legal chambers or by tenants such as the Landed Estates Court. It is actually

Figure 76 Photograph of rear of No. 7 Henrietta Street, showing toilet block addition, 1981.

quite unlikely that Meade removed any staircases, except possibly from No. 13. In fact, much like Thomas Vance, Meade seems to have made substantial alterations to the buildings, installing new floors and supporting partitions, in an attempt to make them 'model' tenements. In a 1914 inquiry, an architect named George O'Connor who was familiar with the tenement problem, specifically pointed to Meade's actions in Henrietta Street, where 'he formed the houses into the flat system, and improved them generally'. Another witness testified that almost no other tenement owner had carried out improvements like Meade and that 'Alderman Meade's experiment' was proof that 'something useful could be done' with tenement property.[74]

There is also physical evidence of Meade improvements, some of which are still visible today. For instance, at the rear of No. 7, there is a full height toilet tower that was added by Meade at some point after his purchase of the house, providing a WC and bathroom to each floor. At No. 3, Meade seems to have added a similar two-storey free-standing structure at the rear.[75] These toilet blocks were a massive improvement over the arrangements in many of the city's other tenements, where large numbers of tenants shared one or two outdoor 'privies' in the backyard. While city bye-laws stipulated that tenements had to provide one toilet for every twelve inhabitants, in practice this ratio was rarely achieved. In 1914, Dublin Corporation made the formal admission that 1,161 tenement houses in the city (out of a total of 5,322) had 20 or more people to only one WC. In one case, in a tenement at No. 10 Francis Street, 107 inhabitants shared only two toilets. City inspectors repeatedly stated that no self-respecting woman in a tenement house would use a public WC located in a backyard, and that these facilities were only used by men, being seen as disgusting and threatening places.[76] Thus, the sanitary arrangements provided by Meade were substantially better than tenements in other streets.

It should not be surprising that Alderman Meade took steps to provide better than average facilities in these tenements. Meade had a consistent record as a philanthropist with an interest in affordable urban housing. In addition to being a trustee of the Sick and Indigent Roomkeepers Society, Meade had also been appointed the director and chairman of the Association for the Housing of the Very Poor when it was founded in 1898. At a special Public Health Congress held that same year, Meade publicly argued for the granting of 'special terms' to Dublin Corporation (such as free sites, or freedom from city rates), to allow them to build houses for the 'very poor'.[77] Meade was later to be a leading member of the Public Health Inquiry in 1900 highlighted for the link between substandard housing and disease.[78] Meade was well versed in the problems facing Dublin's poor, as he had many years' experience in building working-class housing in the city. Meade's father had been one of the first contractors to build for the Dublin Artisans' Dwellings Company, constructing an early housing scheme in Buckingham Street in 1877. Under Alderman Meade, the firm went on to complete a number of similar projects in Rialto (1895–9) and at the Guinness Trust blocks in Bride Street (1893–1901).[79] Meade was a popular civic figure: during his time as mayor, he presided over the introduction of electric lighting in the city, the improvement of drainage, as well as the plans for a new fruit and vegetable market. He was also popular among Dublin's organized labour, with the Dublin United Trades Council praising his time as mayor and offering their support if he was to seek a third term, complimenting him as a good employer and an honest politician.[80] Meade would thus seem to have had a considerable reputation within Dublin as a businessman, philanthropist and civic politician.

While Meade, like Thomas Vance, may have been a successful public figure, both men reflected the unsavoury and hypocritical nature of Victorian capitalism: living in the suburbs but making their money from investments in the city centre, campaigning for better working-class housing but still profiting from tenements. To

Figure 77 Cartoon of a Dublin slum owner, *The Lepracaun Cartoon Monthly*, November 1907.

modern eyes, it might seem surprising that neither man's political career suffered as a result of their owning tenements. Yet the reason for this is simple: owning a tenement was not necessarily seen as disreputable at this time. A frequent argument (put forward by landlords and officials alike) was that the city's housing problem was the fault of 'middlemen'. In fact, the city's long-serving chief medical officer, Charles Cameron, once described them as 'the curse of Dublin'.[81] And it is certainly true that 'middlemen' were an issue in the tenements that sprang up in Henrietta Street from the 1880s. An inquiry in 1885 heard how 'there are eight or ten houses in Henrietta Street sublet at the present time at rents which are three times greater than the sum which the landlord gets from the middlemen; if they were worked *en bloc* the rents could be reduced by at least 50 or 60 per cent'.[82] Again, it was pointed out that the effect of these 'middlemen' was not only to increase the rent paid by occupants, but also to obscure who was responsible for repairs and upkeep.[83] One journalist who investigated Dublin's tenements in 1906 described how 'the tenants cannot tell exactly who owns that old ruin; all they know is that there is a Mister something with pencil in his ear calling every Monday morning for the rent.'[84]

While these 'middlemen' undoubtedly had a harmful effect on the housing market, this is not to say that the owners of the property were blameless. Owners like Meade or Vance might prefer to run tenements that maintained certain standards, but at the end of the day, they were businessmen in search of a return on their investment. In 1913, a former lord mayor recalled how Thomas Vance had once shown him his model dwellings in Bishop Street: 'I saw every appliance for sanitation and comfort, but he showed me his rent book also, which recorded a handsome yearly profit'.[85] Following Joseph Meade's death, the sale of his estate revealed that his tenement properties in Henrietta Street returned a gross rental of £1,500 per year. Even with deductions for rates and expenses, this left a considerable profit.[86] Nor were either of these men afraid to evict tenants who fell into arrears, as newspaper reports make clear.[87] While Vance and Meade may not have been 'the worst of the worst', neither were they angels, and this fact was increasingly subject to comment. The behaviour of Meade was the subject of a satirical cartoon, published in 1907 in the pages of *The Lepracaun Cartoon Monthly*. The figure in the cartoon was that of a fat and cruel 'slum owner'. The text of the cartoon refers to him as buying the house for the price of the mantelpiece (an accusation levelled at Meade) and as being the chair for the 'Society for the better housing of the Poor', likely a reference to Meade's philanthropic activities. In the cartoon, women and children clutter the landings, looking out at this man, as one mother declares 'heres ould Shylock'. Descending the rickety staircase of a tenement house, its plaster peeling and floorboards cracked, the slum owner is carting away his bag of 'rack rent', while a 'notice to quit' sticks out of his pocket. It is an image which hints at the resentments and hostility of Dublin's tenement residents towards their landlords, an antagonism that would only grow over subsequent decades.

Worse was to come though. It seems that the death of Meade in 1900 led to a further deterioration of his properties in Henrietta Street.[38] The numbers living in these tenements certainly increased. Taking No. 9 Henrietta Street as an example, in 1901, it was home to 57 people. By the time of the next census a decade later, this had increased to 97 people. It was described how in No. 14, individual rooms had been further subdivided since the death of Thomas Vance in 1889, as 'the tenant of one room had farmed it out in four corners'.[89] Using data provided by the Valuations Office about the street in 1912, it is clear that several of the tenements were downgraded at this point from 'Class A' tenements to 'Class B', including No. 14.[90] This would indicate a lack of upkeep and maintenance, likely due to a lack of supervision. Following Meade's death, his sizeable estate was dissolved, with his son William gradually winding down the business and selling off properties, a process that took until 1910.[91] Following the death of Thomas Vance in 1889, the properties that he had owned were then administered by a trust. Tellingly, Vance's will left sums of money to be paid to local caretakers for the properties, the executors of his will (his son and sons-in-law) being largely absent from Dublin. Yet the trust still controlled property in Henrietta Street into the 1940s.[92] As a result, after 1900, most of the houses in Henrietta Street were likely to have been administered by a solicitor's representative. It is therefore probable that the image of the 'slumlord' that the *Lepracaun* magazine depicted was actually of an agent or an intermediary. The story of Henrietta Street is one of constant change and adaptation. Unfortunately, change can sometimes mean decline. In the 1880s and 1890s, the tenements in Henrietta Street had not been the 'worst-of-the-worst'. Twenty years later, however, the street's residents would have found this cold comfort.

Dear, dirty Dublin?

There were obviously some very considerable challenges to Dublin's housing market. While many placed the blame squarely on the 'middlemen', these 'jobbers' could argue that they had no incentive to make material improvements on these buildings, as there was such a steady demand from the poor for tenement rooms. The economic vulnerability of Dublin's labouring class meant they could not be discriminating. The result was an astonishing spread of tenements. By the turn of the century, there was almost no area of the city in which there were not tenements on some formerly grand street or square. In 1898, one local newspaper ran a series of exposés on the city's slums. A journalist for the paper recalled how, thirty years earlier, much of the city centre had been a genteel business district, while

> the residential portions of the well-to-do classes were evenly distributed between north and south … Now all is changed … The northern residential quarter has gone to ruin – Rutland and Mountjoy Squares alone still fighting a losing battle for respectability. Nine-tenths of the Gardiner estate is hopeless.

Figure 78 'Dublin Illustrated' from *The Graphic*, 17 August 1878. This image depicts the view of Christ Church Cathedral from the river, the observer looking south across the houses on Wood Quay.

On the south side the sign of the lodging house keeper – forerunner of the tenement house owner, is seen on countless windows. The well-to-do tenants have fled and the thronging hordes of proletariat barbarism fill their places![93]

Other, less panicky accounts also reported how tenements were now more common; as one journalist reported, 'it would be interesting to learn if the residents in the aristocratic localities have had any knowledge heretofore of the pestilential and dangerous conditions which exist within a comparatively few feet of the back windows of their homes'.[94] These reports were born out by official statistics. By 1880, over two-fifths of the city's inhabited houses were let out as tenements. Of these 9,800 tenement buildings, over 2,000 were deemed as unfit for habitation, despite containing some 30,000 people.[95]

In 1898, the same over-wrought newspaper correspondent declared that 'the city is rotting – that is the plain way of putting it … Dublin is getting shabbier, dirtier, and poorer year by year'.[96] While this was a stark verdict to be sure, it echoes other people's assessments. In the opening years of the nineteenth century, visitors to Dublin had been largely positive, describing a city that was flourishing, one with flowers in its windows and elegant carriages in its streets; a place that could 'take a high rank amongst the finest cities of the earth'.[97] As the century came to a close, such up-beat assessments were far more difficult to find. In 1891, one French visitor commented on 'Dear, dirty Dublin! Such are the familiar terms … Dear dirty Dublin is nothing more

92 SPECTRAL MANSIONS

than a conglomeration of poor quarters, whose misery overflows onto the doorsteps of the rich'.[98] Yet this was a city that was also said to be undergoing a cultural renaissance during these years. This was the era of the 'Gaelic Revival', the era when W.B. Yeats and Lady Gregory helped launch the Abbey Theatre; these were the years that saw the formation of the Gaelic League and a flood of new clubs and societies. This image of Dublin during the 'Celtic Twilight' has been endlessly romanticized, but only metres away from the trendy cafes and experimental theatres, there existed a different world of poverty and despair. The novelist George Moore, a member of this cultural revival, once described the city's 'weary and threadbare' streets: 'the Dublin streets stare the vacant and helpless stare of a beggar selling matches on a doorstep … We are in a land of echoes and shadows … Shadow, echoes, and nothing more'.[99] Many Dubliners would have agreed with Moore's description of the city as an 'echo' or a shadow of its former self. As the Victorian age drew to a close, Dublin was already a city that many felt was haunted by its past, or perhaps more accurately, by its lost potential future.

Figure 79 John Cooke, Chancery Lane, off Bride Street, 1913.

3

Life and death in a tenement, 1880–1910

For much of the nineteenth century, the people living in Dublin's tenements remain invisible to the historian. So much of what constitutes the historical record for this period is derived from the perspective of the upper classes, with the conditions of the tenements only rarely depicted in art or prose. At the turn of the twentieth century, however, images and reports of the city's tenements became more common. The advent and popularization of photography had much to do with this. Many of the most enduring images of Dublin's tenements are photographs taken in the 1910s. One of these images, of a tenement in Chancery Lane, is particularly haunting. It depicts a small crowd, of both children and adults, standing on the doorstep of a building, many spilling out onto a cobbled street. The various figures stare towards the camera. For many of them, this event was undoubtedly a novelty, perhaps the only time in their lives that a photo of them was taken. When this image was taken in late 1913, Dublin's tenements had already become one of the pressing social issues of the day. The city's tenements represented different things to different people. For city officials, they were a health hazard. For landlords, they were a source of revenue. To moral reformers, they were too often a place of vice, drunkenness and wickedness. For nationalist politicians, they were a symbol of Dublin's loss of political influence. But for the men and women who actually lived in these tenements, they were simply 'home'. To the working class, arguments about the social or political causes of Dublin's housing problems must have seemed rather abstract. A far more pressing set of questions occupied their daily lives: where could they find shelter? An apartment, a room, even a corner to live in? How much would this cost? How would they find work to pay for it? It is all too easy to view the tenements simply as a social 'problem', an issue to be debated and solved. But for thousands, the tenements were where they lived, slept, played, struggled and, quite often, died.

What was a tenement room like?

In 1906, the *Irish Times* ran a series of articles about Dublin's tenement 'black spots'. While the tone of the reporting was condescending at times, the reporter nonetheless provided a vivid description of what these tenement buildings were like. The account opened with a description of how, in most tenements, the front door was left permanently open: 'the hall, which is considerably large, stands wide open day and night and is the favorite concert platform for all the stray cats on earth'. With so many families sharing a house, most tenements were by necessity 'open door' – each apartment had a lock, but the front door of the building was left open. This had the effect of making the stairwells and hallways, in effect, public space. The journalist went on, describing how

> the chimneys nearly all smoke, and there is not a sound window in the whole building. The floors are all hills and hollows; from some of the rooms you can look straight down through the holes and see what is doing in the room underneath; here and there they are patched up with pieces from an old soap box, or they may be only covered with a sack.

The article went on to describe how a single building contained many room types, of varying sizes and on different floors. The smaller rooms on the upper-most floors were generally seen as the worst: 'The better class of workman will occupy a room or two on the ground or second floor; it is the ill-paid, under-fed labourer, with his over-large stock of youngers ... that comes crowding into the top back room'.[1] This journalist went on to describe the rooms on the top floor of a tenement building: 'that is where every shape of disease germ, both physical and mental, is being bred at hot-house speed. That top back room of the Dublin tenement house is the devil's

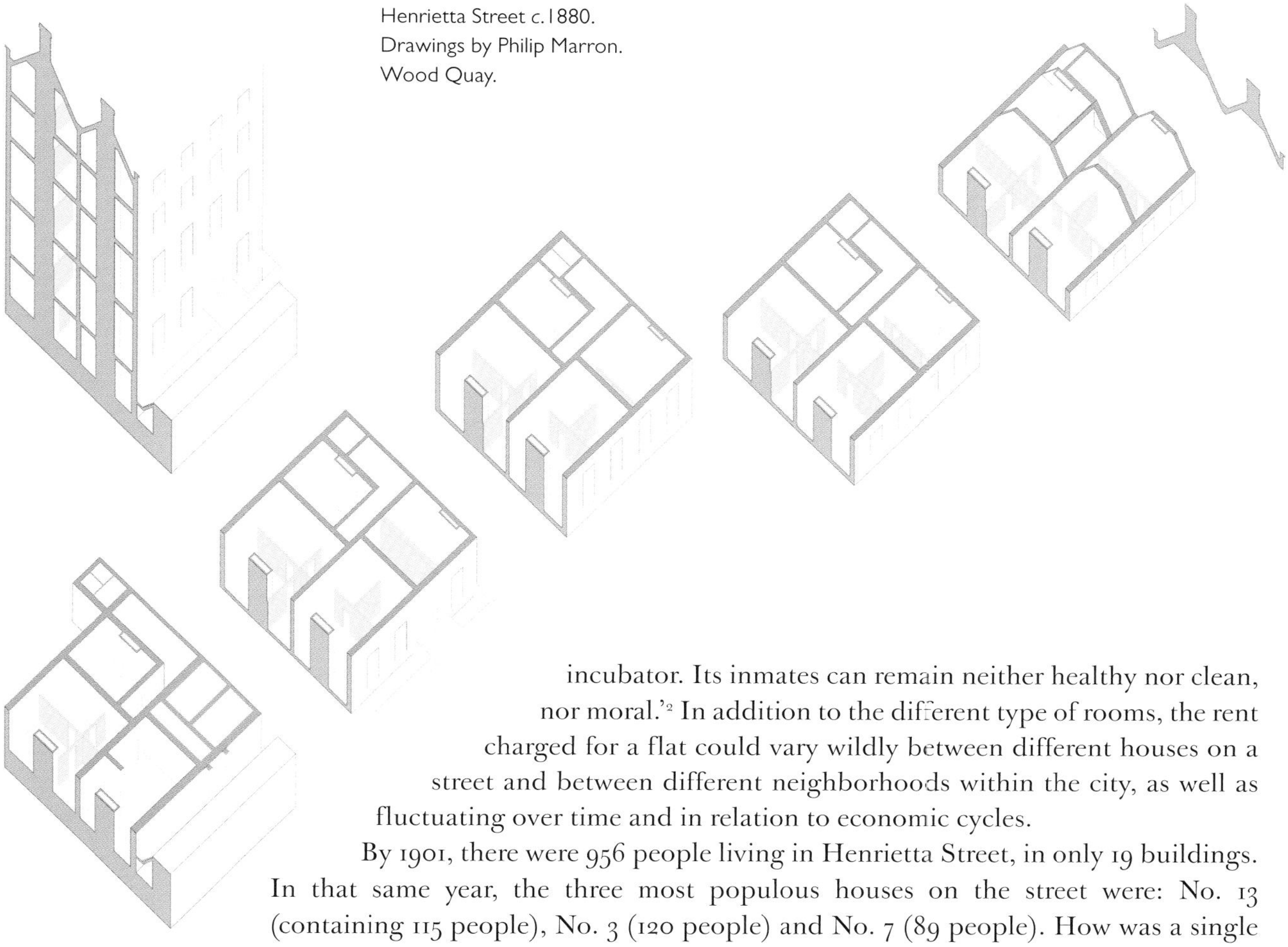

Figure 80 Conjectural re-construction of 14 Henrietta Street c.1880. Drawings by Philip Marron. Wood Quay.

incubator. Its inmates can remain neither healthy nor clean, nor moral.'[2] In addition to the different type of rooms, the rent charged for a flat could vary wildly between different houses on a street and between different neighborhoods within the city, as well as fluctuating over time and in relation to economic cycles.

By 1901, there were 956 people living in Henrietta Street, in only 19 buildings. In that same year, the three most populous houses on the street were: No. 13 (containing 115 people), No. 3 (120 people) and No. 7 (89 people). How was a single house divided to accommodate these large numbers? In the case of Georgian town houses, such as those in Henrietta Street, the building usually consisted of four storeys over a basement. Each of these levels was then divided into multiple apartments. These apartments were described in terms that referred back to the building's original eighteenth-century usage. For instance, the basement floor was referred to as the kitchen, and was usually divided into the 'front' and 'back' kitchen. The ground floor, in addition to the hall, contained a 'front' or 'street' parlour, as well as a back parlour facing onto the garden. The first floor's main rooms were similarly divided, with 'front' and 'back' drawing rooms. The second floor usually contained a series of rooms that were referred to as 'two-pair front' and 'two-pair back', while the third floor or garret would similarly be divided into 'top front' and 'top back rooms'.[3]

In the case of No. 14 Henrietta Street its original eighteenth-century plan comprised a large two-storey entrance and stair hall compartment, and three interconnected

LIFE AND DEATH IN A TENEMENT, 1880–1910

rooms. The ground and first floor comprised two reception rooms, one to the front, and one to the rear, with an adjoining antechamber, off which there was a small private 'closet' tucked behind the secondary stairs which ran from the basement to the third-floor level.

When No. 14 was converted to tenements nineteen separate flats across its five levels were created, one flat in each of the house's eighteenth-century rooms. Looking at the ground floor, we see that the large room at the front of the house (see Figure 80) called the front or street parlour) was subdivided to form a three-room apartment, with the large two-bay rear room (the back parlour room or family dining room) subdivided to form a four-room flat. The ground floor also contains two one-room flats, the one to the rear occupying the 'antechamber' and the other located to the right of the front door, occupying the ground-floor space of the original eighteenth-century entrance stairhall. The original staircase of this house had been stripped out when it was converted to tenements, and (on the ground floor) the entrance hall was divided by a timber-framed partition wall, leaving a dark entrance passage, as well as a small one-room flat.

There was a similar layout of reception rooms on the first floor, with the 'front drawing room' subdivided into a three-room flat, and the 'back drawing room' (originally a formal dining room) subdivided into a four-room flat, with a one-room flat occupying the antechamber room at this level. A three- or four-room flat occupies the first-floor space of the eighteenth-century entrance stairwell compartment. Moving upwards to the two uppermost floors, the second storey (originally a bedchamber floor) and the third storey (originally the garret) each contained two 'front' and two 'back' flats of varying layouts, with between one and four subdivisions or rooms. The individual rooms within each apartment were divided using timber-framed and lined partitions rising to the height of the door in each room, approximately 2.4 metres high. These partitions had evidently been installed by Thomas Vance, who had used similar partitions in his previous lodging houses, and partitions were also to be found in the other town houses on the street and on neighbouring streets.[4]

This illustrated layout of the house can be usefully read alongside notebooks held by the Valuations Office that date from 1912, and which provide descriptions of each of the nineteen apartments in the house. The notebooks provide invaluable information on the form of construction, the plan and dimensions, the physical condition and accommodation arrangements including sanitation provisions (toilets and taps) for many of Dublin's tenements. They provide information on the number of official tenants per flat and the rent they paid. In many entries, including that for No. 14 Henrietta Street, the agents and lessor (the landlord) are also identified. Interestingly, the valuations notebook shows that only thirteen of these apartments were occupied in 1912, with 66 people recorded as resident. This differs from the census of the previous year, which recorded 100 people in the building; a considerable number of those listed on the census were described as lodgers, sub-tenants, or visitors. The earlier 1901 census had already revealed that a majority of the households living in No.

14 had either a 'boarder' or a 'visitor' (likely a boarder the family did not want their landlord finding out about).

The 1912 notebooks also provide a breakdown of the rents for each apartment (see below). Unsurprisingly, the two cheapest flats were located in the basement, with the least expensive being the 'back right' apartment which fetched a rent of 1s. 6d., and which, at the time, was inhabited by two adults and two children. Similarly, the apartments in the upper-most floor (often known as the 'garret') were generally cheaper than elsewhere in the house, with most rented at 3s. 3d. The gross annual rent for the house as a whole was £173, a considerable sum. The building was administered by an agent named Carroll, based at 54 Dawson Street. Carroll was presumably working on behalf of the Vance Estate which still owned the house, although a Commander Heathcote and Dr Beamish, both trustees of the Vance Estate, were listed as 'immediate lessors'.[5] The 1912 valuation describes No. 14 as being clean, thanks partly to the presence of two toilets located at the rear of the building and on the third-floor landing. There were also several water taps, located in the basement and on the third-floor landing.

Apartment location/description	Rent (shillings and pence)
basement, front left	2s. 6d.
basement, back right	1s. 6d.
basement, back left	2s. 9d.
ground floor, front right	3s. 9d.
ground floor, front left	4s. 9d.
ground floor, back right	3s. 9d.
ground floor, back left	4s. 6d.
first floor, front right	4s. 6d.
first floor, front left	4s. 6d.
first floor, back right	3s. 6d.
first floor, back left	4s. 6d.
second floor, front right	4s. 3d.
second floor, front left	4s. 3d.
second floor, back right	3s. 3d.
second floor, back left	4s. 6d.

Apartment location/description	Rent (shillings and pence)
third floor, front right	3s. 6d.
third floor, front left	3s. 3d.
third floor, back right	3s. 3d.
third floor, back left	3s. 3d.

Table 3.1: Rents of apartments in No. 14 Henrietta Street in 1912 (Source: 1912 valuation notebooks, Valuation Office Ireland).

The 1912 valuation notes that while No. 14 had been a 'Class A' tenement, it had been recently downgraded to a 'Class B', with its valuation lowered from £62 to £52. However, despite this downgrade, evidence indicates that Henrietta Street was still not the 'worst of the worst' of Dublin's tenements. In 1914, a survey of tenement families reported that the average weekly rent for a tenement apartment was 3s. or less, and evidence from another inquiry that same year showed that the majority of families paid between 2s. and 2s. 6d.[6] Only the two cheapest apartments in No. 14 (both in the basement) fell into this price range. Admittedly, these were three- to four- room apartments, which always fetched more than the average one-room flat. But taken alongside anecdotal evidence about the conditions in Henrietta Street, it would seem the house was in the mid- to upper-range of tenement accommodation.

Finding the rent was frequently a struggle, and often presented the most serious challenge to a working-class family's well-being. In 1914, it was reported that 30,000 notices to quit were issued in Dublin every year, with the majority of these due to non-payment of rent.[7] Quite often a struggling family might find themselves engaged in a 'night flit', loading up their belongings onto a cart and 'trotting furtively and swiftly through the darkened streets to another wretched habitat ...' A 'flit' was the last straw, 'if a few shillings could be scraped together to pay for the hire of the ass and cart; for, were they to remain, the sheriff's men would be in on the morrow, and their pathetic scraps of property put under the hammer ... towards the arrears of rent'.[8] The inhabitants of Dublin's tenements were highly mobile, frequently moving from one building to another, indicating the economic precariousness of their existence and the lack of security provided by leases and rental agreements. Taking Henrietta Street as an example, in 1901 there were 152 households on the street. A decade later, only sixteen of those families still resided on the street.[9] It is doubtful that the families who left the street during this decade found any improvement in their living situation if they stayed in Dublin. As a later housing inquiry was to hear about Dublin's tenement dwellers: 'the only change they can get is that to a neighbouring court or street, a rise or fall of a few degrees in their condition, or a short space in prison'.[10]

A tenement budget

The amount of rent a family could afford (and their ability to consistently pay it) was obviously dependent on their income. The wages of a Dublin worker could vary depending on their occupation, with highly skilled tradesmen earning as much as 40*s.* a week. For those in regular but low-skilled employment, wages could be between 20 and 25*s.* a week. However, for the army of casual labourers, earnings could be as little as 12 to 15*s.* a week. Keeping these distinctions in mind, it was generally agreed upon that 18*s.* a week was a good estimate of an 'average' weekly wage in the city. Taking 18*s.* as a starting point, an average weekly budget for someone living in the tenements might resemble that produced below. Out of a typical household budget of 18 to 20*s.* a week, the proportion of income spent on rent was between 15 and 17 per cent, which was roughly in line with English working-class budgets

Item	Cost
rent	2*s.* 6*d.*
fuel & light	2*s.* 0*d.*
bread	4*s.* 0*d.*
tea	0*s.* 9*d.*
sugar	0*s.* 8*d.*
milk (often condensed)	0*s.* 6*d.*
butter	1*s.* 6*d.*
potatoes or other vegetable	1*s.* 0*d.*
meat, fish or bacon	2*s.* 0*d.*
Total	14*s.* 11*d.*
weekly wages	18*s.* 0*d.*
Balance	**3*s.* 1*d.***

Table 3.2: D.A. Chart, Typical working-class budget, *Journal of the Statistical Society of Ireland*, 1914.

After rent, the greatest expenditure was food. For those living in the tenements, 'diet' was not a matter of taste or preference so much as it was about the weekly struggle for survival against poverty and illness. For many, their diet was both meagre and monotonous. The most common item in the typical diet was bread, with the two-pound white baker's loaf being the most popular variety in Dublin. A standard breakfast might be white bread and sugared tea. Dubliners derived most of their carbohydrates and sugar from bread, as well as what little protein there was in their diet. The most common vegetables were potatoes, onions and cabbage. Meat was rarely consumed, usually reserved for the main wage-earner in the family, most commonly in the form of bacon, pig's cheek or herrings. Often a family might stretch their limited funds by buying scraps from the butcher or inferior meats that were about to spoil. In the home, perishable goods like milk and margarine were stored in a shaded corner or put in a bucket of cool water. Tea, oatmeal, sugar was sealed in tins to keep out pests. Pieces of gauze were used to cover exposed food from flies. No matter how these goods were stored, there was always problems concerning the quality of foodstuffs. While milk was widely consumed, it was often condensed skimmed milk that had little fat and was thus unsuitable for growing children in need of calories. Milk was commonly diluted and adulterated, with contaminated milk spreading fevers and diseases like diphtheria, tuberculosis and scarlatina. In 1910, an analysis of Dublin's working-class diets was carried out in a study of twenty-one families, with the very poor deliberately excluded. Of these twenty-one 'typical' working-class families, only five achieved the necessary level of protein and all but six of the families were found to have an inadequate intake of calories. The tight budget that many families operated on, as well as the uncertainty about future earnings, meant that the poor frequently purchased commodities like sugar and tea in small quantities, making them more expensive than if bought in bulk. Most families derived the bulk of their calories from shop-prepared bread, instead of porridge or pulses, which were prepared in the home. This was partly due to the difficulties of cooking in tenement houses and the expense of fuel.[11]

With such tight budgets, there was little money left for furnishings or clothes. With so many families living on so little, clothes were often hand-me-downs, with one writer declaring that 'half the population of Dublin are clothed in the cast-off clothes of the other half', while another described how 'the people slept in their clothes … They never washed them – never took them off'.[12] Accounts of the tenements in the early 1900s also comment upon the barren interiors of most rooms, the lack of furniture or material comforts. As one man would later recall about the tenements in this period, although the Georgian exteriors of these buildings 'still managed to preserve some traces of the quondam dignity … their interiors were another matter altogether'. He described how 'the great old rooms' inside these tenements were

> bereft of all furniture save the most miserable makeshifts, with the faded paper of two generations back peeling off the high walls in long ribbons because of the damp; with holes in the flooring so that you had to mind your step, and the laths showing through the broken plaster in the ceilings. What beds! What dirt![13]

Figure 81 John Cooke, Interior of Newmarket *tenement*, 1913.

Figure 82 John Cooke, Interior of tenement, the Coombe, 1913. These images show the grim conditions in older tenement areas in the Liberties, such as the Coombe and Newmarket Square.

Another account from 1913 described how some rooms were

> totally devoid of any sleeping accommodation, a piece of sacking or rags being considered such for a whole family; it was quite exceptional to get a room properly fitted with bed or bedding, table, chairs, or some decent domestic utensils ... the notes of a bird in a cage never sound in the ears of those I visited, and not a flower in the window-sill brightens the tenement room. One copy of the Red Magazine, and that for firelight, was all the printed matter that met my eyes in all the poor dwellings I entered.[14]

Photographic evidence

These written descriptions of Dublin's tenements are confirmed by photographic sources. One source in particular allows us an insight into these conditions, a collection of photographs popularly known as the 'Darkest Dublin' collection, an album of about 100 images now held by the Royal Society of Antiquaries of Ireland. The photographs were most likely taken in September and October of 1913, by John Cooke, honorary treasurer of the National Society for the Prevention of Cruelty to Children (NSPCC) and W.J. Joyce, an officer of the NSPCC. The photographs were taken as part of a government inquiry into housing conditions in Dublin, and about fifty of these images were published as part of the resulting report. However, many more went unpublished, being preserved as a set of lantern-slides.[15]

While not all locations in the photographs have been verified, they do seem to span most of the city, giving a survey of the various tenement neighbourhoods. The images include shots of the 'older' working-class neighbourhoods of the Liberties: Thomas Street, Meath Street, Blackpitts and the Coombe. However, it also includes pictures of the 'new' tenements in the former Gardiner Estate, around Mountjoy Square, Gardiner Street, and Summerhill. There are also a few images of dwellings in the old medieval core of the city, such as Cooke Street and the lanes around Christ Church. Crucially, Cooke's photographs demonstrate the range of building types that could be described as 'tenements'; not only the subdivided Georgian town houses, but the converted stables, overcrowded back courts and cottages. Another striking aspect of the collection is the frequent depiction of waste grounds, confirming what contemporary maps and surveys had indicated about the prevalence of derelict sites in the city.

Cooke's photographs are also remarkable in their depiction of tenement interiors, capturing the terrible conditions that this accommodation entailed. Indeed, the photos are striking in depicting the people who lived in the tenements, not simply the buildings themselves. There is no sentimentalization of working-class life. Arguably the fact that Cooke was essentially an amateur photographer meant he was less likely to 'stage' shots. While a few of the images seem to have been arranged, with the people in shot organized or positioned, most are candid pictures of everyday life, with

Figure 83 (above) John Cooke, Engine Alley, Meath Street, 1913.

Figure 84 (right) John Cooke, A view of Church Street, 1913.

LIFE AND DEATH IN A TENEMENT, 1880–1910

Figure 85 John Cooke, Faithful Place on Lower Tyrone Street, 1913.

all its dismal realities. One set of these images show the lack of furnishing or comforts in a tenement in Waterford Street (see figs. 88, 89). This street was once known as Upper Tyrone Street, and no longer exists. It ran from Marlborough Street to Lower Gardiner Street.

Who lived in the Henrietta Street tenements?

In establishing some basic facts about the people who lived in Henrietta Street, we are lucky to have two 'snapshots': the censuses of 1901 and 1911. While neither census is entirely comprehensive (the 1911 census is slightly more detailed), they nonetheless provide the best insight we have into the nature of the tenements on a street-by-street basis. The Irish census differed from that distributed in Britain in several ways. Crucially, the Irish census included a question asking the religion of every person in a household, something which was not included in the British form. In 1901, the majority of those living in Henrietta Street (88 per cent) were Roman Catholic. Of the remaining 12 per cent (112 people) the bulk were members of the Church of Ireland (85), followed by those who were members of the Church of England (22). Thus, Anglicanism accounted for most of the Protestant presence

Figure 86 (right) John Cooke, Waste ground and ruins near Chancery Street, 1913. This photograph shows the ruined sites at the back of the houses in Chancery Street.

Figure 87 (below) John Cooke, Faddle's Alley, off Dowker's Lane, 1913. This image shows the backyard of a family living in Faddle's Alley, in the Blackpitts area.

Figure 88 John Cooke, Interior of tenement at 8 Waterford Street, 1913.

Figure 89 John Cooke, Interior of tenement at 8 Waterford Street, 1913.

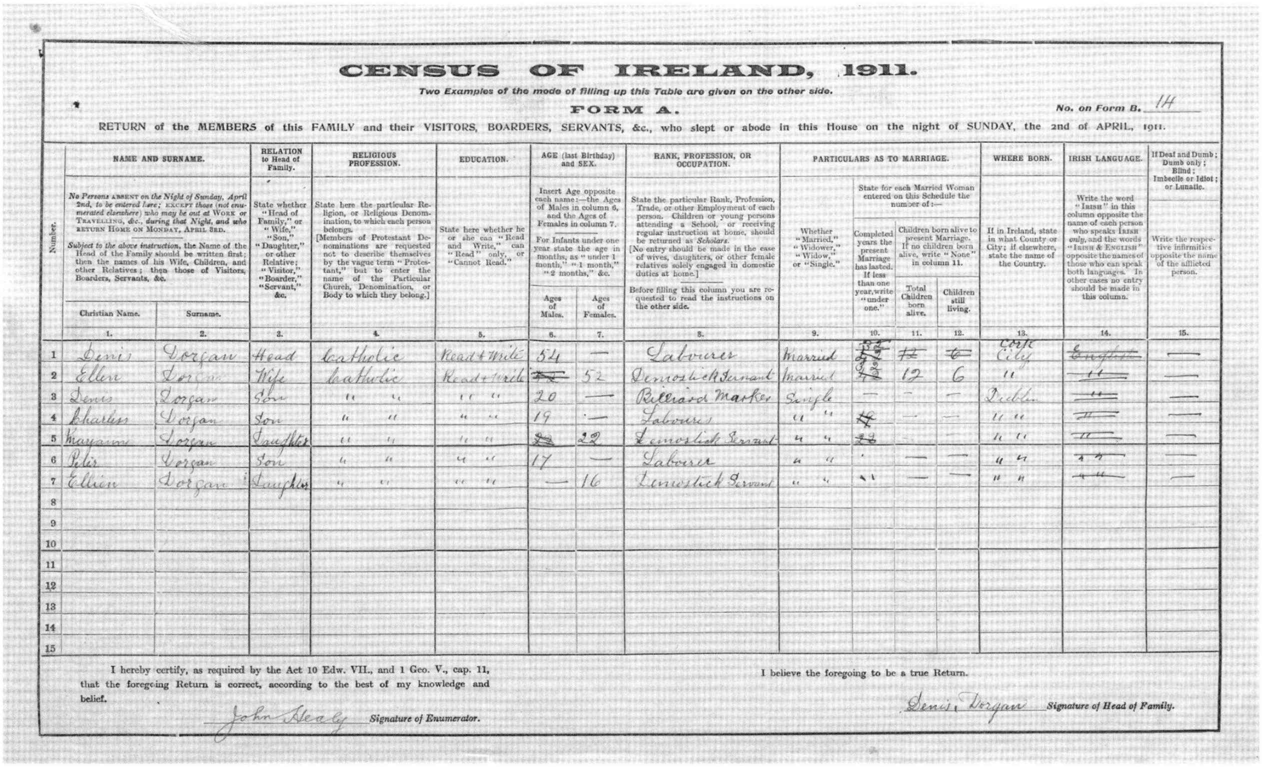

Figure 90 Census enumerator's form for the Dorgan family in No. 14 Henrietta Street, taken from 1911 Census.

on the street. There were, however, a small number from other denominations: two members of the Plymouth Brethern (a Protestant evangelical movement which had originated in Dublin in the 1820s), as well as one Wesleyan Methodist, and two Presbyterians.

The census also provides information about 'place of birth', allowing us to get a sense of where the street's residents were from. In 1901, the majority of those living in Henrietta Street (73 per cent) were native Dubliners.[16] Of those Irish residents who were non-Dubliners, the majority came from Leinster, although there were several from the other three provinces. What is striking is the forty-six people in Henrietta Street who were born outside of Ireland. Half of those born outside Ireland were from England, particularly English industrial towns like Manchester, Leeds and Halifax. Another seventeen people came from Scotland, mainly Glasgow and nearby textile towns. This would suggest that Dublin still had significant ties to Britain via economic migration to manufacturing centres.

However, by far the most revealing category of information the census provides is that concerning occupation. What did Henrietta Street's residents do for a living? It seems that the street was representative of the wider Dublin economy, with a heavy emphasis on low-skill and casual labour. By far the most common jobs on the street were 'general labourer' and domestic servants. In 1901, the single-largest category of employment on the street was 'laundress', due to the 45 women working in the laundry at Our Lady's Home, run by the Daughters of Charity at Nos. 8, 9, and 10. Industrial or factory work accounted for only a small proportion of people in Henrietta Street (less than 5 per cent of those who were employed). In 1901, just under 10 per cent of Henrietta Street's residents worked in the construction trade, in trades such as carpentry and brick-laying. Small manufacturing, mainly clothing, accounted for just over 8 per cent of those employed in Henrietta Street, with tailoring and dressmaking accounting for the bulk of this. However, there were a good deal more working in the low-skill carrying trades, such as porters or servants, or in the low-skill end of transport, such as 'car drivers'. Taken as a group, these low-skill and unskilled workers account for just under 18 per cent of the working adults in Henrietta Street in 1901. This ignores numerous adult males living in the street who did not give any description of occupation, meaning the unskilled contingent is most likely substantially higher.

What emerges from these various numbers is that Henrietta Street was a relatively representative sample of Dublin's occupation structure, in that it demonstrated a relative weakness in industrial employment. In 1911, a quarter of the city's adult males were employed in unskilled 'general labour', such as the carrying trade and casual labour on the docks.[17] This meant that the workforce was extremely vulnerable to victimization by employers, low wages, long hours and periodic unemployment. The city economy's reliance on transport and distribution, as well as the dominant industries of brewing and distilling, meant a high proportion of workers were casual, often discharged in slack times. Periodic unemployment was often built into many occupations with seasonal periods of slack work being a feature of tailoring, dressmaking and the building trades. The records of Dublin's workhouses and the city's prisons also serve to give us an insight into the occupation of those in Henrietta Street who were vulnerable to unemployment and poverty. As with the census, these sources provide a diverse range of occupations, from fish dealers to mattress makers. However, they also reinforce how vulnerable those who were general labourers in the carrying trades were to poverty. Among those who found themselves in a Dublin prison between 1885 and 1906, giving Henrietta Street as an address, just under 40 per cent were general labourers. Similarly, in the workhouse, 'general labourers', servants and 'char women' together accounted for 46 per cent of those who gave a Henrietta Street address in this period.[18]

It was not just the male workforce who suffered from Dublin's weak economy. For the city's working women, the lack of any large sources of industrial employment meant fewer opportunities compared to most British cities. The proportion of women engaged in distribution in Dublin, 'dealing' particularly, was far in excess of most British cities. Other low-skill casual occupations for women were obviously domestic servant, but also 'charwoman' or washerwoman. Indoor domestic servants represented 40 per cent of all female employment in Dublin in 1901.[19] Again, Henrietta Street was broadly in line with the city as a whole. Of the 202 women on Henrietta Street who reported an occupation in 1901, the largest group was 'laundress' (45 women), again due to the Daughters of Charity. After that, the most common occupation was in clothing manufacture, with 30 women described as 'tailoress', seamstress or dressmaker. Another 23 women reported their occupation as domestic servants, while another 12 reported their occupation as either 'machinist' or 'factory worker', indicating some opportunities for industrial employment. Indeed, there were a few instances of women working in jobs that would have traditionally been considered male roles. For instance, in No. 14, a young woman named Kate Carpenter worked as a 'French Polisher' (this was a type of wood finishing that involved many thin coats of shellac). Interestingly, Kate's father and brother worked in unskilled jobs, as a building labourer and a messenger. The issue of female employment also brings up the question of household structure and the number of families in which a woman was the main breadwinner. Taking the 1901 census and examining the household structure of the 152 families on the street, 31 of these households explicitly return a woman as head of the family. In No. 14, one such household was led by a thirty-year-old Hester Moran, a mattress machinist who supported her elderly mother, as well as her own three children. The building was also home to Catherine Caffrey, a biscuit packer who supported her parents and her two brothers, as well as her sister and her two children. Women were a crucial part of the working life of Henrietta Street and the city as a whole.

Children in the tenements

Henrietta Street was a young street: in 1901, the average age was twenty-three and a quarter of those living on the street were under ten years of age. Conversely, it was rare to reach old age: those over the age of 65 accounted for only 1 per cent of the street's residents at the beginning of the twentieth century. The result was that children were a very big part of day-to-day life in Henrietta Street. In 1907, one newspaper described how Henrietta Street continued to be a popular location with children:

> In winter the street is given over to crowds of boys rushing about whilst playing a kind of football. In summer the favourite game is 'tip-cat' which seems to consist of throwing up into the air, and then hitting vigorously down the street a piece of wood, known I believe, as the 'cat'.

The article went on to note that these children also made use of the grounds of the King's Inns: 'these gardens are every day swarming with children, for whom they furnish a safe and admirable playground'. Such descriptions give us an impression of the type of games that these children used to play, an insight into how young people from the tenements had fun and enjoyed themselves. However, for middle-class observers, the 'perpetual playground' of the street was a dangerous thing. In the words of one journalist from the *Irish Times*:

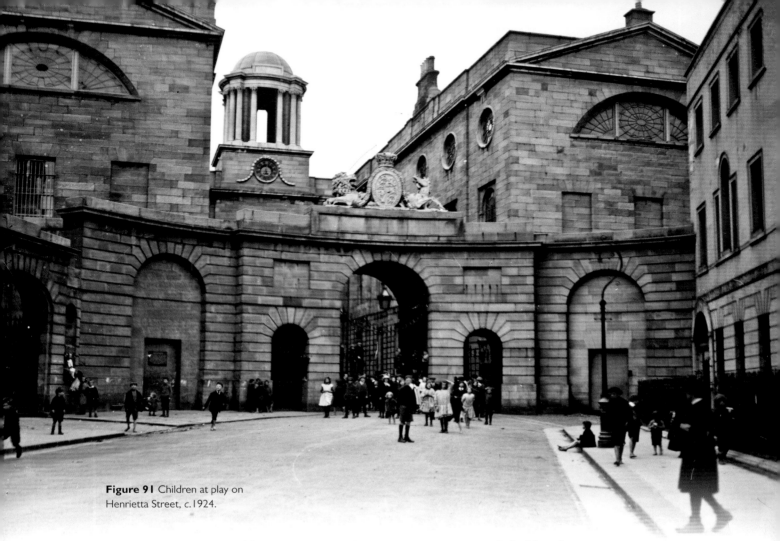

Figure 91 Children at play on Henrietta Street, c.1924.

> the future citizen of five or six years, whose parents are poor ... [is] obliged to take his recreation after school hours either in the street or on tenement stairs ... The open recreation spaces, which relieve the congested houses in fine weather, do not supply the place or recreation halls, or children's gymnasia, where a friendly controlling influence could be exercised ... which is so necessary for city children.

Even bleaker was the verdict of a representative of the National Society for the Prevention of Cruelty to Children (NSPCC) who argued that the conditions inside the tenements were so bad that 'the children are better out of them ... it would be very much worse to leave those children in their tenement houses in the evenings than in the streets'.[20]

In 1901, the vast majority of children on Henrietta Street were reported as 'schoolchild', with no children under the age of 14 reported as working. Most of these schoolchildren probably attended the nearby national school in King's Inns Street. However, there were also several nearby 'ragged' schools, schools run as philanthropic projects by religious orders. In nearby Lurgan Street, a Protestant school run by the Irish Church Missions had been active since 1853. Controversial due to its Protestant evangelism, it nonetheless provided both education and material aid to those living in north Dublin's tenements. Not to be outdone, Catholic charitable schools sought to provide an alternative, with several nearby Catholic 'ragged' schools (renamed St Brigid's schools), in North Anne Street and Halston Street. One of the most important distinctions between 'ragged' schools and the national school system was the provision of food and occasionally clothing within the ragged schools. Until 1914, national schools did not provide meals to students, while simultaneously enforcing strict rules of attendance, which did not allow a sufficient break for students to return home for a meal. In practice, however, many national schools got involved in providing their students with food and clothing, despite disapproval from the Commissioners of National Education. It is perhaps significant that the national school closest to Henrietta Street, in King's Inns Street, was one of the schools most heavily involved in providing aid to students, attesting to the area's poverty.[21]

Figure 92 Bill Doyle, Children playing on Henrietta Street, 1960s.

While every child in Henrietta Street under the age of fourteen was recorded as attending school, for older children it was a different story. In 1901, two-thirds of those aged 14 to 17 were employed. A consequence of Dublin's widespread poverty was that children often had to help supplement their parents' income. According to a witness to a state inquiry, child labour was a direct result of Dublin's lack of well-paying jobs: 'the fact that we have so few industries in the city, that the whole of the family are dependent upon the earnings of one member of the family, and, therefore, the amount of wages upon which they have to live is exceedingly small'.[22] In Henrietta Street, many of the teenage children worked as messengers, while several were assistants to tradesmen such as cabinetmakers, upholsters and plumbers. Others worked in the clothing line, as assistants to tailors or dressmakers. While the work was undoubtedly gruelling, it was better than the fate of those who worked as street hawkers, selling bootlaces, matches, flowers or newspapers. At least if one gained some skills by assisting a tradesman, their teenage occupation might lead to steady employment.

Charity and poor relief

Despite the additional income that children could bring into a household, low wages and periodic unemployment left little margin for savings, meaning that an injury or illness could bring disaster. All too often, families would have to resort to borrowing to keep themselves fed or to make rent, perhaps seeking help from neighbours and family, or short-term credit from a local store or dealer. If these options were exhausted, there was also the local pawnshop, of which there were a sizeable number in Dublin. The pawnshop was a familiar aspect of working-class life; as one observer commented, 'many households in this city have, as a regular feature of their weekly routine, an extensive pawning on Monday and redemption on Saturday'.[23] The city's medical officer similarly noted: 'No inconsiderable number of the poor get out of their beds, or substitutes for them, without knowing when they are to get their breakfast, for the simple reason that they have neither money nor credit. They must starve if they have got nothing which would be taken in pawn'.[24]

What options did the poor have if they could not find employment or if they fell sick? The state did provide some minimal relief. Since 1838, when a new Poor Law was applied to Ireland, poor relief was administered by an area's Poor Law Union. In Dublin, the Corporation was the public health authority but it was the Boards of Guardians of the North and South Dublin Poor Law Unions that administered assistance to the poor. This aid was in the form of 'indoor relief', that is, via admission to a workhouse. The workhouse was one of the most feared institutions in nineteenth-century Dublin. While it provided a basic level of welfare, the regime within its walls was purposely designed to be brutal, in order to deter all but the neediest. But for the sick, elderly, disabled and abandoned wives and children, it was often the only option. Once within the confines of the workhouse, families were separated into different sections: able-bodied men and youths over 15, able-bodied women and girls over 15, the infirm (of both sexes) and children of both genders under 15.

In Dublin, there were two workhouses, one for the South Dublin Union at James Street, and for the North Dublin Union in North Brunswick Street, near Grangegorman. Workhouse records reveal that due to its proximity, Henrietta Street residents who sought refuge in the workhouse tended to go to North Brunswick Street. Theoretically, those who were admitted to the North Dublin Union and were diagnosed as having mental disorders were supposed to transfer to the nearby Richmond Asylum. However, many of those found to be suffering from mental illness were left with the general workhouse population. Workhouse inmates were forbidden from having alcohol, playing cards

Figure 93 'Street arabs', children on the street, Dublin, 1900.

Figure 94
The Grangegorman complex, twentieth century. In the centre of the image is the North Dublin Union Workhouse, with the Richmond Lunatic Asylum to the left of it and the Richmond Penitentiary to the north.

or dice or having certain types of food not allowed by the authorities. Punishments were meted out to those who were caught with contraband, using profane language or feigning sickness to avoid work. The able-bodied of both sexes got up at 5:45 a.m. and after a breakfast from 6:30 to 7, worked from 7 a.m. to 6 p.m., with a one-hour dinner break at noon. Work was brutal and monotonous. Common tasks included breaking stones or oakum picking (unpicking old ropes into fibre). Women might additionally be employed in tasks such as sewing or needlework. The only days when inmates were allowed rest were Sundays, Good Friday, and Christmas Day.

Many who entered the workhouse did so for very short stints, perhaps only a few weeks or months. Many spent only a few days, using the workhouse as short-term relief when faced with eviction or lack of accommodation. For some women and their children, it might have been used during a husband's absence or in cases of domestic abuse. Henrietta Street provides at least one example of the way in which the workhouse could be resorted to for frequent (but short) visits. Mary Ridgeway, a 28-year-old wife of a labourer living in No. 5 Henrietta Street, entered the North Dublin Union Workhouse on six separate occasions in 1904, from June to December, each time entering with her 1-year-old daughter Christina, and each time only staying a few days.[25] For some, the workhouse fulfilled a vital role in the city's medical services. In 1901, the social services handbook of the Church of Ireland described how the workhouse hospital, 'originally

Figure 95 A workhouse scene, with children, Dublin, 1895.

intended to accommodate only the sick inmates of the workhouse, it has by degrees developed in many cases, into the public infirmary of the district'.[26] Again, Henrietta Street provides an example. In 1892, Julia Kenna, a 29-year-old widow from No. 14 Henrietta Street and an epileptic, entered the workhouse hospital with a 1-year-old daughter who died within Julia's first six months there.[27]

While tragic, such a story was common, and reflective of the horrifyingly high mortality rates in Dublin's public institutions.[28] One very vulnerable group that were liable to end up in the workhouse was the elderly. Before the introduction of the Old Age Pensions Act in 1909, there was little in the way of provisions for those who lived to old age. They were reliant on their own savings, the support of relatives, or as a final resort, the workhouse. Yet again, Henrietta Street provides examples. Mary Connor, a 60-year-old widow from No. 16, entered the workhouse in 1895, dying there six years later in 1901. Bridget Doyle, a 74-year-old widow from No. 7, entered in 1894, dying in 1900.[29]

For those who were young and able-bodied, the workhouse was the last resort. The stigma of the workhouse was something most of the 'respectable' poor avoided at all costs and the strict regime within its walls certainly discouraged entry. However, the city was served by several charities that helped provide an alternative. Since the eighteenth century, the non-sectarian Sick and Indigent Roomkeepers Society provided temporary relief for the poor. Since 1818, the Mendicity Institution had also attempted to deliver food, clothing and, when possible, basic employment to the city's neediest, with a focus on its street beggars.[30] Several other groups provided charity to the needy, although most were connected to a religious body of one description or another. Groups like the Association for the Relief of Distressed Protestants provided assistance to the city's Protestant working class, a still sizeable group in the nineteenth century.[31] For the Catholic majority, the largest lay charity was the Society of St Vincent de Paul (SVP), which had 30 branches in the city, distributing relief to some 5,000 families. The Society was particularly active in visiting the homes of the poor; indeed, grants of assistance were usually contingent on a visitation to a person's home. These visitations also offered opportunities to engage in religious work and to observe the family's behaviour.[32]

Figure 96 Drawing of the Sick & Indigent Roomkeeper's Society, Castle Lane. Founded in 1790, the Society is Dublin's oldest still functioning charity.

One of the most critical aspects of charitable activity was the aid provided for pregnant women and young mothers. One notable institution in this respect was the 'Dublin Hospital for Poor Lying-In Women', better known today as the Rotunda. The Rotunda is the oldest continuously operating maternity hospital in the world, but it is also an institution with a longstanding connection to Henrietta Street and the Gardiner Estate. In the mid-eighteenth century when the first Luke Gardiner was developing his lands on the north side, the founder of the lying-in hospital, Bartholomew Mosse, chose a new site for the hospital in 1755, one which would include pleasure grounds which would generate income from public entertainments and visitors' fees. The Gardiners took advantage of this new amenity to lay out what would become Rutland (now Parnell) Square. From its early beginning, though, the Rotunda sought to aid poorer pregnant women.

SPECTRAL MANSIONS

Figure 97 Robert French, Back of the Rotunda Hospital, 1890s.

Mosse often declared that 'the misery of the poor women of the city of Dublin at the time of their lying-in would scarcely be conceived by anyone who had not been an eyewitness of their wretched circumstances … destitute of attendance, medicine and often of proper food by virtue of which hundreds perished with their little infants'.[33]

Mosse was working in the eighteenth century, but a century later, the same challenges faced poor Dublin women who were carrying a child. While the hospitals like the Rotunda and the Coombe (established 1826) continued to provide expecting mothers with help, many women from Dublin's tenements would give birth in their homes or in the workhouse. In the nineteenth century, all new mothers faced the risk of miscarriage, post-natal infection and even death. In 1890, it was revealed that Dublin had the highest infant mortality rate out of any city in the British Isles, with the poor and working class affected worst of all. The overall death rate in the north inner-city was 50 per cent higher than the rate in suburbs such as Rathmines and Rathgar. Most families from Dublin's tenement districts had endured the agony of losing an infant, and had made the sad trek out to Glasnevin Cemetery with a small plain coffin. The 1911 census recorded not only the number of children born to a family, but the number of those children still living. Of those parents from Henrietta Street who provided this information, over two-thirds had lost at least one child, with several families having experienced shocking stories of loss. For instance, in No. 8, the 41-year-old Mary O'Neill had given birth to fourteen children in her life, only one of whom had survived, an 11-year-old daughter named Sarah. As one city official put it,

> there is a popular idea that the children of the Dublin working classes met within the slums are a healthy class ... These fine healthy little creatures are, unfortunately, only the survivors, their less favourably endowed little brothers and sisters have long since passed away, and many even of those able-bodied survivors will, before they grow into adults, in their turn be gradually taken away by disease and death.[34]

In the face of these conditions, the city's charities and hospitals did what they could, but very sadly the largest single category of charity in nineteenth-century Dublin were orphanages. By the 1870s, the city contained forty-four of them, catering for every religion and social class. Most abandoned or orphaned children were cared for by the twenty or so Catholic orphanages or boarding-out schemes, nearly all of which were controlled by female religious orders. Henrietta Street was itself home to a significant charitable institution: the Daughters of Charity. This religious order ran several institutions out of their premises in the street, eventually expanding to occupy Nos. 8, 9 and 10.[35] The first of these was an asylum for discharged female prisoners. The Dublin Discharged Female Roman Catholic Prisoners Aid Society had been founded in 1881 by a lay committee, but in conjunction with the Daughters of Charity. The decision by the Daughters of Charity to locate their refuge in No. 10 Henrietta Street (it had initially been in North King Street) was due to the proximity of the institutional sector in Grangegorman, particularly the Richmond female penitentiary. The Henrietta Street asylum provided these women with a place of residence on arrival and recommendation for jobs. They also provided shelter to those prisoners who would be returning to their homes in the countryside, often escorting them to the train after their stay to ensure they were not 'led astray' by former acquaintances in the city.[36]

The necessity of training women for the workforce was another vital activity undertaken by the Daughters of Charity in Henrietta Street – one that was not simply confined to former prisoners. A night school for factory girls was commenced in 1904 which soon had 100 students, teaching cooking, sewing and domestic work. The activities of the Sisters were expanded, in a physical form, with the purchase of No. 9. Internal doors were opened between the properties, allowing for increased accommodation as well as additional workrooms to give employment to discharged prisoners who did not live in the house, but who were unable to find employment in the labour market, reflecting the depressed economy.[37] One of the employments within the house was laundry work. An extensive laundry was created within No. 10 in 1907, while another was built at the rear of No. 9 in 1911. In addition to the laundry and home, the Daughters of Charity purchased No. 8 for use as a night refuge for poor women, which opened in 1913 and which operated until 1961. In the 1920s, further facilities were added, including a hostel for nuns, business girls and students, as well as a day nursery.[38] One recent historian who has studied the reports and correspondence of the Daughters of Charity, has argued that the home played a

Figure 98 Street view of No. 9 Henrietta Street, 1909.

benevolent role in the lives of the women housed there. The laundry was registered under the Factory Act and thus open to inspection. The Sisters kept in touch with some of the girls and repeatedly provided short-stay accommodation for former residents who found themselves temporarily unemployed. It has been pointed out that former residents wrote grateful letters to the home, which were appended to its annual reports. Another indication that the women had a positive experience was the fact that former residents who found employment often came back to the Home to have their aprons and print dresses made.[39]

The revelations of the last several decades concerning institutions such as the

Magdelene laundries have necessarily shaped our perception of religious charities. There is no denying that the set of institutions that came to be known simply as the 'Magdelenes' were harsh, repressive and morally indefensible. It is important to note that Our Lady's Home in Henrietta Street was not technically a Magdalene laundry, although it did contain a laundry within it. Still, the home had much in common with 'Magdalenes', in that it catered to a largely destitute class of women and enforced a strict system of discipline. Yet until at least the first decade of the twentieth century, these institutions can arguably be described as 'flexible', with the majority of inmates entering and leaving voluntarily.[40] This was certainly the case with the institution run by the Daughters of Charity in Henrietta Street. However, this would later change. It would appear that during the early years of the Free State, the Henrietta Street home became decidedly less 'flexible'. After 1923, it allegedly became a very common institution for female prisoners to be remanded to, as a form of probation in lieu of prison, with women serving sentences ranging from three months to three years. Most of the girls assigned to the home were convicted of petty pilfering, although there were also some infanticide cases.[41]

Crime and punishment

Those living in the tenements might encounter the state via the workhouse, or through the national school system. Others might interact with one of the city's many charities. However, Dublin's poor might also regularly encounter another type of institution: the Dublin Metropolitan Police. It should be stated that Henrietta Street was not necessarily an area with a reputation for crime. However, like any impoverished area it contained its share of social problems. The street itself was occasionally the site of minor crimes or disturbances. For instance, in 1878, two men were arrested for arranging dog fights in Henrietta Street (one of them was later charged for hitting the policeman arresting him). In addition to dog fights, it seems that bare-knuckle boxing matches were occasionally organized on the street, with a newspaper in 1892 reporting how these groups of fighters 'were in the habit of collecting in Henrietta Street night after night, and conducting themselves in a disorderly fashion'. Considering the street's proximity to the King's Inns, such activity might seem surprising. As one lawyer remarked: 'it is surprising that a locality which is the home of law should be the home of lawlessness'.[42] The physical space of the street itself was clearly an often-riotous place, but so too were the interiors of the houses. One of the consequences of buildings being subdivided into so many different apartments was that tenements were mostly 'open door'. With hallways and stairs open to anyone, numerous social problems emerged, such as the use of such spaces for 'immoral' activities. The survival of graffiti on the walls of No. 14 Henrietta Street, forbidding intruders and loiterers, attests to the problems caused by such open access.

Looking at prison registers and surviving arrest records, we can get an idea of what

Figure 99 Graffiti on landing wall of No. 14 Henrietta Street. 'ANY PERSION WHO TAMPERS WITH ANY TING OR WHO IS NOT RESDINT IN THIS HOUSE WIL BE PROSECUTED BY LAW'.

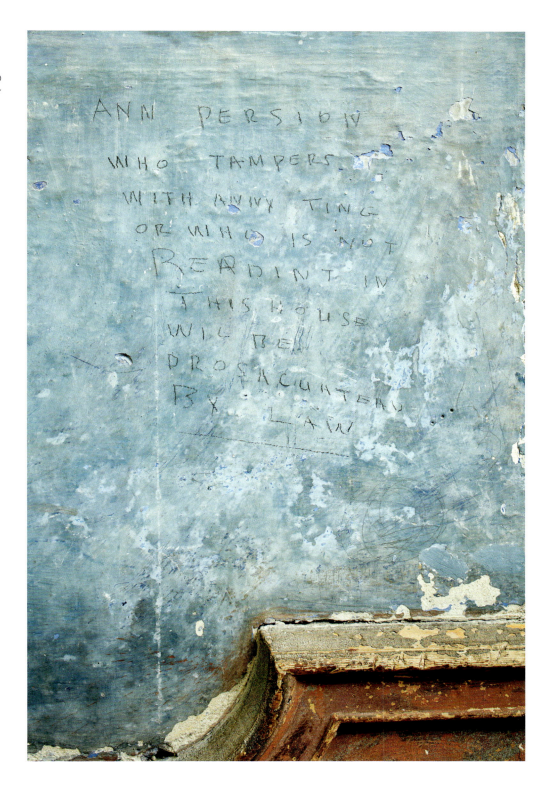

LIFE AND DEATH IN A TENEMENT, 1880–1910

crimes were committed by residents of Henrietta Street in the years 1885–1905.[43] During these years, there were only two serious crimes against a person (as opposed to crimes involving property or 'vice'). In 1898, a 60-year-old woman from No. 2 Henrietta Street, Catherine Gibney, was imprisoned for manslaughter. In 1906, another resident of the street named James Dunne was imprisoned for assault, having stabbed a man.[44] Violent crime was not a frequent occurrence in Henrietta Street, and in this the street was broadly in line with the city as a whole. In Dublin, serious offences (murder, rape, manslaughter, burglary) represented only a small proportion of crimes. Far more common were petty offences, which were 'civil' rather than criminal in nature: breaches of traffic acts, vandalism, drunkenness, loitering. These exceeded 'serious' crimes by over ten times. As a whole, crime was on the decline during the last several decades of the nineteenth century. Irish cities, particularly Dublin, were proportionately more highly policed than British cities. In 1900, the numbers of crimes committed in the Dublin Metropolitan Police district was less than half what it had been in 1870.

A twenty-year sample of prison records (1885–1905) provides an interesting range of offences committed by residents of Henrietta Street: 'breach of railway bye-laws', 'cruelty to a cow', 'ill-treating a donkey', and even 'attempt to commit suicide'. One of the most common categories of offences committed by residents on the street was petty theft, usually of small items of clothing or food. For instance, in 1904, Annie Brady was arrested from her home in 16 Henrietta Street, charged with defrauding a local grocer.[45] There were also several instances of assault, as well as 'malicious

Figure 100
A member of the Dublin Metropolitan Police patrols on Eden Quay, late nineteenth century.

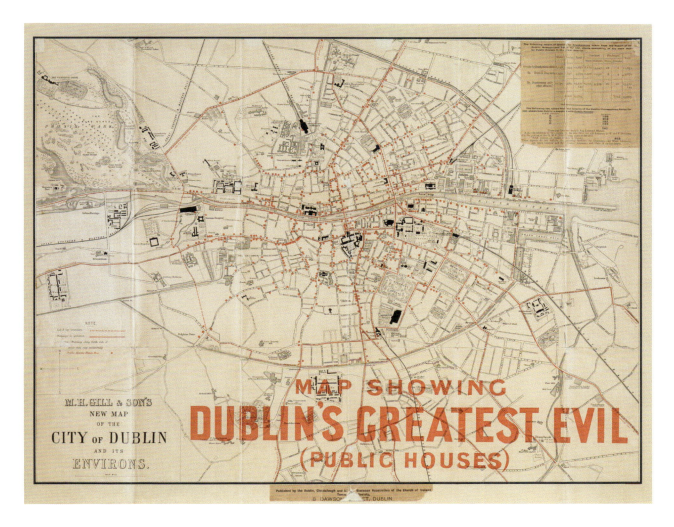

Figure 101

Map showing Dublin's greatest evil (public houses), 1892.

damage' or vandalism. However, by a wide margin, the most common crime among Henrietta Street residents was drunkenness (just over 28 per cent of the sample). This includes 'drunk and disorderly' as well as some more intriguing descriptions such as 'drunk in charge of a horse' and 'drunk and in charge of loaded firearm in a public street'. Looking at just one house on the street, No. 14, we see that half of the entries in prison records for residents of this building were for drunkenness. Once again, the street was broadly in line with the city as a whole. In the year 1899, just over 9,000 people were arrested in Dublin for drunkenness (over a third of them women), and this was actually an improvement over earlier, higher rates.[46] Drunkenness was seen as one of the great social problems of the Victorian age and a constant theme of moralists and religious reformers. Certainly, the work of temperance movements (and more importantly stricter licensing acts) had done much to reduce the number of arrests for drunkenness in the last decade of the nineteenth century. In 1901, however, Dublin had one of the highest rates of arrests for drunkenness within the British Isles. While middle-class observers were rarely sympathetic about the use of alcohol among the working class, some realized that the demoralizing conditions of the tenements and alcohol abuse were linked. In the words of one witness to the 1885 Housing Inquiry: 'if I had to live in the depressed conditions in which the poor of this country live, I too should become a drunkard'.[47] Alcohol was a cheap relief to the depressing realities of working life: the public house provided a refuge from overcrowded living accommodation, the use of spirits or porter might temper a substandard diet.[48]

After drunkenness the other great 'social evil' of the age was prostitution, a crime that similarly obsessed moral reformers. Much like other cities, extreme poverty had encouraged the growth of prostitution in Dublin, likely exacerbated by the presence of a large garrison. In 1901, the police estimated 1,677 women were involved in the city's sex trade, a figure equal to just under 2 per cent of the adult female population (most likely an exaggeration).[49] One of the city's most notorious red-light districts was the area around Montgomery Street (now Foley Street), a district better known as 'Monto' and fictionalized in James Joyce's *Ulysses* as 'Night town'. However, prostitution was not a crime that was restricted to any one part of the city. Henrietta Street, with its proximity to the barracks, was certainly affected. In the years 1885–1905, only one woman living in Henrietta Street was imprisoned for the crime of prostitution or soliciting. This was Ellen Watson, who was arrested in 1886 and again in 1889 for solicitation. However, in many cases, women in the sex trade were not arrested for the crime of prostitution itself, but for other offences that were most likely related, such as drunkenness or loitering.[50] For instance, taking slightly later prison records from 1914, we find the case of Annie Burke, living at No. 16 Henrietta Street. During her time there, Annie was arrested on four separate occasions. While her occupation is described as 'prostitute' in all four instances, only two of these arrests are for soliciting, the other two being for 'drunk and disorderly' and 'assault of a police constable'. Her sentences ranged from seven days to a month.[51]

While it was the brothels in 'Monto' that tended to catch the headlines, prostitution was also carried out by individual women working out of lodgings within tenement buildings. The barrister and politician Tom Kettle recounted once being shown around a tenement by a woman who was working as a prostitute, and who worked out of one of the rooms. Kettle was not there as a client; he was there as part of an investigation into the conditions within the city's slums. The circumstances that this woman lived in shocked him: 'there was a family living in every corner but one of that dilapidated salon. As we approached the prostitute's corner we approached civilization. There was a screen around the bed'.[52] How such women were treated by other tenants is difficult to generalize. A later collection of oral histories from Dublin tenements records how neighbours could be sympathetic to sex workers: 'they were very decent, very kind, the wives'd even say "hello" to them and be friendly enough'.[53] Other sources suggest a more hostile reaction. One man interviewed by investigators into housing conditions in 1914 complained that he wanted the eviction of a woman living in the room above his own as she was an 'unfortunate' (a common euphemism for a woman working as a prostitute), and that he was trying 'to bring up children dacint … and how could he do it with women like that in the house'.[54]

While parents may have done the best they could to raise their children 'dacint', prison registers also record incidence of children from Henrietta Street being incarcerated. The majority of these cases were for minor crimes such as 'loitering', and petty larcenies of objects such as boots, food or small quantities of goods like tobacco. Many were never imprisoned, simply arrested then released with a caution. Using surviving ledgers of the DMP, we get a tiny glimpse into the experiences of young offenders from Henrietta Street. Taking the year 1916, we find that Thomas Loyer and Anthony Kinsella, two ten-year-old boys from No. 14 Henrietta Street, were cautioned after having broken the glass in a fire alarm. Another young man, a 15-year-old named John Shannon from nearby 13 Henrietta Place, was put on probation for the crime of 'frequenting Royal Barracks'.[55] Others were not so lucky as to receive a simple warning or probation. If a young person was arrested, charged, and found guilty, the consequences could be severe. By the beginning of the twentieth century, children were rarely committed to Irish prisons (as they had been in earlier decades), but were instead being sent to a new set of institutions that have since become notorious for their abuses: the industrial and reform schools. Industrial schools had been introduced to Ireland in the nineteenth century and had quickly expanded. By 1921, 7,000 children were detained in these institutions. These schools had a dismal record of providing adequate welfare: 2,623 children died in the custody of these institutions between 1869 and 1913.[56] Only a small proportion of children committed to industrial schools committed any crime, and many of these hardly merited the harsh penalties that residential schools imposed. For instance, in 1916, two young men from Henrietta Street, John O'Reilly and Thomas Keating, aged 11 and 10 respectively, were sentenced to Carriglea Park for four years for the offence of stealing boots.[57] Carriglea Park was an industrial school run by the Christian Brothers, the brutal conditions of which have been documented in the published report of the Ryan Commission.[58] While the bulk of this evidence relates to a later period, it is nonetheless disturbing to consider that two young boys were sent to such an institution for four years simply for stealing boots.

Disease and death

While life in Dublin's tenements was undoubtedly tough, those who had survived to adulthood were the lucky ones. At the beginning of the twentieth century Dublin had the highest death rate per capita in the British Isles, and this was largely due to a high infant mortality rate and the pervasiveness of infectious disease among the city's working class. Dublin's many tenements were a breeding ground for a host

Figure 102
Constance Gore-Booth, Countess Markievicz, 'Visit to a Dublin family during the tuberculosis epidemic', 1924.

of 'zymotic diseases', a category of illness that included all the major killers of the nineteenth century: typhus, typhoid fever, scarlet fever, measles, cholera, diphtheria, and several more. Along with tuberculosis and respiratory illness, these accounted for the extremely high average mortality rate. The link between the prevalence of disease and the overcrowded conditions in tenements was self-evident. In an 1879 report on disease in Dublin, two of the city's medical staff described how

> the crowded and unsanitary living conditions in the tenements, compounded by malnutrition and insufficient clothing ... were aggravated by the high rate of unemployment. Diseases such as typhus, typhoid, smallpox, dysentery, tuberculosis and the dreaded cholera, all had one thing in common – they found an easy and deadly foothold in the poverty-weakened bodies of the inhabitants of the Dublin slums.[59]

Thanks to the records of Glasnevin cemetery, we have a record of seventy-four people from No. 14 Henrietta Street who died over a thirty-eight-year period (1864–1902).[60] Of these deaths, just under half were of children aged five and younger. Three of the infants from No. 14 were either still born or died due to premature birth, while another three died due to vague descriptions such as 'delicacy' or 'disability'. Similarly, another six children died due to 'convulsions'. Convulsions were most probably only the final effect of other conditions or infections, such as dehydration resulting from gastrointestinal problems.⁶¹ After these descriptions, the biggest category of fatal diseases among the children from No. 14 were diseases relating to the lungs: bronchitis, pneumonia and 'phthisis', a lung disease sometimes known as 'wasting sickness' or consumption, but which we know today as tuberculosis. In fact, tuberculosis was also the most common cause of death among adults in this sample, followed closely by bronchitis. Along with ailments such as asthma, whooping cough and inflammation of the lung, respiratory diseases account for roughly half of the adult deaths in No. 14 during these years. Of the remaining adult burials in Glasnevin, the causes of death include several instances of heart disease, stomach cancer, liver failure and 'general debility' (effectively old age). However, adults also succumbed to infectious diseases, with typhoid, measles and diarrhoea each accounting for a single death.

There was an obvious link between the conditions in the tenements and the prevalence of disease. Yet many officials were still unclear how to rectify the problem. This was partially the result of debates within the medical and scientific community. Until the 1880s, disease was widely believed to be caused by 'putrid accumulations of organic matter' and that it was spread by 'bad air' or 'miasma'. On the face of it, this theory made sense when applied to the congested, ill-ventilated housing of the

Figure 103
John Cooke, Tenement interior, Francis Street, The Coombe, 1913.

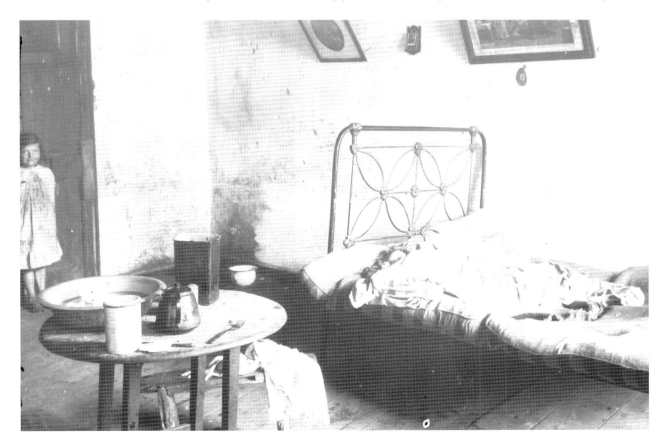

LIFE AND DEATH IN A TENEMENT, 1880–1910

tenements. Therefore, the answer was simply to allow light and air into these districts by opening confined passages of overcrowded buildings, as well as removing 'putrid' matter by ensuring regular 'scavenging' and waste removal. One of the consequences of the belief in 'miasmic' theory was that sanitary reformers were led to expect dramatic improvements from very limited measures, such as whitewashing or the widening of streets. In the latter half of the nineteenth century, public health authorities stressed the need to eradicate disease blackspots, areas vulnerable to repeated outbreaks. It was argued that these so-called 'fever nests' needed to be improved as they posed a health risk to the population as a whole. While a fever outbreak might start in an impoverished house, it could quickly spread to the middle classes. In 1866, new by-laws provided for the regular inspection and cleansing of such dwellings, with Dublin Corporation opening a Disinfecting Department in Marrowbone Lane that included a laundry and medicated baths. The Public Health Act 1875 (extended to Ireland in 1878) gave local authorities even more extensive sanitary powers, which they were not afraid to use. During outbreaks of contagious diseases, the Department could isolate the infected persons, as well as a mandated disinfection and cleansing of their rooms, furnishings, bedding and clothing.

From 1880, Dublin's Disinfecting Department began to tackle the city's many private slaughterhouses and dairies within residential areas, businesses that frequently spewed insanitary by-products into streets and alleys. These businesses were increasingly pushed out of the city centre, and those that remained were subject to regulation. Another significant area of improvement was in the area of refuse collection. During hot summers, discarded rubbish and waste could bring masses of flies swarming around

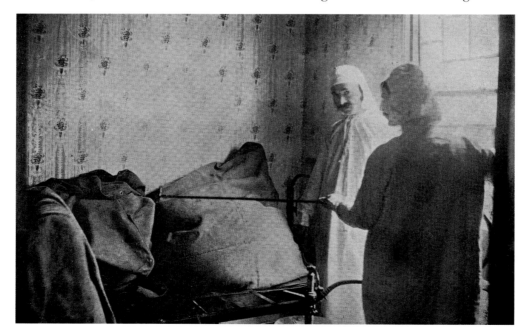

Figure 104
Disinfectors spraying infected premises with disinfectants, 1911.

Figure 105
Dublin Corporation, *The fly peril*, 1914. This was a leaflet distributed by the Corporation's Public Health Committee during the summer of 1914.

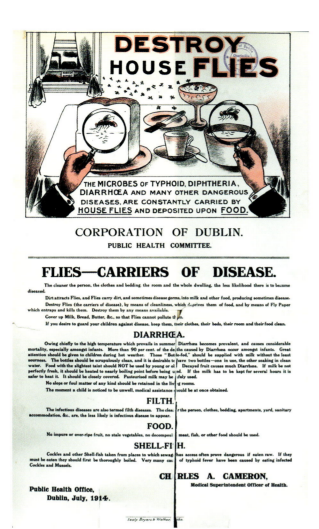

tenement yards and alleys, resulting in the outbreak of illnesses like diarrhoea. By 1900, however, considerable progress had been made in providing the regular removal of house refuse in portable dustbins that replaced ash pits in backyards. Yet the biggest improvement in the city's sanitation was the introduction of a new, clean water source from the Vartry reservoir, completed in 1868. Previously, water had simply been taken from the Liffey or its tributaries. Yet, surprisingly, the new water supply did not lead to an immediate reduction in mortality rates, even from diseases like typhoid fever, commonly spread by contaminated water. This is partially explained by the fact that few tenement families had their own in-house water supply, instead relying on a single outside common tap, as well as still having to carry and store water in infected surroundings, making washing and hygiene problematic. Moreover, despite the growing number of flush toilets, Dublin's main drainage scheme was not completed until 1906; until then the city's sewage simply flowed into the river Liffey, gaining it a reputation as an 'Irish river Styx'. The city's death rate remained high, as serious epidemics could still occur, such as the spate of measles infections in 1899, while an outbreak of smallpox in 1903 killed thirty-three Dubliners. While the numbers dying from typhoid, typhus and cholera were declining, instances of the 'wasting disease' of tuberculosis only peaked in 1904 in Dublin, accounting for 13,000 deaths that year. Sanitary measures might improve conditions but could not eradicate the core problem: widespread poverty. As Dublin entered the twentieth century, the extent of the problems facing its working class, particularly the problem of affordable housing, was all too clear. While it would not be quick or easy, the age of housing reform was finally at hand.

Figure 106 'The tenement – a menace to all', *Puck* (New York), March 1901. The image's caption declares that tenements are 'not only an evil in itself, but the vice, crime and disease it breeds invade the homes of rich and poor alike'.

4

The beginnings of reform, 1900–14

Throughout the western world, the turn of the twentieth century was a time when cities began to tackle the problem of tenement housing. For instance, in 1901, the American Progressive movement succeeded in passing the New York State Tenement House Act. A landmark piece of legislation, it banned the construction of tenements with poor ventilation and sanitation, imposing state regulation on New York's working-class housing stock for the first time. The Act was the result of a crusade by both politicians and social reformers, as well as a considerable campaign in the press. One American magazine, *Puck*, carried a cartoon that depicted a tenement building, from which a series of ghosts issued out of. The caption explained how tenements were not simply a social disgrace in themselves, but that they created a multitude of sins: alcoholism, prostitution, disease, gambling, drug-abuse, crime and (overseeing them all) death. Once again, the metaphor of tenements producing ghosts was a potent one.

This movement for housing reform was present in Ireland as well, albeit progressing at a slower pace. The issue was often subsumed by the larger political context, as the year 1900 witnessed the reunification of the Irish Parliamentary Party (IPP), after a decade of division and in-fighting. The mission of the IPP was to achieve 'Home Rule': a degree of self-government and devolved power for Ireland, with the restitution of an Irish parliament, but the country staying within the empire. The IPP paid significant attention to Dublin and its local politics. After all, if Home Rule was achieved then the city would once again be the seat of a national parliament. Many in the IPP felt that Dublin Corporation would thus provide a model for this new Home Rule parliament.[1] In contrast, Irish unionists felt that an improvement of living conditions in the city could be part of 'killing Home Rule by kindness'. Meanwhile 'advanced nationalists', those who sought full independence from Britain, realized that agitating on housing issues could be part of a larger campaign against British rule. In 1900, however, the ascent of advanced nationalism still lay in the future, and the IPP would continue to win the majority of Irish parliamentary seats until 1918.

The IPP was similarly dominant within Dublin Corporation, with its supporters controlling the city's local government. Many Dubliners, however, increasingly regarded the 'Corpo' as corrupt, dominated by the publicans and petty shopkeepers who also staffed the IPP. Within the municipal council, patronage and insider dealing were the norm, although a movement for municipal reform was (very slowly) beginning to take shape. In 1898, a new Local Government Act had broadened the Dublin electorate considerably. Before this, only about 8,000 people were eligible to vote in local elections, a number that had now more than quadrupled to 36,000 voters. This included 900 women voters who for the first time could cast a ballot in Dublin's municipal elections, if not yet parliamentary elections. In the Inns Quay ward, the division that Henrietta Street was located in, women now represented 24 per cent of the electorate.[2] While this was certainly an improvement in representation, in some regards it fell short. To be eligible to vote, electors had to pay more than 4*s*. a week in rent and have been resident in the same location for at least a year. This disqualified the vast majority of the city's unskilled and semi-skilled workers, living in cheap tenement rooms and moving frequently. Nonetheless, in the twentieth century, the voice of the tenements would demand to be heard.

Disease, death and sanitation

In Henrietta Street, the twentieth century began with the threat of eviction. In No. 9, an unemployed tailor named Timothy Carroll and his family were facing homelessness. Months earlier the family had fallen behind on their rent, and bailiffs had been sent to confiscate most of their furniture. However, this was not enough to pay off their arrears and the landlord, Joseph Meade, pursued an eviction order, scheduled for 21 December 1899. The order had been delayed, however, as one of Carroll's children had died from measles, while another two were in a 'state of collapse'. The public health board intervened, persuading Meade's agent to postpone the eviction. By January 1900, another of Carroll's children had died, while a third was seriously ill with pneumonia. Nonetheless, Meade insisted he was still owed five months' rent and would pursue the family's removal.[3] While the ultimate fate of Carroll's family is unknown, many aspects of their story were all too familiar. Not simply the struggle to pay the rent and the precariousness of low-paid work, but also the threat of disease, especially to children. The turn of the century had been marked by an ever-increasing awareness of the poor state of Dublin's public health, and the dreadful death rates it produced. The city's annual death rate was at least 25 per cent higher than any other city in the British Isles. Dublin had the highest rate of infant mortality of any city in the United Kingdom during the years 1899 to 1913.[4] Dublin was lagging behind not only most British cities, but most of Western Europe. In 1906 an international comparison of urban mortality rates found that Dublin was closer to cities such as Moscow and Budapest. Within Dublin, the poorest areas had death rates that might compare to some of the worst neighbourhoods of Cairo, Moscow or Madras.[5]

These issues were very much in the news in 1900, as a sharp rise in the death rate the previous year had led to an inquiry about the probable causes.[6] The report had been produced by the Local Government Board, and it had canvased the district medical officers. The finished report concluded that the city's high mortality rate was not just the result of periodic epidemics (although this did certainly occur) but of deeper, structural problems in the city. The causes the report gave for the excessive death rate were a depressing repetition of what had been said for decades: the overcrowding in specific districts and the insanitary housing conditions this produced, the shortcomings in sewerage and sanitation, but most of all the staggering extent of poverty within the city. Several years later, Dublin's chief medical officer, Sir Charles Cameron, produced a pamphlet entitled *How the poor live*, in which he flatly stated that 'there are probably no cities in the United Kingdom in which so large a proportion belong to the poorest classes as is the case in Dublin'. Cameron was also clear that it was the horrendous mortality rates among those at the bottom of society that produced the high overall death rate: 'I do not believe that in any English town a high death rate in one fourth of the population could have the same effect on the general rate'.[7] With such a large proportion of the city's population living in a state of perpetual malnourishment, fatal disease would always be an intrinsic part of life in the tenements.

Which is not to say that there had been no attempts made to improve things. In the last several decades of the nineteenth century there had been some very real achievements in terms of urban sanitation. For instance, in 1880 'dry privies' (outhouses without a flush system or water) had been the norm, with the city containing only 743 water closets. Within a couple of years, the number of water closets had risen to 15,000.

In the 1890s, Dublin Corporation carried out some impressive infrastructure projects, such as its main drainage scheme, which enormously improved the disposal of sewage from the inner city. The regular removal of rubbish and refuse had also improved, with portable dustbins replacing the ash pits that been the standard in most large houses. The number of city bins more than doubled in the two decades between 1894 and 1914. The Corporation had also gotten tougher on insanitary houses and cellar dwellings with a noticeable increase in closures of both after 1899.[8]

Yet for all these efforts, urban disease and mortality rates had not improved, a fact frequently commented on by writers and satirists. The cartoon opposite, taken from the *The Leprecaun Cartoon Monthly*, illustrates many problems facing the city. Invoking the well-known nickname of 'dear, dirty Dublin', the cartoon is subtitled 'Wanted: a Public Health Department'. In the image, the female personification of Dublin brandishes a scroll reading 'Highest Death Rate in Europe' to a dissipated figure representing the Public Health Department. Surrounding the two figures are the names of the diseases facing Dublin's poor: 'consumption', 'typhoid fever' 'diphtheria'. While the cartoon points to the old targets of open sewers, rotten vegetables, and private slaughter houses, there are also some new targets. Namely, 'Cork Hill' (the home of Dublin Corporation) and, emblazoned on a tenement building, 'City Fathers, Slum Owners'. The cartoon demonstrates a new, more strident tone to the calls for sanitary reform that were emerging.

Figure 107 (above) The Sanitary Sub-Officers of the Corporation of Dublin, 1909.
Figure 108 (opposite) 'Dear, dirty Dublin', *The Lepracaun Cartoon Monthly*, December 1908.

The extent of the tenement problem

Any attempt to improve Dublin's sanitation would have to contend with its substandard accommodation. As early as 1880, a report on the city's sewerage and drainage pointed out that 'public sanitary works and main sewers will be of little avail if these tenement houses are left in their personal neglected condition'.[9] The health problem caused by the tenements could not be solved by sanitary controls, however strenuously applied. Improved sanitation might treat some of the worst symptoms but it could not eradicate the core issue. Even the closure of insanitary houses and cellars might only make the supply of cheap housing even scarcer, exacerbating the situation. A real solution would require the construction of large quantities of new housing, at rents the poor could afford. For several decades, there had been a lack of speculative building in the city. Between 1891 and 1911, the population of Dublin grew by just over 20,000. Yet only 2,600 new dwellings had been added to the city's housing stock, an average of only 130 new homes per year. Even in the surrounding suburbs, there was comparatively little built for a working-class budget, forcing Dublin's workers to make do with the existing stock of house. In 1911, out of an estimated working-class population of 194,000 in Dublin, only 32,000 lived in purpose-built new houses. Meanwhile the majority of the working class were consigned to live in tenement houses, in squalid and overcrowded conditions.[10]

While knowledge of this issue wasn't exactly new, the full extent of Dublin's tenement problem had been laid bare by a series of reports after 1900. The 1911 census was particularly noteworthy, as it revealed that just under 24 per cent of the city's population lived in one-room tenement dwellings. This type of accommodation was not unique to Dublin of course, but that such a large proportion of the population lived in the lowest class of housing was unusual. In comparison, in Manchester and Liverpool, the proportion living in one-room tenement accommodation was only 6 per cent and 2 per cent, respectively. The closest comparison to Dublin was the neighbourhood of Finsbury in London, where the figure was 14.8 per cent, followed by Glasgow at 13.2 per cent.[11] Whereas in most cities one-room tenements constituted only a small proportion of the total working-class housing stock, in Dublin they housed close to quarter of the population.[12]

The result was that large sections of the city were in noticeable physical decay. Again, this was hardly news. As discussed in a previous chapter, the deterioration of tenement buildings was commented upon as early as the 1870s. However, by the twentieth century, no amount of patching or superficial repair could disguise the damage done to the material fabric of these houses. In 1911, it was estimated that around 1500 of the worst tenement buildings (containing over 22,000 people) could be defined as being totally unfit for human habitation.[13] Tenement owners increasingly resorted to last-ditch efforts to maintain the structural integrity of their investments, such as inserting supporting struts on walls. This practice seemed to be widespread. Dublin Corporation even urged the police to ban heavy vehicles from the city centre, for fear of vibrations leading to house collapses (a fear that was sadly all too real).[14] The dire physical conditions of Dublin's tenement houses even produced satirical cartoons, such as the one reproduced below.

Providing affordable housing

Why had so few homes been built for the working class? There are several answers. First, it needs to be remembered that before the 1920s, municipal authorities throughout the British Isles were hesitant to intervene directly in housing markets. Instead, they favoured incentives to private or philanthropic endeavours, usually in the form of favourable loans. Many city councils in the nineteenth century had been convinced of the ability of philanthropic capitalism to tackle the evils of overcrowding and insanitary housing. The dominant ideology of 'laissez-faire' economics maintained that there was no substitute for the all-knowing and benevolent free market.[15] Many Victorians also believed that poverty was the result of the moral failings of the poor, and therefore providing housing would undermine the will of the poor to be self-reliant and remove the incentive for them to 'morally reform' themselves. However, neither 'laissez-faire' nor 'moralism' were entirely coherent or all-encompassing ideologies, and neither fully explains the situation in Dublin. Instead, the explanation can be found in several external factors restricting the provision of public housing. First, the tight financial restrictions and limited tax base which Dublin Corporation relied on. The exodus of the city's middle and upper classes to the suburbs had drained the city of tax revenue and restricted its options in pursuing new projects. Dublin Corporation was repeatedly frustrated in its attempts to annex

Figure 109 'Doomed at last', *The Lepracaun Cartoon Monthly*, January 1913. This cartoon depicts the very real phenomenon of external supports being used to prop up structurally unsound tenement buildings.

Figure 110 David Jazay, Ellis Court, Benburb Street, 1992. The flat complex at Benburb Street was the first Dublin Corporation housing scheme, constructed in the 1880s.

these townships, although in 1900 some new areas like Kilmainham, Drumcondra and Clontarf were added. Yet the largest and wealthiest suburbs, Rathmines and Pembroke, remained independent and outside of the Corporation's jurisdiction. If these areas had been added, they would have helped provide additional land for building working-class housing. But more importantly, they would have brought large numbers of middle-class citizens into the city's tax base. Similarly, if the city boundaries had been extended to include all the townships, this would have added to the city's valuation, enhancing its ability to borrow money for new projects. In 1900, a Conservative government in Westminster had refused to include Ireland in a Housing Act that would have removed borrowing limits for city councils building municipal housing, a measure which would have greatly benefitted Dublin. This was the first time in thirty-four years that Ireland had been deliberately excluded from British urban housing legislation.[16] Without the desired boundary extension the Corporation's only option seemed to be to levy further taxes upon its already limited base, an option that produced stiff opposition and protest from Dublin ratepayers.[17]

While the provision of public housing on any significant scale was slow to emerge in Dublin, the city's Corporation nonetheless became a significant player in the urban housing market. Due to the strict financial and legal limitations that it operated under, the Corporation's interventions were initially limited. It was not until 1884 that the formal approval was granted for the Corporation's first housing scheme at Benburb Street, at the time known as Barrack Street due to its proximity to the Royal Barracks (now Collins Barracks). It was a plain, even austere, design. Particularly on city-centre sites where the land costs were high, there was a need for cost-cutting measures to keep rents down. The Benburb Street project was a four-storey building, containing 144 small flats that ranged from one to three bedrooms. Alongside the flats, the site included a 72-bed lodging house, aimed at providing for single adults who could not afford a flat. (It would continue to function as a Corporation-run lodging house for elderly men into the 1970s.) In Benburb Street, the flats were aimed at those who could not afford dwellings provided by private companies, with rents as low as 1s. 6d. a week. However, there were problems almost immediately. The blocks had been built to low construction standards, with near-constant repairs and improvements needed. Even more harmful was the street's pre-existing reputation for prostitution and vice. As early as 1837, a publication described how

> it is known to every officer whose regiment has been quartered in the Royal Barracks at Dublin that their vicinity has long been cursed with a line of brothels and low public-houses called Barrack-street, and filled with the most abandoned crew of rogues and prostitutes which even all Dublin, with its unhappy pre-eminence in that species of population, can produce.[18]

Dublin Corporation's attempt to provide cheap housing in an area with long-standing social problems may have been well-meaning but ultimately misguided. Moreover, the Benburb scheme was not the only instance in which Corporation housing failed to achieve its design. Between 1900 and 1911, the Corporation constructed a series of apartment blocks in Brides' Alley, adjacent to Iveagh Trust housing. However due to high site costs and foundation works, rents were set at high levels and the Corporation curtailed some of its plans for the scheme. In 1904–5, the Corporation constructed an even larger estate of five-storey tenements in Foley Street, the heart of the red-light district of 'Monto'. Again, the Corporation had attempted to house the very poor by providing 460 cheap flats, most a single room plus scullery and WC. However, the estate soon earned a reputation for vice and squalor, with the Corporation being forced to rent rooms at loss-making levels.[19]

Previously, during the 1890s, Dublin Corporation had also experimented with a different strategy of building self-contained cottages, such as at St Joseph's Place, Clonliffe Street and Blackhall Place. After 1900, when the city's boundaries were extended to certain neighbouring suburbs, the Corporation constructed cottages at

Figure 111 Newspaper image of Foley Street flats, *Evening Herald*, 24 June 1977.

Drumcondra (1903–4), Clontarf (1904–5) and Inchicore (1905–10). After 1908 and the introduction of new housing legislation, the Corporation increasingly built self-contained cottages on cleared inner-city sites.[20]

Significantly, the Corporation was not the only body active in Dublin's housing market. Several private and philanthropic bodies had also been building homes aimed at the working class. Several of these companies have been described as 'philanthropy at five per cent', representing a business that was still for-profit, even if their goals were ultimately benevolent. The Dublin and Suburban Workmen's Dwellings Co., commenced in 1890, was run on these lines but by 1914 had built only 288 houses for 1,600 inhabitants. The activities of the Guinness (Iveagh) Trust are well known, with impressive works at Kevin Street, Bull Alley/St Patrick's Cathedral, and Bride Street to name a few.[21] Some large businesses constructed housing for their work forces, usually close to their work and of generally superior quality. For instance, Guinness constructed apartments in Rialto and then in Belview, on the fringes of the brewery complex. Similarly, several railway companies built worker accommodation, as in Inchicore, where the Great South Western Railway Company built large numbers of houses.[22] However, by far the most important company of this type was the Dublin Artisans' Dwelling Company.

The Dublin Artisans' Dwelling Company

First set up in 1876, the Dublin Artisans' Dwelling Company (DADC) played an important role in the provision of working-class housing for the next several decades, helping to shape the look of much of the modern city. The DADC was the product of a conference organized by the Dublin Sanitary Association, a group which itself was a reaction to a series of epidemics that broke out within Dublin's slums in the 1870s. The DADC was thus part of a wider movement for healthy and affordable housing. It was to be the only sizeable semi-philanthropic housing body in Ireland. It

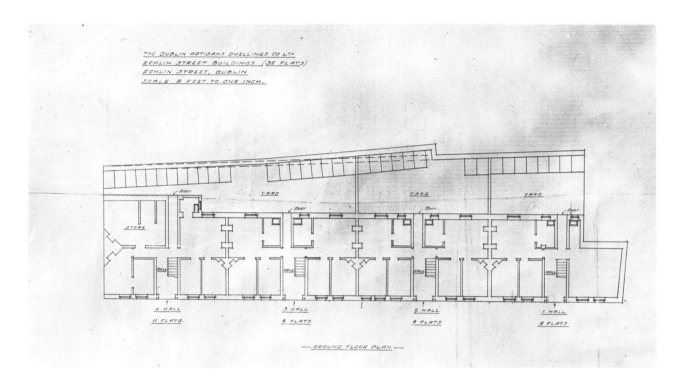

Figure 112 Plan for the Dublin Artisans' Dwelling Company buildings at Echlin Street.

is important to note that the DADC was not designed as a charitable institution. It was a joint-stock company, run for profit. The company's capital was raised through issuing shares, with investors promised reliable dividends, albeit at a reduced rate of between 4 and 5 per cent. Its shareholders included some of the most prominent members of Dublin's business elite, including Sir Arthur Guinness (1st Baron Ardilaun), his brother Edward Guinness (1st earl of Iveagh), William La Touche, William Findlater and John Jameson. However, free-market principles notwithstanding, the DADC benefitted from state assistance in several ways. It received public loans at interest rates better than the general market rate, as well as leasing several sites from Dublin Corporation for very favourable amounts (so favourable in fact that the Corporation lost money).

The DADC's first projects took inspiration from the British tenement model, constructing multi-storey apartment blocks at Buckingham, Echlin, and Dominick Streets in the north-east of the city between 1876 and 1888. However, the company soon abandoned these multi-storey designs for schemes comprised of one- and two-storey cottages, such as their projects in the Coombe and Plunkett Street during the 1880s. This paved the way for more extensive schemes in Rialto and Harold's Cross, before the acquisition of a twenty-six acre site in Stoneybatter, which would become one of the company's largest and best known projects, the Manor Place Scheme (1901–8).

The DADC had a number of standard house designs that they reused ('Type A', 'Type B', etc.), which made construction more efficient and cost-effective. Even

Figure 113 G & T Crampton, Part of a housing scheme of 700 houses for the DADC, 1903–6. This image shows the Oxmantown Road in Stoneybatter.

in a single project like Stoneybatter, the apparent repetitive layouts masked some surprising variation of design. The DADC exercised considerable control over their tenants, ensuring prompt collection of rent and swift eviction for repeated non-payment. The company was careful to prevent overcrowding by employing caretakers who not only collected rent, but also reported on the occupants and recommended new tenants they considered 'suitable'. For instance, newly married couples were not allowed to remain living in the house of their parents, although they would get first preference for new rental property as it became available.

While the company's houses were considered to be of very high quality, a repeated criticism was the level of rent that it charged. The high rents were a result of the high building cost and the low density of the cottage estates, meaning that the DADC was only able to rehouse better-paid workers. The standard rent for a single-storey dwelling ranged from 6s. to 8s. a week, putting them out of the reach of most 'general' or unskilled labourers. As the *Irish Builder* pointed out in May 1903:

> It is obvious no poor man can pay the rents demanded by the Artisans' Dwellings Company, running, as they do, up to 10s. a week, we believe, a sum, needless to say, beyond the means of a workingman, even though he be a tradesman in receipt of good wages. The houses ... are in many instances, we are informed, let to people of a totally different class, such as commercial clerks, and so on.

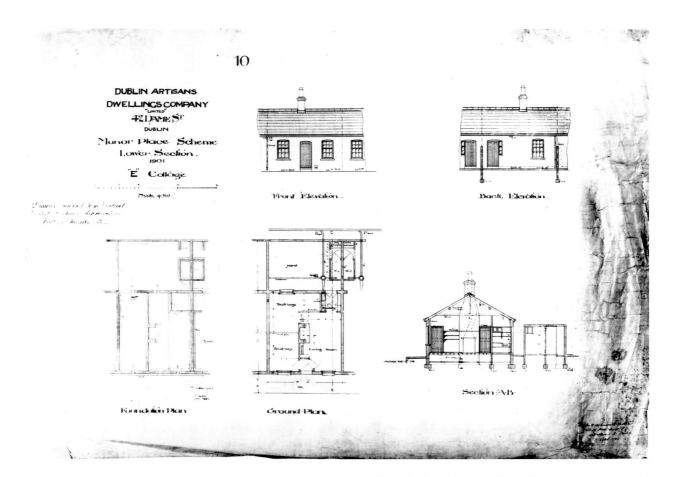

Figure 114 Dublin Artisans' Dwellings Company, Blueprints for Type 'E' Cottages, 1895.

This was true, as the 1901 census confirmed that clerks, police officers, and the highly skilled predominated many of the company's estates. However, the company justified this by arguing that there was a 'filtering up' effect, as the better-paid workers moved into DADC homes they would free up dwellings for the worse-off. While this conclusion was questionable, the DADC were nonetheless the main provider of new working-class housing until the early twentieth century.[23] The concepts of subsidized social housing and direct state intervention was still not sufficiently evolved. Working-class housing schemes were expected to be at least self-financing, if not actually profitable.

Moreover, despite the best of intentions, the number of new houses built in the city, whether by the Corporation or the DADC, fell far short of what was required. By 1918, the Corporation had built over 2,000 dwellings, roughly split between flats and cottages. Over almost four decades, the DADC had on average erected less than 100 houses a year. To put this in perspective, in 1914 it was estimated that between 15,000 and 20,000 houses were still urgently needed.[24] This failure to adequately provide urban, working-class housing was in stark contrast to the progress made in *rural* Irish dwellings in the same period. Nearly 50,000 cottages for agricultural labourers had been built between 1883 and 1921, at a cost of 8.5 million pounds, mostly with the help of subsidies from the British exchequer. The years 1910–11 alone saw 6,223 rural dwellings completed. Irish rural labourers were occasionally described as 'among the best housed of their class in Western Europe'.[25] The shortcoming of the private housing sector in Dublin becomes even starker when the city is compared to Belfast, where house-building ran at a rate of around 1,000 units a year in the 1880s. In the 1890s, the annual average was nearly 2,000 dwellings, with a peak of 4,500 dwellings constructed in 1898.[26] These new houses were built specifically for the working classes. Although laid out in monotonous terraces, they were a 'two-up-two-down' design of good quality, constructed out of red brick and slate roofs. Houses were carefully graded in size at rents between 2*s*. 6*d*. and 5*s*. per week. What was important was that they catered for all sectors of the working class. As the *Irish Builder* remarked about Belfast, 'No city in the kingdom has a better supply of smaller modern suburban houses of very moderate rents'.[27] Sadly, the same could not be said for Dublin.

Municipal housing: cottages or blocks?

In the early years of the twentieth century, it was clear that thousands of people living in tenements needed to be rehoused. The risk posed by the tenements was not only disease, but of physical breakdown. In fact, it was the collapse of a tenement in Townsend Street in 1902, a collapse that killed one person and injured many more, which prompted a special housing conference the next year. The 1903 conference was only the first of a series of housing conferences held in Dublin over the next several years, but it was nonetheless a landmark. Attended by local MPs and members of the Corporation, this was when the municipal authorities finally got serious about the prospects of massive slum clearance and rebuilding. While it was obvious that the Corporation would have to intervene in the housing market on a large scale, it was still unclear as to what form this intervention should take. There were several options. One possibility was to build tall, high-density blocks of flats within the city centre. Examples like the Iveagh Trust flats had shown that this option could be done well, with plenty of light and ventilation, leaving workers close to the centre of town and their place of employment. However, there was also the option of rehousing workers on the city's borders in small houses (usually referred to as cottages). There was a certain appeal to this option, as building tracts of low-density housing on the outskirts (where land was cheaper) made such a project more affordable. However, detractors pointed out that this would separate people from their work, as well as imposing higher travel costs. The same critics claimed that the 'suburbanization' of workers would serve to only relocate the slums, not to cure them, while simultaneously creating large desolated areas within the city centre.[28] Nonetheless, this suburban solution won out in 1903 and, in many ways, it continued to be the overarching policy of the Corporation for the next several decades.[29]

Figure 115 'Town planning (latest scheme)', *The Lepracaun Cartoon Monthly*, July 1914.

TOWN PLANNING (Latest Scheme
MOTTO—" EXCELSIOR!"
Certainly! Abolish the tenements. Each family a cottage. Suburbs being too far for workers, central ground rent too dear, there being no charge for sky space, the higher the air the purer, we'll build the cottages on top of each other.

The cartoon opposite satirizes the two contrasting options for working-class housing provision, depicting workers' cottages as being stacked like inner-city tenement blocks.

To make these workers' cottages a reality, the Corporation, aided by the Irish Parliamentary Party, sought new legislation to enhance their powers. The Housing of the Working Classes (Ireland) Act of 1908, known as the Clancy Act, made some significant strides forward.[30] It extended the power of compulsory purchase to Irish city councils, as well as lifting limits on municipal borrowing (a measure that had been previously denied in 1900 and 1903). It also made it less profitable for slumlords to own tenements, as the owner was now obliged to keep the properties in habitable condition; if he did not the municipal authority was empowered to demolish the premises, the costs of the demolition being placed on the owner. The Clancy Act was passed at a time when private entities like the DADC were building few houses, meaning that the local authorities were now almost the only builder of new and affordable housing. Crucially, the act created a direct government subsidy for urban housing, although it amounted to only £6000 a year. Nonetheless, this at least established a precedent of state subsidy for urban housing.[31]

The politics of housing and labour

The years immediately after the Clancy Act, those leading up to the First World War, were a time when urban reform was in the spotlight. This was partly due to a new and assertive labour movement in the city. While organized labour had made gains in local politics after 1900, these had been modest. In the early years of the century, labour candidates in municipal elections tended to get assimilated into the nationalist politics of the Irish Parliamentary Party.[32] The IPP was very good at curbing any opposition to its dominance, effectively portraying itself as sufficiently attentive to 'labour' interests. The rhetoric of the IPP blamed the Act of Union as the major cause of all of Ireland's problems, and this was a belief shared by most trade unionists. Any deviation from the nationalist party line could be painted as a form of treason. There were occasionally challenges to the Party's dominance, such as the socialist James Connolly's unsuccessful campaign to win a seat on the City Council in 1903. However, such opposition was rare.[33] This all changed in 1908, however, with the arrival in Dublin of James Larkin. Larkin, like Connolly, represented a new form of trade unionism, one that was not based around the older craft trades, but that included semi- and un-skilled labour. Originally from Liverpool, Larkin's first experience in Ireland had been in organizing Belfast's dock workers, where he had led an unsuccessful strike. Having then come to Dublin, Larkin would go on to found the Irish Transport and General Workers' Union (ITGWU) in January of 1909, drawing members from a range of industries including unskilled labour, eventually reaching a membership of more than 24,000 workers by the start of 1913.[34] Right from the start Larkin's tactics and personality alarmed employers and career politicians. Larkin ascribed to a doctrine known as syndicalism, the idea that workers could gain control over the economy (and eventually the government) by direct means such as a general strike. For Larkin, the weapon of the sympathetic strike could be used to cripple Dublin's capitalist class, as well as help create a common sense of class identity among workers. Whereas the Irish Parliamentary Party had been able to assimilate earlier labour leaders, the socialism of Larkin and Connolly was something different entirely.

In 1911, Larkin had founded a newspaper, *The Irish Worker*, as a pro-labour alternative to the capitalist owned press. It was notable not only for the quality of its content, but

Figure 116 Masthead of *The Irish Worker*.

also the spotlight it shone on the living conditions of Dublin workers. In November 1911, the paper devoted an entire front page to 'Facts about Dublin', while subsequent issues aggressively called out members of the Corporation for their failure to address the housing crisis in the city.[35] Even more pointedly, Larkin and his allies were willing to challenge the dominance of establishment politicians at the ballot box. In January 1912, seven candidates (including Larkin) ran for seats on Dublin Corporation, running on a programme that emphasized labour issues, but also housing conditions. They promised that a Dublin under Labour would no longer be a place where 'the children of our class [are] murdered by their unhealthy surroundings'.[36] Despite the venomous campaign against them by the right-wing press, Larkin and four of his colleagues won seats on the Corporation, although Larkin was later debarred due to an earlier criminal conviction. By 1913, the party now held ten seats. Although they were massively outnumbered by the IPP, they still represented the second-largest group within the municipal government. If nothing else, they had upset the cosy monopoly of the IPP in local politics.[37]

The Irish Parliamentary Party therefore had plenty of incentive to try and reassert its dominance over the Irish labour movement. One way of doing this would have been to demonstrate that it could make progress on working-class issues like housing. There were widespread accusations that the Party (and by extension Dublin Corporation) were 'in the grip of the slum landlord'.[38] There was some compelling evidence to support this claim. For instance, when a tenement had collapsed in Townsend Street in 1902, killing one person, the building was revealed to have been owned by a city Alderman, Gerald O'Reilly. Despite the building having been condemned as unsafe, a building inspector (possibly prompted by O'Reilly) had got the condemnation reversed. Despite such shocking negligence, this tragedy did not affect Alderman O'Reilly's career: he was elected lord mayor in 1908.[39] In this regard, O'Reilly resembled Joseph Meade, the owner of most of the Henrietta Street tenements who had served as lord mayor twice during the 1890s. Clearly, the ownership of tenement property was no barrier to advancement in municipal politics. Moreover, the tragedy in Townsend Street would not be the last of this type of incident, with another tenement collapse in 1909, this time in North Cumberland Street. The response of the Corporation was again staggeringly inadequate and complacent: they merely imposed higher standards of workmanship when supporting struts were placed against insecure houses.[40] Two years later, yet another collapse, this time of several tenements in North King Street, seriously injured two men, one of whom later died. By this time, even the conservative *Irish Times* was demanding an official inquiry into the competence of Dublin Corporation, pointing out that 'the slums of Dublin will still be there whether we get Home Rule or not'.[41] Increasingly, the figure of the 'slum owner' and their dominance of Dublin's public life was being blamed for the city's sorry state. Once again, the cartoonists of *The Lepracaun* provided a powerful visual metaphor of the city in the clutches of the 'insanitary monster' that was the slumlord.

DUBLIN'S INSANITARY MONSTER.

The Congress of the Royal Institute of Public Health, which opens in Dublin on August 15, includes in its programme a series of papers on the Housing Problem. It is to be hoped that a visit to the Dublin slums—largely the property of members of the Dublin Corporation, who weep crocodile tears over the lot of the poor while they are robbing them—will not be omitted.

God sends his creatures light and air
And water open to the skies.
Man locks him in a stifling lair
And wonders why his brother dies.

[We reproduce this cartoon by the late Thomas Fitzpatrick, which appeared in "The Lepracaun" of August, 1911, as it represents the present condition of the city under the all-powerful slum-owner.]

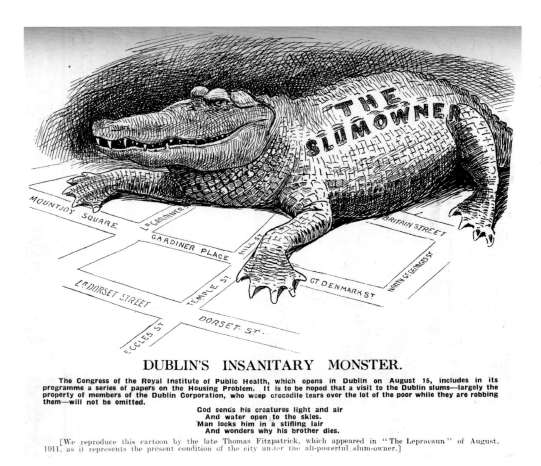

Figure 117 'Dublin's insanitary monster', *The Lepracaun Cartoon Monthly*, August 1908. The cartoon depicts the monster of the 'slum owner' lurking over the streets of the north-east of the city, including the former Gardiner Estate.

Figure 118 (opposite) Front page of *The Daily Sketch*, 5 September 1913. The headlines of a London newspaper days after the Church Street disaster.

Dublin Housing Inquiry

The issue of Dublin's tenement owners and their links to the Corporation would be pushed into the spotlight as the result of yet another tragedy. On 2 September 1913, two tenement houses in Church Street collapsed, killing seven people. Among the dead were two children, aged 4 and 5, while another eight residents were seriously injured. While there had been similar tenement collapses before in the city, this time there was sufficient outrage to force an official investigation.

The chief secretary's office was requested to set up a public inquiry into housing in Dublin, an inquiry that would be carried out by the Local Government Board, a branch of the Dublin Castle administration. It was also a body that had a history of conflict with Dublin Corporation. The LGB had a fraught relationship with most councils, as its principal remit was to keep them in order and investigate possible wrongdoing. It also had the authority to curb their rating power and could also refuse requests for borrowing powers. Any investigation by the LGB into Dublin Corporation was likely to be controversial.

Why Should Women Be Afraid Of The Dublin Police?

DAILY SKETCH

FRIDAY, SEPTEMBER 1913.

Telephones—Editorial and Publishing: 6678 Holborn.
Advertisements: 2972 Holborn.

LONDON'S BEST PICTURE PAPER.

London: 46-47, Shoe-lane, E.C.
Manchester: Withy-grove.

DUBLIN A CITY OF HOMELESS PEOPLE AND GRIEF-STRICKEN PARENTS.

Hanna Dignam and her "home."

A Capuchin friar prays with the bereaved and gives absolution.

Old Mary Dunne, now homeless.

Searching among the debris for imprisoned victims buried underneath tons of masonry.

Thomas Devlin with his wife and child, and Bessie Smith (inset), a cripple whom he saved.

There was nothing left of the house but the walls—and a few ornaments.

When the two tenement houses in Church-street, Dublin, collapsed scenes of anguish and of horror were witnessed. Many of the victims were crushed almost beyond recognition, and mothers were wild with grief when their little ones were dug out of the piles of stone and mortar in which they had been engulfed. Priests tried to console the bereaved, who lost both friends and houses, and comfort the dying. Even strong men joined with them when they offered up prayers for the repose of the souls of the humble victims.

Printed and Published by E. HULTON and CO., LIMITED, London and Manchester.—FRIDAY, SEPTEMBER 5, 1913.

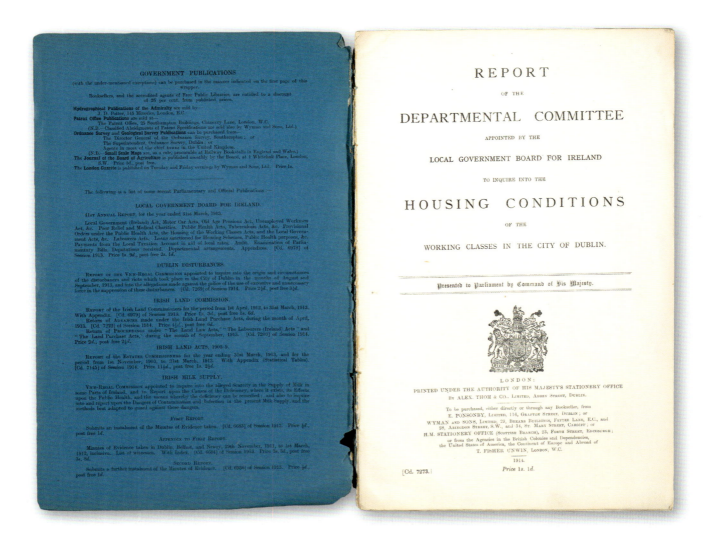

Figure 119 Front cover, *Report of the Departmental committee appointed by the Local Government Board for Ireland to enquire into the housing conditions of the working classes in the city of Dublin*, 1914.

The Dublin Housing Inquiry sat for 17 days in November and December 1913, hearing evidence from 76 witnesses from a variety of backgrounds. Around a quarter of witnesses were members of Dublin Corporation; another quarter were corporation officials; another quarter could be classified as social reformers or housing experts – the remainder represented either private interests, various church bodies or labour organizations. Notably, no one who actually lived in one of the city's tenements was called to give evidence. The eventual report produced by this inquiry was a lengthy and extremely detailed account of the city's housing problems. While much of what it said had been said before, it was nonetheless a significant document. It clearly spelled out the seriousness of Dublin's housing problems, combining graphic testimony with the clarity of statistics relating to the city. It provided extensive documentation concerning the finances of the existing corporation housing schemes, the rents paid in

Figure 120 Cartoon of Sir Charles Cameron, *The Lepracaun Cartoon Monthly*, September 1906.

existing tenements, the incomes of their inhabitants, as well as the costs of rehousing those in substandard accommodation.[42]

As expected, the committee of the Inquiry took aim at the role of Dublin Corporation, particularly the Corporation's failure to effectively enforce sanitary regulations. It criticized the chief medical officer of health, Charles Cameron, for failing to enforce sanitary regulations. This was a criticism which was hardly fair and which did not recognize the very real achievements of Cameron, or the extremely limited resources he had access to. For over half a century, Charles Cameron had been a prominent figure in the debates over Dublin's health and housing. Having been appointed Dublin's chief medical officer for health in 1880, he spent the next four decades in charge of the Sanitary Department of Dublin Corporation.

Throughout his career, he helped ensure that sanitary inspections of domestic and industrial buildings became more widespread, in an attempt to force the closure of the worst and most insanitary buildings in the city. Cameron had introduced a regular street-cleaning and refuse-collection service, helping to abolish backyard ash pits and 'dry privies'. He consistently advocated for the provision of running water and flush toilets for every Dubliner, although this was not achieved during his lifetime. Cameron was also a professor of hygiene and chemistry in the Royal College of Surgeons in Ireland, contributing to debates over the nature of infectious disease, particularly among the poor. He applied the latest science in analytical chemistry to detect the adulteration of food, something that seriously harmed the working class. He was a prolific author, publishing numerous reports and papers on sanitation, nutrition and housing reform. In 1885, Cameron was knighted for his services in the cause of public health, subsequently being appointed as the president of the College of Surgeons in Ireland, and later as president of the Royal Institute of Public Health.

Yet despite these achievements, in 1913 Cameron became the target of intense criticism, particularly his perceived willingness to allow landlords to skirt regulations. Were these criticisms fair? One of the charges against Cameron was that he authorized tax rebates to the owners of tenements, rebates that were only supposed to be granted if significant improvements had been made to the building. Cameron was accused of granting these rebates to landlords who had not made any such improvements, including several owners who were city aldermen. Against this accusation of corruption, Cameron argued that his department had actually refused most of the applications for rebates, while simultaneously defending those that were granted, as he believed they helped keep the rent in such buildings at a reasonable level for those who needed cheap lodgings. Moreover, Cameron could point out to some significant achievements, including the closure of many unhealthy tenements and cellars. Cameron conceded that his officers struggled to always enforce sanitary regulations given the weak sanctions that the law provided them. If Cameron was guilty of lax regulation of standards in the face of special interests, he had also been vocal in advocating the provision of public housing, which he saw as the solution to the underlying problems of the city. In truth, many of the 'revelations' of the 1913 Inquiry had been known to city officials for years, Cameron was merely a convenient scapegoat. While the Inquiry damaged Cameron's reputation, he would defend himself in print, retaining the office of chief medical officer for Dublin until his death in 1921.[43]

However, the housing inquiry took aim at more than just Charles Cameron. It focused on Dublin Corporation in another way, by scrutinizing its members. It was revealed that at least 16 members of the Corporation owned tenement properties. The report stated that 102 tenement houses in Dublin (out of a total of 5,322) were owned by Corporation members. The majority of this property was owned by three people – Aldermen Corrigan, Crozier, and O'Reilly. Between them they owned a total of 61 properties, mostly tenements and a few small cottages. All their properties were deemed to be in poor repair by the inquiry. Even more scandalous was the issue of tax rebates. Owners of tenements could obtain tax rebates if they demonstrated that they had materially improved a previously substandard building. It seems that a large number of these type of rebates had been granted to members of the Corporation who owned tenements, despite many having failed to make the required improvements. Depressingly, despite the publicity given to these revelations, the majority of these tenement-owning members were successfully re-elected in the next local government elections in 1916.[44]

The housing inquiry did more than simply illustrate the extent of the problem, it also put forward possible solutions. The 1914 Report was significant because it provided a detailed and realistic estimate of what would be required to achieve 'the complete breaking up of the tenement system as it exists'. It proposed the building of 14,000 new housing units, to be built on the city's outskirts, keeping with proposals from previous housing conferences. However, for these new cottages to have any real

Figure 121 'Tumbling tenements or, shelling the slums', *The Lepracaun Cartoon Monthly*, March 1914. This cartoon was critical of the potential effect of the housing inquiry's report, fearing it would simply 'end in smoke' rather than significant action.

effect, they would have to be built by the Corporation and not left to 'philanthropy at five per cent'. It was the most extensive and ambitious proposal that had ever appeared and it was explicit in stating the need for substantial state assistance, in the form of 100 per cent loans from government. The estimated cost of this proposal was £3,500,000 – equivalent to ten times the total spent by the Corporation on housebuilding over the previous thirty years.[45]

When the housing inquiry's report was published in January 1914, there was an immediate backlash from a range of commentators. The Corporation claimed that it had been unfairly slandered by the Local Government Board, a body, it claimed, that had actually prevented it from tackling the city's problems. The nationalist majority on the Corporation denounced the report as having been an expensive and impractical waste of time, and simply another example of 'Britain's malign interference in Irish affairs'.[46] It was pointed out that the Inquiry had not probed in to the Local Government Board's own role in the housing crisis, nor were any other municipalities subject to similar scrutiny. Nonetheless, Dublin's municipal council responded by passing a resolution in April 1914, stating that city officials were prohibited from owning any tenement property. Those who did so were urged to sell them immediately, as well as stating that this was a condition for any future promotion within the Corporation.⁴⁷ The outcome of the report, with its demands for state assistance, came at an inconvenient moment for the Irish Parliamentary Party, and Irish nationalists in general. In the words of Mary Daly, 'there is something incongruous in proclaiming their desire and fitness for Home Rule while simultaneously requesting special financial assistance from the British Treasury'. In fact, a deputation of southern mayors even met with John Redmond to ask whether housing grants would still be available from the British government despite Home Rule, which Redmond assured them would be the case. For unionists, the housing inquiry proved that nationalists were incapable of self-government. The Unionist MP George Touch, writing to the London *Times*, declared

> Dublin has Home Rule in Municipal affairs and the town council is controlled by Nationalists. This has prevailed for fifteen years. At the end of that period Mr Lloyd George is able to say that housing conditions are the worst in Europe. What an object lesson in Nationalist rule.⁴⁸

Locked Out: labour and housing

The housing inquiry's report was tied up in the city's tense political situation. All the more so, as the inquiry had occurred during one of the most significant and bitter industrial disputes the city had ever seen: the infamous 1913 Lockout. Between August of 1913 and February of 1914, a coalition of more than 400 employers had come together to try and destroy the Irish Transport and General Workers' Union. The employers had been organized by William Martin Murphy, the owner of the *Irish Independent* and director of the Dublin United Tramway Company, among many other businesses. A deeply conservative man, Murphy was horrified by the syndicalism of Larkin and the threat of the 'new unionism' he represented. The lockout began when Murphy and his fellow employers offered their workers an ultimatum: sign a pledge disowning the ITGWU or resign. When workers refused, they were locked out from their place of an employment. As a result, 15,000 people were put out of work, with an additional 10,000 being laid off as a result of the dispute. Many more casual labourers and street vendors, who were not unionized, also faced deprivation because of the knock-on effects of the dispute. At the height of the lockout nearly a third of the city's working population was reliant on charity to get by.

The 1913 Lockout was more than an industrial dispute; it became a political contest between capital and labour, that was occasionally played out in the streets. On 31 August, the police attacked a crowd gathered to listen to a speech by Jim Larkin, despite an order from the authorities banning the meeting. The police baton charged the crowd, injuring hundreds, while two trade unionists were beaten to death. Another young man later died as a result of his injuries.

Figure 122 Photograph, *Irish Life*, October 1913. This image shows a crowd of strikers, with barefoot boys holding up *Daily Herald* sheets reading 'Murphy Must Go!'

The tenements were a key part of the lockout. It was only two days after 'Bloody Sunday' that the tenements in Church Street collapsed, which had prompted the housing inquiry. The day after the collapse in Church Street, the *Freeman's Journal* was reporting that 'The ITGWU turned the "housing issue" into an active element in class relations, and for explicitly political purposes'.[49] A later commentator observed that 'Labour advocates were not slow to see in this Church Street calamity a splendid object lesson of the evils of Dublin capitalism'.[50] By the beginning of the next year, the Dublin Labour party urged in its manifesto for Corporation elections to 'VOTE FOR LABOUR and SWEEP AWAY THE SLUMS'.[51] Other groups attempted to use the issue of housing to deflect from the grievances of labour. In this sense, the tenements became the scapegoat for the larger economic problems in the city. The conservative *Irish Builder* argued that 'decently housed men would never have fallen such a complete prey to mob-oratory' of figures like Larkin or Connolly.[52] William Martin Murphy's paper, the *Irish Independent*, was eager to shift the spotlight onto housing issues as the cause of the lockout, rather than any fault on the part of the employers. In one issue, it

proclaimed that 'the heather of revolt against intolerable conditions has been dried in the twenty thousand single tenement rooms of Dublin. Syndicalism set the heather on fire'.[53] James Connolly pointed to the new public concern about the slums as 'one of the fruits of the strikers of Dublin had won'. Even the Catholic hierarchy was voicing concern about the link between the slums and the spread of labour militancy. In February 1914, they issued a pastoral calling for sweeping housing reform in Dublin.[54] In a similar vein, the recent disturbances in the city impressed upon the middle classes the need for housing reform. The motivation for providing affordable working-class housing was no longer financial or philanthropic, but due to the fear of social unrest.

Despite this new awareness of social problems, it did not resolve the lockout. The workers and employers settled into a war of attrition over the winter of 1913–14. The odds were always on the side of the bosses, as hunger and desperation forced many

Figure 123 Joseph Cashman, Baton charge of the Dublin Metropolitan Police during the Dublin Lockout, 1913. This image depicts the events of the 'Bloody Sunday' riot of 31 August 1913, in which two people were killed.

Figure 124 (left) Ernest Kavanagh, 'Dublin labour war', 1914. This cartoon depicts Larkin using the 'labour war' to shine a light on Dublin's social problems.

back to work. Although some stuck it out until May, Murphy and the employers could claim a victory. But it was a bitter triumph. In the course of the twenty-two-week struggle, five people had died and hundreds had been injured, with the city's economy and trade dislocated. The employers had lost nearly two-million-man days of work, as well as somewhere in the region of £1 million. The locked-out workers had suffered loss of wages, lack of food, the threat of imprisonment and the reality of police brutality. One of the results of the lockout had been the creation of the Irish Citizen Army, a paramilitary group of volunteers from the ITGWU for the defence of workers from the police. Just as the collapse of tenements had produced an inquiry into housing, the riots during the lockout also produced a separate government inquiry. This investigation into the confrontations between the city's workers and the police painted a picture of a separate underworld of poverty and desperation lurking just beyond the open doors of the city's tenements. The testimony of several police

constables recounted how they feared to enter the tenements when rioters ran into them, with one constable narrowly escaping with his life after passing the door of a tenement in Beresford Place.⁵⁵

Hidden Dublin

The inquiries of 1913–14 seemed to confirm the impression that the tenements were an alien world, hidden from the 'respectable' city. They described in detail a world that had previously only been hinted at by journalists and reformers. 1914 also witnessed another landmark description of the city, albeit of a very different type: the publication of James Joyce's *Dubliners*. Joyce had written this collection of short stories nearly a decade earlier, and the Dublin that Joyce depicts is the city as it was in 1904 (the same year that he would later choose as the setting for his masterpiece *Ulysses*). While Joyce came from a comfortable middle-class background, as a young man he witnessed the social decline of his family due to his father's drinking and poor management of money. Joyce exposed a world that had rarely been depicted in Irish literature: that of Dublin's petit bourgeois, its small shopkeepers and tradesmen, its clerks, moneylenders and bank officials. It was a world of pubs and drab offices, of rented rooms, boarding houses, and homes in less-than-fashionable neighbourhoods. *Dubliners* contains only a few references to those struggling underneath. None of the action takes place in a tenement, and the city's poor and destitute feature only in fleeting roles at the edge of the main narratives, described merely as 'ragged boys' or 'the rough tribes from the cottages'. However, the reality of Dublin's poverty is a constant, if unseen, presence in these stories. The fear of poverty and an awareness of the precariousness of their situation pervades most of the characters, whatever their social background.

Figure 125 (opposite) 'La misère à Dublin', *Le Miroir*, 23 November 1913. This image, published by a French newspaper, was taken during the height of the 1913 Lockout and shows two young boys sleeping rough in a doorway.
Figure 126 (right) Portrait of James Joyce, 1915.

Joyce's depiction of Dublin and its social problems has shaped the popular memory of this era. Yet, by 1914, whether it was in fiction or in the pages of government inquiries, almost every observer recognized that the city's poor desperately needed help. While the most obvious measures were slum clearances and the construction of public housing, what was also needed was a systematic approach to urban development. The city needed a town plan, a blueprint for future growth. Several years earlier, the pioneering town planners Patrick Geddes and Raymond Unwin had arrived in Dublin. Both were advocates of low density working-class 'garden villages', and together they called for a comprehensive city plan for Dublin.[56] The two men acted as housing consultants to Dublin Corporation, as well as helping to create the Civics Institute of Ireland. As it turned out, 1914 was a big year for town planning in Ireland, with the Civics Institute staging its first exhibition in late July of that year. Interestingly, the exhibition took place right next door to Henrietta Street, in the Linenhall Barracks and on the grounds of the King's Inns. In the various promotional material for the exhibition, the motif of Dublin as a 'Phoenix of Cities' was emphasized. The idea was that the city could recover from its recent social and political disturbances, and tackle its challenges head on. The catalogue for the exhibition began with a foreword that proclaimed that 'bad housing affects the entire community, touching the individual, the family, the neighbourhood, and corrupting the social and civic life of the whole city'. What was needed, it argued, was to 'increase amongst all classes the sense of civic responsibility, and to unite them in a fixed resolution to wipe out the shame of our towns and cities by making them towns and cities of homes, not of tenements.' While the event may not have achieved this lofty goal, it did seem to have been a success as an attraction. It reportedly received 9,000 visitors on its opening day, while special trains were run to bring in visitors from outside the city, with some stores running special 'exhibition sales' for its duration.[57]

Despite a strong public interest, the civic exhibition was forced to close prematurely due to the dramatic events in Europe: on Tuesday, 4 August, Britain declared war on

Figure 127 Lilian Davidson, Poster for the Civic Exhibition, 1914.

Germany. The First World War had begun. In the gardens of the King's Inns, the last day of the exhibition was made free to the public. In response, crowds of people from nearby tenements, including those in Henrietta Street, flooded into the grounds and stole away most of the unsecured furniture, most likely to pawn it or to use it for fuel.[58] It was a poignant moment. While the future of the city was being debated by the wealthy and the town planners, while Europe lurched into world war and Ireland's hopes of Home Rule were being shelved, Dublin's tenement dwellers were engaged in the more prosaic and constant war for daily survival.

Figure 128 'Who fears to speak of Easter Week?' A Republican poster commemorating the Rising, 1916.

5

Henrietta Street and the Irish Revolution, 1914–23

At the end of the eighteenth century, Dublin had been at the centre of debates over the Act of Union. More than a century later, the city would be at the heart of the struggle to end the Union between Ireland and Britain. The events of the years 1914 to 1923 have come to be known as the Irish Revolution, a process which included world war, insurrection, insurgency, and, ultimately, civil war. As the prospective capital of an independent Ireland, Dublin was the stage on which many of the key events of this revolution played out. For most Dubliners, the most dramatic changes were the product of the First World War. Whether it was service in the ranks or suffering the loss of a loved one, the Great War touched everyone. For many, the fight for independence drew them

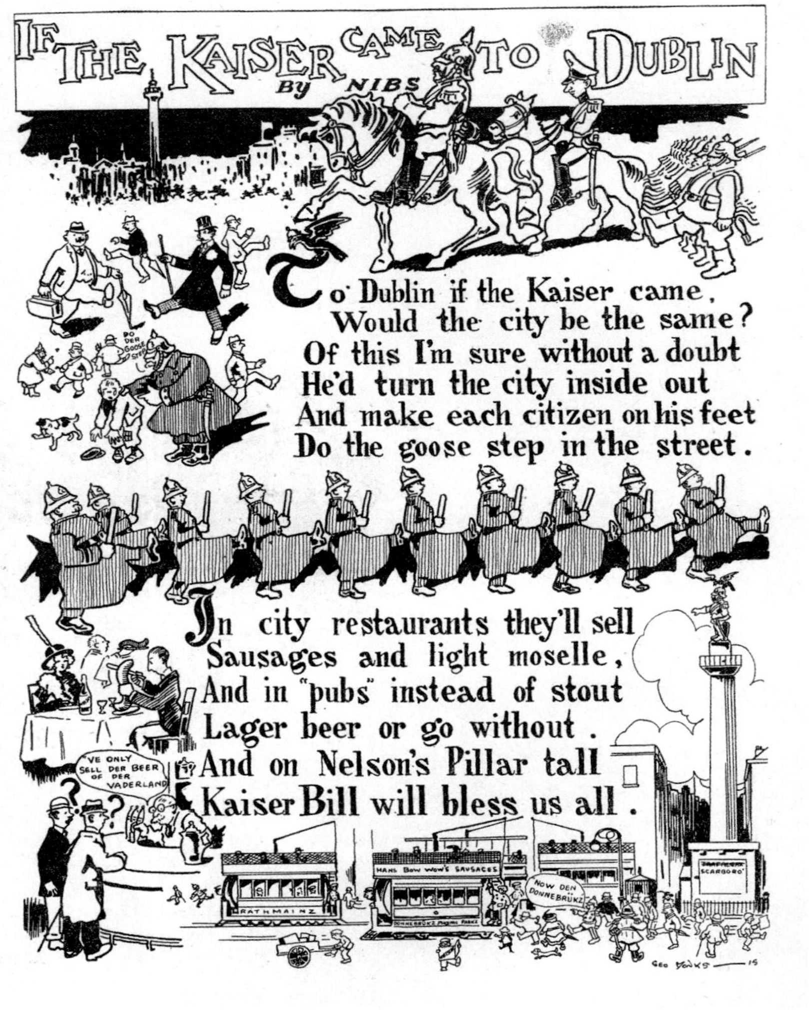

Figure 129 'If the Kaiser came to Dublin', *The Lepracaun Cartoon Monthly*, February 1915. This cartoon, although humorous, indicated genuine anxiety and anti-German sentiment.

into new political allegiances and struggles, in complex and sometimes divisive ways. Yet, as one historian has observed, despite 'all the headline-grabbing events, putting bread on the table was still the most important priority for most'.[1] While the years after 1914 were transformative, the challenges facing many Dubliners remained the same as they had always been. The issue of affordable housing was a constant throughout this period, although the onset of war in 1914 threatened to bring municipal construction to a halt. While the housing issue had always been a political one, after 1916 it became more controversial than ever. Despite some significant, if limited, innovations in the provision of working-class housing, the years of the Irish Revolution did not witness the resolution of Dublin's tenement 'problem'. Yet the Revolution nevertheless affected the residents of the city's tenements in profound and dramatic ways.

The First World War

The lockout had seen Dublin gripped by a war between classes, but within months of its end the city was gripped by a new war between nations. Working-class Dubliners, having fought on the picket lines, would soon find themselves recruited to fight on the front lines. The Royal Dublin Fusiliers and several other regiments found Dublin to be a fertile recruiting ground. An estimated 35,000 Dubliners fought in the war, with unskilled workers representing 41 per cent of these recruits (and as much as 55 per cent of infantry regiments).[2] The city's workers, still reeling from the industrial dispute of the previous year, were volunteers largely out of economic necessity. In the spring of 1915, it was claimed that some 2,500 members of the ITGWU had enlisted. One officer in the 16th Division commented that many of the men signing up were 'real toughs ... Larkinites enticed to join the colours by the prospect of good food and pay, which was welcome to them after months of semi-starvation during the great strikes of 1913 and 1914'.[3] Few, if any, of these men could have anticipated the type of modern industrial warfare that awaited them.

On the home front, Dubliners experienced the effects of the war in multiple ways. On the whole, the First World War saw a substantial reduction of unemployment in Ireland. Unlike Belfast though, Dublin lacked substantial heavy industry, and

Figure 130 Cartoon, 'Employers and recruiting', showing the figure of 'starvation' forcing workers into the army. Taken from *The Leader*, 26 September 1914.

Figure 131 The Parkgate Street munition factory, c.1915–17. The rear wall of this factory was adorned with paintings of the Union Jack as well as a flag with the Irish harp. Note the text: 'The man in the trenches wants shells, Irish shells'.

it did not benefit as greatly. However, the war benefitted Irish farmers whose food stuffs were in high demand and Dublin, as a conduit between rural Ireland and the British markets, stood to gain from this. For instance, by 1915, Dublin's cattle market was handling record numbers on their way across the Irish Sea. However, such gains were overshadowed by the damage done to the city's alcohol industry. Restrictions on brewing and distilling were introduced under the Defence of the Realm Act, reducing employment in the city. In 1917, the payroll for the alcohol industry was half what it had been in 1914.[4] However, there were some new war industries in Dublin, notably munitions, with the government's National Shell Factory in Parkgate Street producing half a million shells by 1918. Just as in Britain, the departure of so many male workers opened up new employment opportunities for women, with 1,000 female employees in the Parkgate factory, and another 300 in the privately owned plant run by the Dublin Dockyards Co. These women could earn up to £3 a week, a substantial amount that was higher than the wages of most building workers, to say nothing of the earnings of casual labourers. The numbers of both women and men in the city's workhouses fell in the course of the war, while the death rate for the city also slightly dropped.

Many working-class householders benefitted from separation allowances – payments made to the wives of soldiers at the front. For those living in Dublin's tenements, separation allowances probably accounted for the second-largest source of income, after labourer's wages.[5] The wives and widows of soldiers who received such

168   SPECTRAL MANSIONS

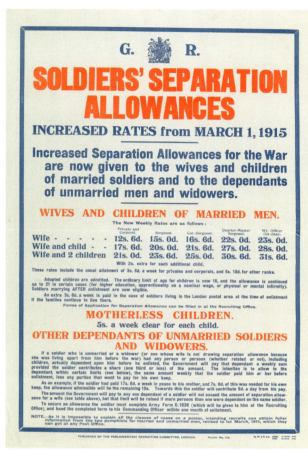

Figure 132 Schedule of separation allowance, 1915. The separation allowances were on a sliding scale, with additional sums per child but also depending on the rank of the soldier (private, sergeant, etc.).

payments came to be known as 'separation women', a term sometimes used to malign them for a variety of reasons, including perceived immorality. The sums that dependants could receive were significant, especially when one remembers the low-paying nature of most employment in Dublin. In February 1915, the separation allowance for the wife of a soldier was 12s. 6d. a week, with an additional 5s. for the first child, 3s. 6d. for the second, and 2s. for the third and each subsequent child. In a city where the vast majority of labourers earned as little as 18s. a week, these were considerable sums.

Yet there were detrimental effects as well. Inflation and shortages were a serious problem, with wages struggling to keep pace with prices. Black bread ('war bread') became a staple of Dublin's diet, while increases in the price of milk were a recurrent concern. While the price of a pint of milk might sound like a trivial issue, it was the cheapest form of protein available on a working-class budget and crucial for childhood development. The price of a pint of milk more than doubled between 1916 and 1917, with government eventually banning milk exports and imposing a price ceiling. It was not just food but fuel also, with a shortage of coal imports resulting in high prices. By 1917, coal cost as much as the weekly rent in many homes. As a result, some hospitals reduced the temperature on the wards, while many businesses closed early to conserve fuel.[6]

Fatalities

The most profound way the war affected Dubliners was in the loss of loved ones at the front. Next to Belfast, Dublin was one of the main recruitment centres in the country and many young men from Henrietta Street enlisted. While the local regiment, the

Figure 133 'College Green, Dublin', *The Lady of the House*, Christmas Annual, 1915. This depiction of the city during the First World War was undoubtedly a cheery one, conveying continued activity and bustle.

Royal Dublin Fusiliers, had their depot in Naas, they also had a battalion stationed in the Linenhall Barracks, only a stones-throw away. Census data from the decades before the war indicates a strong tradition of recruitment into the British army from the street. For instance, in 1901, No. 8 Henrietta Street was home to Patrick Masterson, who had fought in the Indian Rebellion of 1857. Across the street in No. 12, Terence

Harty had served in South Africa during the Second Anglo-Boer War. In other cases, information provided on the census reveals that some residents were the families of soldiers. In 1901, No. 8 was home to the family of Mary Gleeson whose children had all been born in parts of the British Empire that suggested a military connection: Hong Kong, Singapore and South Africa, while two of her other children had been born in Tipperary and Limerick (both towns with substantial barracks). Her eldest son, John, was described as 'soldier' in 1901, although his age is given as 14.[7]

No previous war could compare to the mass slaughter of the First World War. Out of a population of 4.4 million people, there were roughly 200,000 Irish combatants and approximately 30,000 Irish fatalities. No other war or conflict had ever involved so many Irishmen, with the war producing seven fatalities for every thousand persons. While not as high a rate as some parts of the UK, it nonetheless represented a shocking death toll for such a small country. One estimate of Dubliners killed in the war puts the number at just over 6,500, although the real number is likely higher.[8] Nearly everyone had a relative or a friend at the front. For instance, the reports of the high number of casualties suffered by the Dublin Fusiliers in the Gallipoli campaign had a palpable effect on the city.

Figure 134 Photograph of John Brogan, which he used as a postcard to his mother in Henrietta Street.

In Henrietta Street, several men would enlist, and were fortunate enough to survive the conflict. John Brogan, who had lived in No. 14, enlisted in the Scottish Rifles, and had worked at the nearby Broadstone station for the Midland Great Western Railway. While stationed in France, Brogan wrote a postcard to his mother who still lived in Henrietta Street. The postcard is a photo of Brogan himself, resting his foot on a German shell, while in his note he boasted that he was 'in full fighting order in this photo'. Tragically, while Brogan would survive the war and return to Ireland, he was later killed during a training session at the army artillery range in the Glen of Imaal.[9]

Another resident of No. 14 Henrietta Street was Anthony

 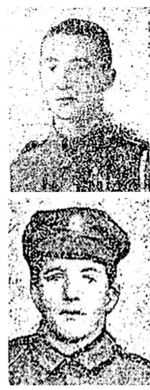

Figure 135 (far left) Photograph of Anthony Morrell.
Figure 136 William Dyer (top), died of his wounds, 21 September 1918, and his brother Thomas Dyer (bottom), killed in action, 28 September 1918. *Saturday Herald*, 26 October and 16 November 1918. Their parents, John and Teresa Dyer, lived in No. 14 Henrietta Street.

Morrell, who enlisted in the Royal Dublin Fusiliers when he was only 15, presumably having lied about his age. Anthony would survive the war, coming back to Ireland and living until 1949.[10]

Number 14 was also home to Patrick Ennis, a casual labourer and father of two who, like Morrell, enlisted in the Royal Dublin Fusiliers during the summer of 1914, going on to fight in both Gallipoli and the Somme, surviving the war to return to Henrietta Street where his young family lived in a single room. Next door, in No. 13, John Horrigan had similarly joined up in 1914, later being taken as a prisoner of war at Loos, but surviving and returning to the street after the war.

Others were not so lucky, with several families in Henrietta Street mourning the death of a father, a son, or a brother. In No. 3, John and Ann Keating lost their son Francis, who died in the Battle of Messines in June 1917. Patrick and Mary West, at No. 16, lost their son Peter (aged 18) at Ypres, where he died fighting with the Royal Irish Rifles in June 1915. One family, the Dyers of No. 14, experienced the heartbreak of losing more than one son. Their son Thomas had fought valiantly at Ypres, but was killed in action in September 1918. That same month, his brother William was killed fighting with the Shropshire Light Infantry in Greece.[11]

Some in Henrietta Street would mourn the loss of a sweetheart or boyfriend. For instance, living in No. 12, Ellen 'Cissie' Dorgan would mourn the loss of Jack Appleby, who died fighting in Cambrai, France in December of 1917. In her memorial card for Jack, Cissie lamented the loss of a potential future she might have had with him:

> The hardest part is yet to come,
> When the warriors all return.
> I'll miss among the cheery crowd
> The face of my dear one.
> When last I saw his smiling face
> He looked so strong and brave
> I little thought how soon he'd be
> Laid in a soldier's grave.

While Jack left what little money he had to his mother, his will stipulated that his prayer book and pocket book be given to Cissie. Given the circumstances of his death (no body was ever recovered) it is unlikely she received these items.[12]

The Rising

The above stories are only a few examples, and many other families in Henrietta Street experienced the death of a loved one because of the war.[13] How did they make sense of this loss? Every family was faced with finding consolation and, if possible, meaning in the death of a loved one. In a country where insurrection was about to transform and complicate political loyalties, this could be especially challenging. The First World War had broken out at a time when the question of Irish self-government had led to a dramatic polarization within Irish politics. This included a militarization of everyday life, which had begun even before 1914 with the phenomenon of paramilitary Volunteering. Volunteering had begun among Ulster unionists. However, it was soon imitated by southern nationalists, leading to the creation of the Irish Volunteers in late 1913. Soon, the events of the 1913 Lock out would lead to the creation of another group, the Irish Citizens Army, a smaller socialist militia. By mid-1914, as many as 300,000 people were enrolled in one of these groups, while many women had joined one of the auxiliary groups, such as Cumann na mBan. Following the outbreak of the war, many of the Irish Volunteers joined the British army, a controversial issue which split the movement. Despite opposition from labour leaders, many of the working-class radicals also found themselves enlisting, perhaps more out of economic necessity.

However, among the radicals and advanced nationalists who remained in Dublin, plans began to gestate for a rebellion against British rule, a rebellion whose date was set for Easter of 1916. The Rising shocked those who lived through it and has transfixed historians ever since. Arguably the turning point in putting Ireland on the path to independence, its effects on Dublin city were enormous. In the space of less than a week, somewhere in the region of 480 people lost their lives. While estimates

of the death toll vary, it seems that more than half the fatalities were civilians. Over another 3,000 people were wounded or seriously injured, again mainly civilians. The Rising had taken place in the centre of a busy civilian city. The British army had brought in the 'big guns', with heavy artillery fire decimating the city centre. In such circumstances, the human cost of 'collateral damage' was bound to be high. While Henrietta Street did not directly witness any fighting, some of the surrounding areas were the scene of intense fighting during Easter week. The nearby Linenhall Barracks, where an unarmed garrison had surrendered to a group of Volunteers, was destroyed after a fire was set inside. Ironically, the fire had an adverse effect for the Volunteers, as it had the result of illuminating the area, making it difficult for rebels to move at night without attracting British sniper fire. Photographic depictions of the nearby Church Street area attest to the extent of the fighting and resulting damage.[14]

One former resident of Henrietta Street would play an interesting role in the Easter Rising: Rosie Hackett. While Rosie had been born in Prebend Street, on Constitution Hill, she later lived with her second husband Patrick Gray in Nos. 13 and 14 Henrietta Street before then moving to Old Abbey Street. Hackett was a remarkable figure. She had been a factory worker in Jacob's Biscuits in 1909, and had been swept up by the new labour militancy in the city, enrolling as a member of Larkin's ITWGU. In 1911

Figure 137 Sackville Street in flames – a photograph taken by a *Daily Sketch* photographer under fire, May 1916.

Figure 138 Linenhall Barracks, Dublin, shelled, 1916.

Figure 139 The wreck they made of Church Street, Dublin, 1916.

Figure 140 (above) Members of the Irish Women Workers' Union, Liberty Hall.

Figure 141 (left) Photo of an older Rosie Hackett, *Fifty Years of Liberty Hall*, 1959.

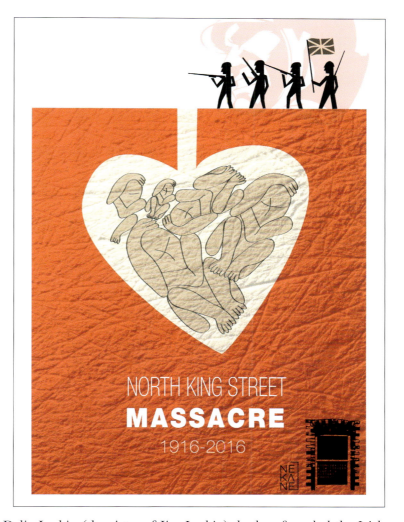

Figure 142
Nekane Orkaizagirre/ Stoneybatter & Smithfield People's History Project. Poster commemorating the 100th anniversary of the North King Street massacre, 2016.

Hackett, alongside Delia Larkin (the sister of Jim Larkin), had co-founded the Irish Women Workers' Union (IWWU). During the 1913 Lockout she had help mobilize the Jacob's workers to strike in solidarity with other workers; she was also active with her colleagues in the IWWU in setting up a soup kitchen in Liberty Hall. Rosie later became a member of the Irish Citizen Army and would be closely involved in the 1916 Rising, being part of the battalion in St Stephen's Green and the Royal College of Surgeons. She had also been involved in the printing of the Proclamation of the Irish Republic in Liberty Hall. After the Rising, Rosie continued to be prominent in the IWWU, being a leading figure in the city's trade unionism and social activism for the next several decades. She died in July 1976, aged 82, and in 2014, a new bridge across the Liffey was named the Rosie Hackett Bridge in her honour.[15]

Hackett was a remarkable figure, and her participation in the 1916 Rising saw her at the centre of some of the fighting. For others, the Rising was a brutal or horrific experience. One of the most shocking incidents that Easter occured just around the corner from Henrietta Street, in North King Street, where civilians were killed in cold blood by British forces. The area had seen some of the fiercest fighting of the Rising and the South Staffordshire regiment had taken heavy losses clearing the area. On the Friday night/Saturday morning, troops broke into several houses, shooting and bayonetting sixteen civilian men and boys whom they accused of being rebels. In several instances, the bodies of victims were concealed by British soldiers under the floorboards of abandoned buildings, not being discovered until weeks later. At the time, these killings were overshadowed by the dramatic fighting at the GPO and incidents of military excesses elsewhere.

In addition to firefights and bombardment, the withdrawal of the police from the streets allowed for large-scale looting of grocery shops and department stores. The *Irish Independent* reported that

> when darkness set in on Easter Monday the lawless element in the city set themselves out for loot … the revolutionaries in the GPO did their best to stop the looting, and fired blank shots at intervals over the heads of the mob. Nothing seemed to frighten them.[16]

The recent discovery of Dublin Metropolitan Police register logs (now available online) sheds some light on the profile of these looters.[17] While those subsequently

Figure 143 Girls gathering firewood after the Rising, 1916.

Figure 144 Business as usual: a newsvendor resumes business amongst the ruins, 1916.

Figure 145 East side of Sackville Street from O'Connell Bridge, 1916.

charged for looting had a diverse range of occupations, married women and widows comprised over half of the offenders. The next largest group were those with no occupation and many of the looters were recorded as having no fixed abode. There was also a smattering of those in skilled trades and small shopkeepers. Nonetheless, some of the more eye-catching images concerning the Rising's aftermath were of those scavenging rather than looting, particularly for debris that could be used for fuel (an important commodity in a time of coal shortages).

1916 and the housing crisis

Following the surrender of the rebels, reactions in the city were mixed, although shock and confusion was perhaps the most common feeling. While we do not have an all-encompassing opinion poll, some broad generalizations can be made. It seems that much of the city was initially hostile to the rebels, although a minority certainly admired their resolve and bravery. Some, however, were appalled by the Rising,

Figure 146 The front page of the *Sunday Independent*, 30 April–7 May 1916 edition.

Figure 147 View of the ruins north of Sackville Street, 1916.

particularly those with family members fighting at the front. The so-called 'separation women' were notably hostile towards the rebels. A caricature of the separation women as drunk, disorderly and unpatriotic emerged, an image that was unfair. The Rising had coincided with the first anniversary of the Battle of Saint-Julien, where the Dublin Fusiliers had suffered heavy casualties. Many of the women who jeered at the rebels were probably widows, sisters or mothers of the dead. Nonetheless, the separation women's fate was sealed in the collective popular memory. However, early on, the contempt for the rising came from several sources. For instance, the press, particularly William Martin Murphy's *Independent*, condemned the Rising in strong terms.

As debates emerged over what had caused the Rising, many observers pointed to Dublin's housing conditions as a possible source of grievance. In the official British report on the Rising, special attention was paid to the 'housing conditions of the working classes in the city of Dublin [which] might have accounted for an underlying sense of dissatisfaction with existing authority'. General John Maxwell, the commander of the British forces during the Rising, told the British cabinet much the same, blaming the state of the city's tenements for widespread discontent.[18] The playwright George Bernard Shaw, in a typically acidic commentary, asked why, oh why, didn't the artillery knock down half of Dublin while it had the chance? Think of the insanitary areas, the slums, the glorious chance of making a clean sweep of them! Only 179 houses [destroyed] and probably at least nine of them quite decent ones. I'd have laid at least 17,000 of them flat and made a decent town of it![19]

In 1916, many Dubliners would have failed to see the humour in Shaw's comments, but he had a point. While the Rising could not be explained in purely economic terms, the housing problems was clearly a source of grievance and disaffection. In the same way that the 1913 Lockout brought the city's social difficulties into the spotlight, 1916 refocused attention on the housing problem.

The outbreak of the war in 1914 had acted as a brake on the construction of municipal housing, with funds drying up and building materials becoming difficult to obtain. In 1915, the housing expert of the Local Government Board had reminded Dublin Corporation that due to the war, 'claims on public resources', even for urgent matters like housing, had to be subordinated to the war effort. The Dublin Castle administration seemed totally complacent about the issue, repeatedly attempting to turn off the tap of public funds for housing. However, despite a moratorium by the British Treasury on such spending, the Corporation nonetheless instigated some significant projects during the war years. Construction took place on the McCaffrey Estate in the Mount Brown/Kilmainham area. There were significant 'slum clearance' schemes, most notably in Church Street during 1916–17, the site of the horrific 1913 tenement collapse.

The Corporation undertook further housing schemes at Ormond Market, St James' Walk and Spitalfields in 1917–18, providing a mixture of cottages and flats.

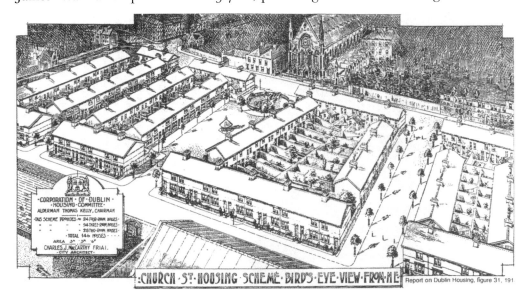

Figure 148 'Church St housing scheme bird's eye view', 1918. This is a view of the housing scheme looking across from the north-east, with the church of St Mary of the Angels in the background.

These years also saw the Corporation purchasing the site for Fairbrothers Fields, near the Tenterfields area of the Liberties. While the plans for this site dated back to 1912 (and would go through several further revisions), its eventual construction in the 1920s would be enormously significant. The damage inflicted by the 1916 Rising constrained the abilities of Dublin Corporation to pursue such schemes. In the aftermath of the Rising, the chief of Dublin's Fire Brigade estimated the damage as being somewhere in the region of £2.5 million – a massive sum. Not only did funds have to be diverted to city centre reconstruction, but the loss of income from rate-payers whose property had been destroyed further hampered new projects. Plans by the Corporation to raise loans on the American market ultimately came to nothing. For its part, the British government sought to use the housing issue to curb Irish disaffection. By mid-1917, Dublin Castle began to drop some of its objections to further housing developments, with the Local Government Board drafting plans for war-time loans to the Corporation for this purpose. However, by the following year, political events began to overtake such gestures, with the ascent of more advanced nationalists like Sinn Féin leading to increased tensions between the LGB and local authorities.[20] The year 1918 also marked the publication of a new report on the city's housing which restated the magnitude of the crisis facing the working class. It confirmed that matters had only worsened since the 1913 Housing Inquiry, with nearly 30 per cent of Dubliners living in fourth-class housing and just under 16,000 Dubliners living in one-room tenements (nearly a third of which could be classified as unfit for habitation). It proposed the construction of 16,500 suburban cottages, the renovation of 3,800 existing tenements and the provision of a further 13,000 city dwellings. Once again, even the most pragmatic assessment of Dublin's housing demonstrated the need for large-scale building.[21]

Post-war Dublin

The end of the First World War was celebrated throughout Ireland, with reports in Dublin of cheering crowds 'jazz dancing' down Grafton Street. Yet the aftermath of the war was not entirely celebratory. Between the armistice in 1918 and the summer of 1920, over 100,000 veterans of the Great War returned to Ireland as civilians. Many returned mutilated or disabled, while even those who had escaped physical harm often bore deep psychological scars. While it is impossible to estimate the numbers of disabled men living in Ireland after the war, the numbers must have been considerable.[22] Moreover, demobilization also introduced a new and deadly disease – the so-called 'Spanish Flu'. One of the great unsung horrors of these years, this pandemic emerged in the final stages of the war, preying on a malnourished population whose immune systems were worn down. This flu may have killed as many as 50 million people worldwide. While only 2.5 per cent of those who caught the flu died, it was highly contagious. In Ireland as many as 800,000 people were infected (one in five of the total population), with the disease killing over 20,000 people in little over

Figure 149 Victory parade going down Westmoreland Street, 19 July 1919. The figures in the foreground are sitting atop the front of Trinity College, while the view below is of the crowds along Westmoreland Street.

a year. To put this in context, this is at least four times the number of people killed in Ireland as a result of political violence between 1916 and 1923. The Spanish Flu spread quickly through civilian and military transport networks. Dublin, as a point of disembarkation for troops, was badly hit. Just under 3,000 deaths in Dublin County could be attributed to the flu in the course of 1918–19.[23]

While Irish veterans had shared the experiences of British soldiers, their return to civilian life was different, more closely resembling those European countries where national borders were now being redrawn and fought over.[24] In the years following the armistice, there were very real fears that unemployed veterans might be drawn into the military wing of the Irish republican movement, now known as the IRA. This coincided with a wider concern among British politicians that the post-war United Kingdom should provide 'homes fit for heroes'. It was feared that if the millions of demobilized servicemen returned to the same social deprivations of the pre-war period, they might be attracted to radical socialism. In this sense, the provision of public housing was 'insurance' against social revolution. In Ireland, this fear of communism or 'Bolshevism' was allied to opposition to Irish nationalism. In April 1919, the Irish chief secretary addressed the British parliament on the issue of housing, declaring that 'Filth, squalor, congestion, rack-rents … They are the allies of death and disease, of immorality and vice all over the world. But in Ireland they are that and something more. They are the allies of Bolshevism and Sinn Féin'.[25] As a result, in August of that year, the 1919 Housing (Ireland) Act was passed, with a programme to build 50,000 new dwellings, many intended for the accommodation of ex-servicemen. In the Dublin area this resulted in the construction of a housing estate at Killester, in the northeast suburbs. The forty-acre site there had been donated by Sir Henry McLaughlin, a wealthy unionist building contractor. Under the sponsorship of the Local Government Board, teams of ex-servicemen were employed in building 247 cottages, of a generally high standard, although with accompanying high rent. The estate was administered by the Irish Soldiers, and Sailors, Trust, although relations between the trust and the tenants would later break down. While well-meaning, these 'homes fit for heroes' were a drop in the ocean compared to the scale of the housing crisis in Dublin, a fact reflected in the 18,000 applications for homes in the Killester estate.[26]

By 1920, the post-war housing campaign was coming up against the reality that British rule in Ireland, at least outside of Ulster, was increasingly under threat. The end of the First World War had also witnessed the destruction of the Irish Parliamentary Party as a political force, and the ascent of Sinn Féin as the new voice of nationalist Ireland. Despite being proscribed in September of 1919, Sinn Féin won overall control of 72 out of 127 local authorities in Ireland, sharing power with Labour in another 26. These Sinn Féin-controlled bodies included Dublin Corporation, where the imprisoned Sinn Féin MP Thomas Kelly had been elected the new Lord Mayor. In July 1920, the British-backed Local Government Board had announced that all financial assistance would be withdrawn if the authority of the British government was not accepted and the Local Government Board itself recognized. However, the majority of local authorities instead switched their allegiance to the underground Dáil Éireann, which had set up its own Local Government Department. It was this challenge to the legitimacy of the Local Government Board, and British authority more generally, that explains the relative lack of activity under the 1919 Housing Act in Dublin. By 1921, only about 800 houses were built in the country under the Act.[27] At any rate, the question over public housing was to be overshadowed by the political events of the next several years.

The War of Independence

The Irish War of Independence (1919–21) was a conflict that had both urban and rural components. While much of the war took the form of guerrilla actions in the countryside, Dublin remained a key theatre of operations. For republicans seeking to challenge the power of Dublin Castle, inhibiting the safe movement of the authorities in the capital, challenging them for control of the streets, was crucial. It was vital for the republican side to create a space in which the alternative administration of the Dáil could function. As the centre of organized labour, the opening up of links with Dublin's trade unions to promote boycotts and passive resistance was of great importance to Sinn Féin. Dublin also experienced some of the highest fatalities in the country during this conflict, second only to County Cork. Between January 1917

Figure 150 Thomas Bryan (standing) in his Volunteers uniform, 1917–20.

and December 1921, just over 300 people were killed in Dublin city and county, half of whom were civilians.[28]

Henrietta Street was occasionally near the action. For instance, in June 1920, a daring IRA raid took place on the nearby King's Inns. A group from 1st Battalion IRA had decided to attack a military guard house located in the King's Inns building. They had a man on the inside, Jerry Golden, a law clerk who had used his position to scan the layout of the guard room. On the day, Golden gave the signal to two groups of men positioned in Henrietta Street and on Constitution Hill. The raid went off without a hitch, the men easily overpowering the guards and making away with a considerable number of arms, including ten rifles, several revolvers, a Lewis machine gun, and a large quantity of ammunition. The young Kevin Barry was part of the raid, and it was described how he exited the King's Inns while humorously wearing a soldier's helmet that he had taken, brandishing a machine gun as the group made their get-away. One member of the raiding party recalled how 'in the excitement of the raid many men had lost count of time … many thought the distance down Henrietta Street increased tenfold and all were relieved to get into other thoroughfares'.[29]

Among those carrying out this raid was a young man from Henrietta Street: Thomas Bryan. Known by his friends as Tommy, Bryan had grown up in No. 14, the son of James and Mary Bryan. Tommy had been educated by the Christian Brothers in North Brunswick Street, before training as an electrical engineer. Bryan was one of three siblings, and was close to his sister Bridget, who was a member of Cumann na mBan. Tommy was also politically active, joining the Irish Volunteers before going on to join the IRA's 5th Battalion in Dublin. As a result of his activities, he had some close brushes with the authorities. On one occasion, when delivering dispatches as part of his duties, he was stopped by the Auxiliaries, a paramilitary unit of the Royal Irish Constabulary. Fearing that a search would find the dispatches on his person, Tommy threw his bicycle at the Auxiliaries and ran into a nearby pub, escaping through the back door. However, at this time, when a bicycle was purchased, the name and address of the buyer was recorded in a ledger alongside the bicycle's serial number. To prevent the bicycle being traced, some of Bryan's comrades broke into the bicycle shop and stole the incriminating records.

Bryan's luck would soon run out. On 21 January 1921, Tommy was part of an IRA ambush on Crown forces, attacking them near the Tolka Bridge in Drumcondra. While the military did not suffer any casualties, one of the IRA-men was killed and another five captured, including Bryan. He was subsequently tried by court martial. Found guilty, Thomas was one of ten men sentenced to death and hanged by the British military in 1920–21. At the time of his arrest, Thomas had only recently married his sweetheart, Annie Glynn. While imprisoned, Bryan remained stoic in the face of death, writing to his sister that 'I'm well prepared to die and am not one bit upset'. However, he feared for his wife, who was pregnant with their first child: 'I don't mind death in any form but naturally my thoughts stray to my dear little wife, for as she truly said some time ago, its our women who suffer the most'.[30] Tommy would see Annie a final time, just days before his execution on 14 March 1921. As one IRA captain, Sean Prendergast, would recall: 'The sense of tragedy that surrounded these young IRA men who were awaiting death was felt in IRA circles in Dublin: their execution on March 14th, 1921, came as a staggering blow to us. It was a big price to pay for freedom'.

The bodies of Bryan and nine of his comrades were buried in Mountjoy Prison. Despite years of requests by family members, the bodies of the 'Forgotten Ten' would remain in Mountjoy for eighty years. In October 2001, the bodies of these men were exhumed and reburied with state honours. In the immediate wake of Bryan's execution in 1922, his family would struggle. Tragically, Annie would lose their child only a few months later. She would subsequently move into a tenement room in Mountjoy Street, relying on charity from the White Cross before being granted a state pension. She died in 1930, aged just 30, due to heart failure caused by tuberculosis. Tommy's parents, as well as his two sisters, continued to live in a flat in 14 Henrietta Street. They too applied for a state pension, being described as 'absolutely in want', due to several family members suffering from chronic illnesses. His sister Bridget would die in 1934 while her own application for a pension was being considered. Kathleen Lynn, the doctor and Sinn Fein activist, wrote to the minister for defence, stating that Bridget had waited 'vainly' for a pension she well deserved: 'she gave her all'.³¹

Figure 151 'Thomas Bryan, died for Ireland March 14th 1921', James Kirwan Collection, NLI.

For most Dubliners, the War of Independence was experienced as a grim and unglamorous struggle. For many civilians, the most obvious impact of the conflict was the introduction of a curfew in 1920, lasting from midnight to 5 a.m. (it was then brought earlier to 8 p.m.). The curfew was more than an inconvenience, it nearly killed the entertainment industry and badly hit shipping, with dockers often refusing to work during curfew hours. The prevalence of British army patrols and checkpoints gave the city the feeling of being under siege, enhanced by the reinforcement of public buildings with sandbags. There was the presence of the notorious 'Black and Tans', a special reserve force of the Royal Irish Constabulary, who (like the similarly notorious Auxiliaries) were mainly comprised of British army veterans, a group totally unsuited to civilian policing. Their frequent stops and searches amounted to harassment, while the city was also disproportionately hit by internment. Arrests of suspects could be made on very little evidence and once again Henrietta Street was not immune. In the

Figure 152 Dublin's latest terror, *Daily Sketch*, 5 April 1920. This photograph shows a civilian in Dublin being searched by the military.

wake of the notorious incidents of 'Bloody Sunday' in November 1920 there was a raid by authorities into the houses in Henrietta Street, resulting in the arrests of nine men from Nos. 3, 5, and 7.³²

Even for those not directly caught up in the fighting, the city could be a dangerous place during these years. Indeed, the very banality of violence is often striking. In October 1922, a young newsboy from No. 16 Henrietta Street, Francis McCauley, was shot in the leg by a man who he had tried to sell a newspaper to. The man, irritated, had brandished a revolver at the boy to chase him off, with the gun then going off.³³ In a Europe that was awash with guns after the First World War, such incidents were all too common. A year earlier, in March 1921, several children from Henrietta Street were seriously injured when they were caught in the crossfire between a British army patrol and members of the IRA. On 30 March, as several military cars approached the corner of Henrietta Street and Dorset Street, two bombs had been lobbed at the vehicles, with the soldiers stopping and exchanging shots with their attackers. Some children had been playing in the street at the time, and several were injured by splintering wood and broken glass. One of the injured children was named as Lizzie Buchanan from Henrietta Street.³⁴ Little 'Lizzie' Buchanan would later go on to marry and become Mrs Elizabeth Dowling. Mrs Dowling and her family lived in No. 14 Henrietta Street from 1940 to 1975, with Elizabeth being one of the last women to live in the building as a tenement. A recreation of Mrs Dowling's flat is part of the present museum at No. 14.

Civil War

While the War of Independence nominally came to an end with the calling of a truce in July 1921, it was not the end of hostilities. Sporadic attacks and raids by the IRA continued into the following year. However, far worse fighting was soon to commence as a result of the Anglo-Irish Treaty. The Treaty was ratified by the Second Dáil on 7 January 1922, by a margin of 64 votes to 57. While the Treaty led to the creation of the Irish Free State, it also created deep divisions. The Treaty partitioned (or at least copper-fastened the partition of) the country, with Northern Ireland as a separate state remaining in the United Kingdom. Meanwhile, the new Irish Free State in the south would exit the UK, but remain in the British Commonwealth as a dominion. Because of these conditions, a number of republicans rejected the agreement as a betrayal. These anti-Treaty forces mounted a military resistance to the Free State, and the country erupted into civil war. Dublin, for the most part, stood by the Treaty, although there was a significant anti-Treaty presence in the city. In the general election that took place in June 1922, pro-Treaty Sinn Féin polled better than their anti-Treaty opponent in almost all of the Dublin constituencies.[35] The Dáil had maintained a higher degree of control over the IRA in Dublin than it had elsewhere, with the result that when the national army was formed in 1922, it was built around the Dublin Guard and brigades over which it exercised the most control. While most of the IRA commanders in the provinces declared against the Treaty, the headquarters staff in Dublin mostly stayed loyal to the new Provisional Government. This was to prove crucial to their future success.

Figure 153 The Four Courts during the battle of Dublin, July 1922.

The Civil War formally commenced in June 1922, following the seizure of the Four Courts building by anti-Treaty republicans. On the 28th of that month, the Free State army attacked the building, with the siege ending with an explosion which destroyed much of the building, including the contents of the nearby Public Records Office. Several blocks away, another detachment of those opposed to the Treaty had occupied north-eastern sections of Sackville Street (now O'Connell Street). After eight days of fighting, with at least 80 people killed, the anti-Treaty forces in Dublin surrendered, although some slipped out of the city to join their comrades elsewhere. The opening battle of the Civil War had been a victory for the new Free State, which had retained control of the capital, an important logistic and psychological advantage. While Dublin would not escape further violence during the Civil War, after July 1922, the bulk of the fighting took place elsewhere. However, for the second time in only six years, a large chunk of the city centre had been reduced to ruins, while its citizens looked uneasily towards the future. By 1923, Dublin was a capital city once more, but one that would continue to struggle to come to terms with the preceding decade of upheaval.

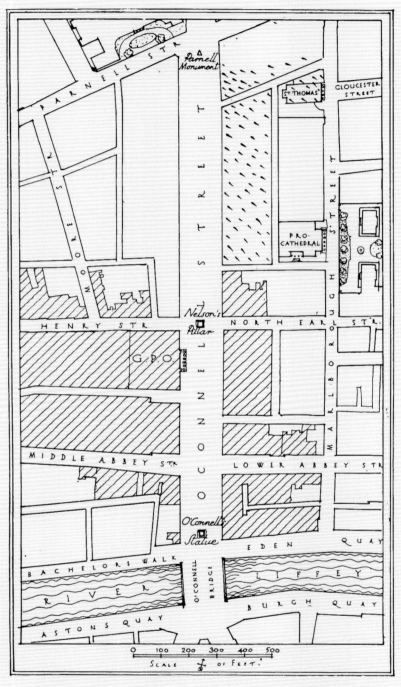

The damaged areas in the neighbourhood of O'Connell Street. The hatched portions were destroyed in 1916 and the dotted portions in 1922. The destruction of St. Thomas' Church and the frontage in O'Connell Street will allow Gloucester Street, to be carried through.

Figure 154 Map showing area of Upper Sackville Street damaged in the Civil War, *The Irish Builder*, 1923.

Epilogue:
Dublin of the future?

While the Irish Revolution was an incredibly important period, in a certain sense what is remarkable is how much did *not* change – at least at first. True, by 1923 you could see many of the new symbols of the Free State government: its flag, the national army, a new police force.[1] Despite jokes to the contrary, the new state did not merely change the colour of the post boxes. Yet there was a remarkable continuity in the social problems that faced Dublin. Despite the dramatic fighting that had taken place in the city, particularly around the Four Courts and Sackville Street, mere yards away in places like Henrietta Street, things remained as they had always been. Revolution and Civil War could rage, but it sadly seemed that Dublin would always have its slums. The intractability of the city's tenements and their associated social problems was confirmed in 1926 when a new census took place, the first since 1911. All of the problems revealed in the previous census were still there. Almost half of the city's population lived in dwellings of only one or two rooms, while over 23 per cent of the population lived in accommodation with four or more people per room. The city had seen some moderate improvements in infant mortality, but it was still much higher than elsewhere in the country, as well as being higher than almost every British city. In 1918, it had been estimated that at least 16,500 new homes were required, along with the remodelling of near 4,000 of the 'better' tenements. The task at hand was essentially to rehouse 40 per cent of the city's population, at an estimated cost of £8,640,000. This was a task that even an established and financially secure government would have struggled with. In the 1920s, with the Irish Free State struggling to establish itself in the wake of the Civil War, this task seemed insurmountable.² In the meantime, Dublin's workers continued to endure substandard housing conditions, as the promises of earlier calls for reform seemed to falter.

Figure 155 Cartoon, *The Capuchin Annual*, 1940. The cartoon expresses the disillusionment of many in Dublin with the continuing tenement problem in the twentieth century.

SLUM LANDLORD: "Yeh! Shove in another three families, Mike, the agitation's died down."

Housing was not the only issue for the new government in terms of building. The repair and reconstruction of damaged sections of the city took priority, with a desire to make Dublin a fitting capital for the new state. Yet even in this, the emphasis was on budgetary restraint. There was no grand statements or major improvements in the rebuilding of upper Sackville Street, although a new city architect used legislation to enforce some degree of uniformity on new buildings. Nor would there be a purpose-built government complex in imitation of London's Whitehall. If the government of W.T. Cosgrave had any strong idea about Dublin's redevelopment, it was to concentrate government offices and the parliament as closely as possible, as cheaply as possible. The Dáil remained in the former premises of the Royal Dublin Society in Leinster House, while the Royal College of Science on Merrion Street soon housed the main ministries.

Figure 156 Map of proposed road works: Patrick Abercrombie, Sydney Kelly & Arthur Kelly, *Dublin of the future: the new town plan*, 1922. The orange lines indicate existing roads to be widened, as well as entirely new thoroughfares.

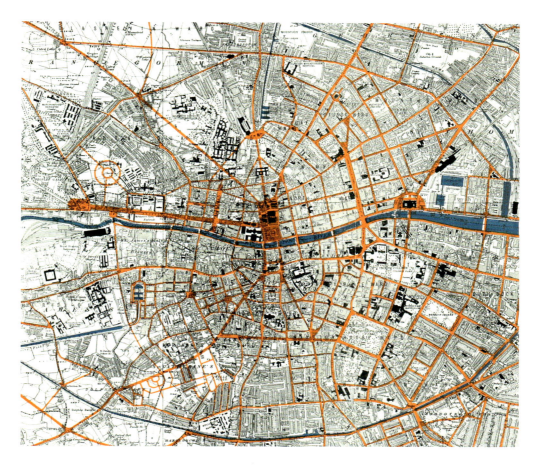

It is telling that a new building for a state ministry would not be commissioned until 1939, with the Department of Industry and Commerce in Kildare Street.

In terms of local government, Dublin Corporation contented itself with renaming existing streets and bridges, rather than constructing new ones. In June 1921, a report prepared for the city council provided a list of streets named after British royalty and lord lieutenants that could be renamed. Among the proposed changes, it was suggested that Henrietta Street be renamed 'Primate's Hill', a suggestion that was, quite frankly, confusing. The idea was to remove 'Henrietta' because it was allegedly a reference to the wife of an eighteenth-century lord lieutenant (the duke of Bolton). But if an association with the 'Ascendancy' was the problem, then 'Primate's Hill' was hardly much better. The primate was the ecclesiastical head of the Church of Ireland, and a member of the Protestant Ascendancy and a notable undertaker of the crown's business in the eighteenth century. Nothing seems to have come of this bizarre suggestion. Interestingly, some other proposed changes did not go ahead either, such as the renaming Mountjoy Square as Tom Clarke Square, or Fitzwilliam Square as Oliver Plunkett Square (although these at least made sense in terms of patriotic credentials).[3]

EPILOGUE: DUBLIN OF THE FUTURE?   195

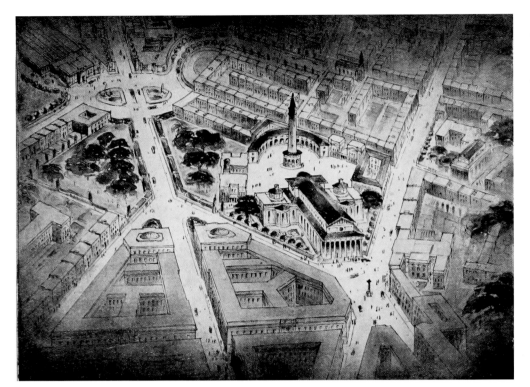

Figure 157 Sketch showing suggested cathedral site at the head of Capel Street, Abercrombie, Kelly & Kelly, *Dublin of the future: the new town plan*, 1922. In this plan Henrietta Street would have been demolished to make space for the cathedral's courtyard, although the King's Inns are still present.

Yet for all of the caution of these years, there were some quite radical ideas being floated about Dublin's future. Notably, in 1922 a report entitled *Dublin of the future* was published. The report was the brainchild of Patrick Abercrombie, a British town planner who had won the Civics Institute of Ireland's competition for a Dublin town plan back in 1914. In the intervening years which it took to get published, much had changed, a fact that Abercrombie acknowledged; arguing that it was precisely because of the 'recent change in national circumstances a new epoch has begun'. Abercrombie's plan was nothing if not ambitious. It called for a large-scale intervention, with new thoroughfares and traffic hubs, combined with new bridges and public buildings. Some idea of how extensive this plan was can be seen in one of the maps, illustrating the various new and widened roads being proposed.

Abercrombie's plan aimed to impose a rational order on the city, in some ways harkening back to the ethos of the Wide Streets Commissioners of the eighteenth century, or the nineteenth-century renovation of Paris under Baron Haussmann. It planned a new complex of cultural buildings north of the river, accompanied by the pulling down of large numbers of residential streets. A taste of the plan's boldness is apparent if one looks at what was suggested for Henrietta Street. It proposed the demolition of the street and its surrounding area, while preserving the King's Inns. In the place of the demolished buildings there would be a national cathedral and its plaza, complete with a 500-foot-high campanile, crowned with the figure of

Figure 158 Harry Clarke, 'The last hour of the night', *Dublin of the future: the new town plan*, 1922.

St Patrick. The surrounding arcade would contain busts of Irish saints and famous Irishmen.

These suggestions were obviously dramatic. Although, oddly, the best-remembered image of the plan is not any of the maps or sketches of proposed buildings, but instead the report's frontispiece. Created by the artist Harry Clarke, the image is entitled 'The last hour of the night'. It is quite literally a haunting image, depicting a demonic ghoul towering over Dublin. On the left-hand of the image are three iconic Dublin buildings which had been burnt, each during a different phase of the Revolution:

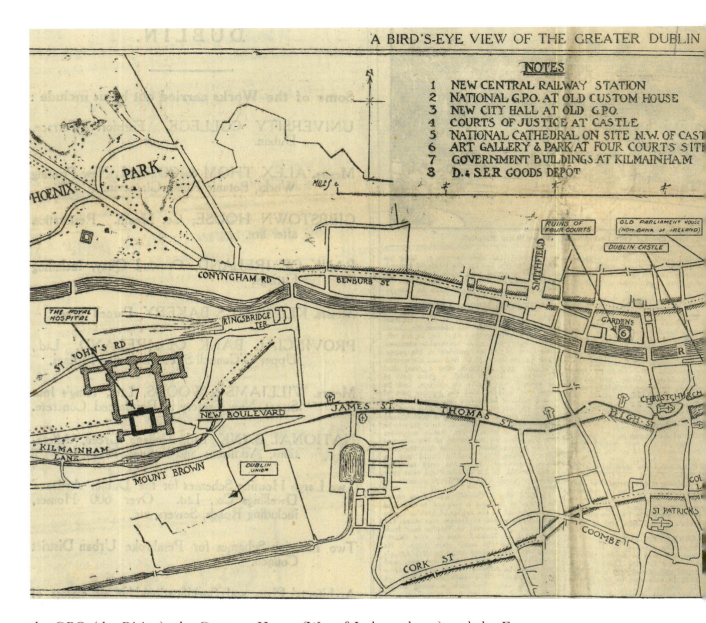

the GPO (the Rising), the Customs House (War of Independence) and the Four Courts (Civil War). Yet on the opposite side, the ghoul has his hand outstretched to a dilapidated town house, now in use as a tenement, its residents standing outside in the streets. The tenements depicted on the right-hand side of the image overshadow the historic ruins on the left, perhaps suggesting that Dublin's social problems were of a greater magnitude than even the political conflicts of the Revolution. Tellingly, the public buildings depicted by Clarke would all be repaired by 1931, yet the problem of the city's tenements would remain for far longer.

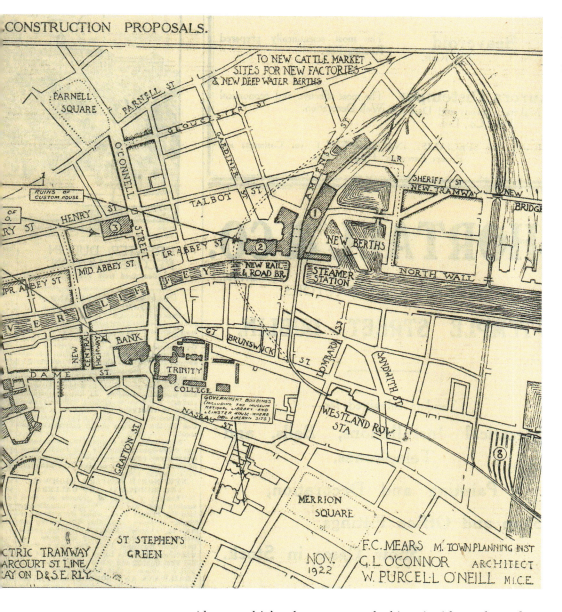

Figure 159 'A bird's-eye view of the Greater Dublin reconstruction proposals', December 1922.

Abercrombie's plan was not lacking in ideas about how to resolve the city's tenement problem. Part of the plan called for new 'extra urban' districts in Crumlin, Cabra and Drumcondra, where 60,000 of the city's poor were to be rehoused in new working-class suburbs. It suggested that these neighbourhoods be linked to the city by high-speed trams, bringing workers to their employment at low-cost fares in ten or twelve minutes. As utopian as all this was, Abercrombie's plan was nonetheless a fascinating vision of an alternative Dublin that was never to be. As David Dickson has commented, 'it would have taken a military dictatorship and Guinness millions to realize this plan'.[4] Yet its audacity inspired a generation of architects and city officials, keeping the concept of town planning in the public eye. In fact, a year after the publication of Abercrombie's plan, an alternative plan for the city was put forward by the Greater Dublin Reconstruction Movement. This movement had been founded the previous year with the aim of promoting good planning for the new capital, feeling that Abercrombie's plan was out of date. What they instead suggested was to relocate the Oireachtas westwards, in a new building located on the grounds of the Royal Hospital in Kilmainham. The new parliament buildings could be connected to the city via a new highway. Along this route, they proposed that a

Figure 160 David Davison, stair hall in 14 Henrietta Street, 1981.

number of important public buildings could be repurposed to serve the needs of the new state. For instance, the Four Courts would be turned into a municipal art gallery, Dublin Castle would become the new courts of justice, and the GPO would become the new city hall. Like Abercrombie's plan, it also envisioned a new national cathedral, only in this case it would be located on a site adjoining Christ Church.

The Greater Dublin Reconstruction Movement's plans attracted a lot of attention, not all of it positive. Most government ministers found the ideas impractical, while it was pointed out that the plan failed to provide any coherent scheme for how to rehouse the thousands of people living in substandard accommodation. Intriguingly, it seems there was at least one other proposal which did turn its attention to the tenements, particularly those in Henrietta Street. Oliver St John Gogarty, an author and one-time friend of James Joyce, recalls an unusual encounter in London in the 1920s, when he was at a dinner party with Lady Islington. Lady Islington was a notable interior decorator and it seems that on a recent visit to the city, she had been 'delighted with Dublin, which is the largest Georgian city extant, and it was this Georgianism that attracted her'. Having heard that much of Henrietta Street had once been purchased by Alderman Meade for only £900, she became interested in acquiring the property. Gogarty plainly states that 'she instructed me to buy Henrietta Street for her'. Gogarty,

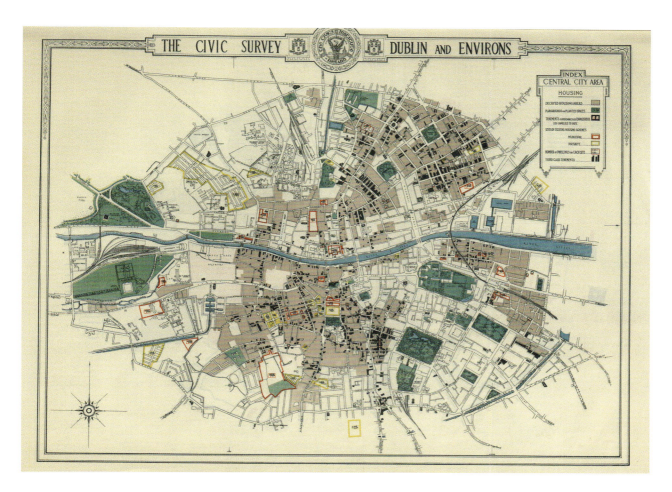

Figure 161 *The civic survey of Dublin and environs, 1925.*

sensing he might get stuck as an intermediary and be left 'with a slum on my hands', put Lady Islington in contact with a Dublin architect who inspected the houses on her behalf. The architect reported back that the buildings had been 'the habitation of slum dwellers for so long, the wood work was impregnated with acrid odours which could not be got rid of, so the houses were useless for anything but tenements'. Gogarty comments that this report effectively ended any 'visions of fashion being revived, and of the north side of the city coming again into prominence'. [5]

It is an amusing anecdote, but for those who still lived in these houses it was hardly a laughing matter. The mid–1920s once again saw confirmation of the extent of the city's problems with the publication of the Dublin Civic Survey in 1925. The survey's analysis of the city's condition was stark, particularly in regards to housing. As it stated:

> Housing in Dublin today is more than a 'question' and more than a problem – it is a tragedy. Its conditions cause either a rapid or slow death. Rapid

EPILOGUE: DUBLIN OF THE FUTURE?

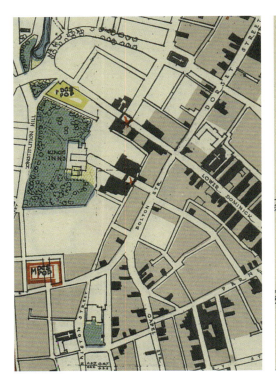 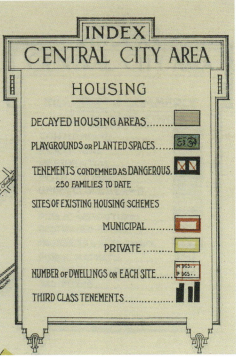

Figure 162 (left) Detail showing Henrietta Street and surroundings, *The civic survey of Dublin and environs*, 1925. Note that the buildings in the street are denoted as third-class tenements, including several marked with red crosses which indicate a tenement condemned as dangerous.

Figure 163 (right) Index to map of central city area, *The civic survey of Dublin and environs*, 1925.

when the houses fall upon the tenants, as has already happened, – slow when they remain standing dens of insanitation.

While the survey was cautiously optimistic about the potential of Dublin as a restored capital, it was also clear that rehousing the poor was a priority as 'no town planning scheme for Dublin is worthy of consideration which does not deal primarily with the vexed question of the housing of the working classes'.[6] The survey included maps of 'decayed housing areas', including those condemned as dangerous. A quick look confirms that not much had changed since previous surveys in 1914 or 1918, with the Gardiner Estate still the worst affected part of the city. Henrietta Street was at the centre of an area of decayed housing, with several of its own buildings marked as condemned.

Depicting the tenements

For many, the city's tenements would become a symbol of the shortcomings of independence. The 1920s were a time when artists, particularly playwrights, tackled the issue of Dublin's slums. These were the years when Sean O'Casey produced his iconic depictions of Dublin's working class, in plays such as *The shadow of the gunman* (1923), *Juno and the Paycock* (1924) and *The plough and the stars* (1926). O'Casey's plays

202   SPECTRAL MANSIONS

Figure 164
A.P. Wilson, *Victims*, published in *The Irish Worker*, 21 December 1912.

have since become a staple of Irish theatre. Yet he was not the first to depict Dublin's tenements on stage. In 1912, the very first depiction of Dublin's tenements took place in Liberty Hall, in a performance of a one-act play entitled *Victims*. The play was both performed and watched by members of the city's working class, being a production by the Irish Workers' Dramatic Club, a group founded by Delia Larkin to provide edifying entertainment for workers in the evenings. The play had been written by Andrew Patrick Wilson, an actor and writer who was active in radical theatre in both Ireland and Scotland. *Victims* tells the story of a couple, Jack and Anne Nolan, struggling to make ends meet in a city characterized by chronic unemployment and unscrupulous slumlords. It is a powerful appeal for class solidarity, with one character arguing that 'If you get the sack my friend … You will be a victim as well as me then. We are all victims … we cannot fight profit-mongers if we fight one another. One victim tearing another victim and all in the sacred name of profit.'

Andrew Wilson, the man who wrote *Victims,* also wrote *The Slough*, first staged in the Abbey Theatre in 1914. Despite the Abbey's association with depictions of rural life (such as the infamous staging of the *Playboy of the Western World* in 1907), the theatre also had a strong repertoire of urban plays.[7] Between 1914 and 1947, the Abbey would stage at least eleven plays set in the city's tenements. In 1917, the theatre premiered *Blight: the tragedy of Dublin*, a play by Oliver St John Gogarty and Joseph O'Connor. The play took aim at the myopic greed of the wealthy, and expressed many of Gogarty's own views concerning the role of the tenements in causing poor health and disease. Gogarty was a surgeon and medical campaigner, later serving as a member of Seanad, where he spoke on public health issues, arguing that what was needed was better investment in public housing. Both *Blight* and *The Slough* took aim at urban power brokers, not only landlords but municipal politicians, the Corporation and church leaders. However, plays in the Abbey did not always apply a serious analysis to Dublin's social problems. The tenements (however awkwardly) could also be the setting for farce. In 1922, the Abbey staged Matthew Brennan's *A leprechaun in the tenement*, a work that would today be described as 'problematic'; it lapsed into offensive buffoonery which was criticized at the time and has ensured it has not achieved any lasting impact. The fact that it was staged at all probably says more about the instability and confusion of the theatre during the Civil War period.

The Abbey was not alone in staging plays about the tenements. In 1939, the Gate premiered a play entitled *Marrowbone Lane* by Robert Collis. Collis was a doctor who was appalled at the conditions in which the working class continued to live. The play is a claustrophobic portrayal of the daily struggle for survival in the tenements, also depicting the horrors of Dublin's infant mortality, something Collis was well acquainted with as a paediatrician. *Marrowbone Lane* was successful enough to ensure an extended run and underwent a revival in 1941 at the Gaiety. Collis used the success of the play to spearhead a new charitable trust, the Marrowbone Lane Fund, aimed at improving the lives and treatment of those with cerebral palsy.

Figure 165 Set photograph from Robert Collis, *Marrowbone Lane*, 1939.

In subsequent decades, the tenements remained a potent theme for authors. For instance, one of the most successful works of historical fiction set in Dublin was *Strumpet City* by James Plunkett. Published as a novel in 1969, an early version of the work had debuted as a stage play in 1958 before going through several revisions and adaptations. Set during the 1913 Lockout, *Strumpet City* tells multiple intertwined stories, with several of the main characters living in the fictional tenement of Chandler's Court. When the book was adapted into a successful television drama in 1980, the producers chose to use Henrietta Street as the setting for Chandler's Court. At the time of filming, many of the houses in Henrietta Street had only recently ceased to be used as tenements, making for a clash of historical fiction and contemporary reality.

> These bricks were returning once more to dust, one by one these walls would bulge outwards, crack, collapse into rubble. They were despised and uncared for, like the tenants they sheltered, who lived for the most part on bread and tea and bore children on rickety beds to grow up in the same hardship and hunger.
>
> James Plunkett, *Strumpet City* (1969)

Figure 166 Still from the television adaptation of *Strumpet City*, RTÉ, 1980. The image shows the actors on Henrietta Street which was used as the setting of Chandler's Court.

Garden cities

While Dublin's tenements would transfix playwrights and authors, the issue also preoccupied successive government administrations. In the 1920s, although Cumann na nGaedheal were unenthusiastic about increasing social spending, they were at least aware of the need to address the housing issue. In a 1924 address, the president of the Executive Council, W.T. Cosgrave, stated that the housing crisis

> directly or indirectly affects every aspect of national life, and until it is settled there will be no genuine peace or contentment in the land. For no populace housed as many of the people of Dublin are, can be good citizens, or loyal and devoted subjects of the state.⁸

The 1925 Civic Survey had recommended the policy of suburbanization, building affordable housing on the outskirts of the city, a policy which had been a staple of Dublin planning since the housing conference of 1903. It was now to be implemented in a much more significant way. For instance, the decade saw the fruition of the scheme at Fairbrothers Fields, on the edges of the Liberties, a project which had been long in the making. The plans had undergone a redesign in 1917–18, reducing the proposed density of dwellings per acre, and had been heavily influenced by the British urban planning movement, particularly 'Garden City' ideas.

The 'Garden City' or Garden suburb idea was the notion that one could integrate the best aspects of both urban and rural living, and by doing this provide a beneficial atmosphere for the working class. The concept called for a low-density greenbelt where workers would be free from the harmful influences (both physical and moral) of the inner city. One of the most prominent advocates of the Garden City movement was Raymond Unwin who, along with Patrick Geddes, had been brought to Dublin in 1914 by the Civics Institute of Ireland. The project in Fairbrothers Fields was, in a sense, the first real application of the ideas of figures like Unwin and Geddes. While clearance of the site commenced in 1917, a lack of committed funds stopped progress. Work was then restarted in 1921 using short-term loans, with the estate eventually being completed under a grant from the new Free State Government, under its 'Million Pound Scheme'. This was a fund enabling local government to construct new dwellings, usually for the purpose of owner-occupancy rather than rental. In fact, Fairbrothers Fields was used as a pilot scheme whereby new houses were sold to tenants who were then charged via a weekly 'pay-back' system in lieu of rent. This marked the beginning of a larger shift by the Corporation towards the ideal of owner-occupancy, an idea that would define the outlook of successive governments.[9] The houses at Fairbrothers Field were built to remarkably high standard, with the Dublin Building Trades Guild playing a notable part in this. Built in three stages between 1921 and 1927, the scheme consisted of 334 five-room cottages with parlours and another 82 four-room non-parlour houses. While the project may have been the first example of the garden suburb ideal in Ireland, it was soon overshadowed by another scheme, the 'jewel in the crown' of the Corporation's suburban estates: Marino.

Located just north of the city centre, the Marino site had been the focus of the planners Geddes and Unwin in 1914, with a detailed proposal for the project drawn up by the assistant city architect Horace O'Rourke in 1919. While the War of Independence had prevented construction, O'Rourke's designs were reconsidered by the Corporation's Housing Committee in 1922, with the site being expanded. Constructed between 1923 and 1929, the entire scheme comprised 428 houses of three to five rooms, with a low density of twelve houses per acre and great care paid to the overall layout The scheme was designed according to a landscaped master plan that included lots of green space. There were also efforts to provide variation in the layout and design of the houses, avoiding a repetitive or drab feel to the neighbourhood.[10] These designs show some of the different plans for the houses, including the types 'A', 'B', and 'C'. The variation in the elevations and layouts of the houses in Marino were a significant part of the scheme's visual appeal.

Marino was the closest Ireland ever came to the Garden suburban ideal. Like Fairbrothers Fields, the houses were of a high quality, with virtually all the dwellings being substantial five-room plus parlour cottages, with separate bathrooms. However, the very quality of the houses highlighted a central flaw in the plan: places like Marino could only cater to the better-paid workers, not those most in need of rehousing. Much like earlier schemes by philanthropic bodies like the Dublin Artisans' Dwellings Company, Marino was aimed at the skilled working class, those in better-paid, steady

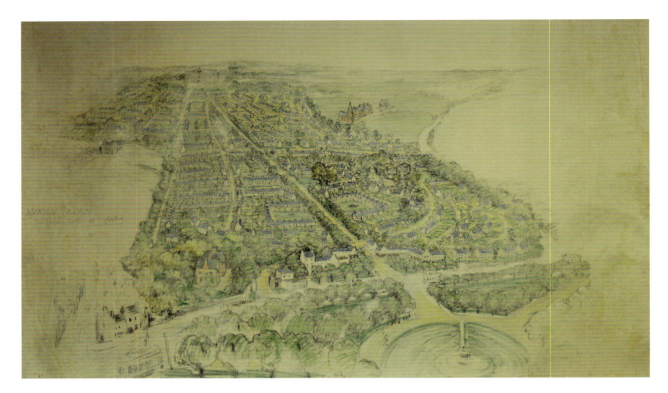

employment. But Dublin remained a city in which low-paid and casual labour represented a considerable portion of the workforce. The homes in Marino were not intended for long-term renting but were instead meant for tenant purchase, albeit financed through several new schemes. City officials had come to argue that providing houses for the better-off workers was still a useful activity thanks to what they called 'filtering-up'. This was the idea that by relocating the more secure workers, the less well-off could move into the dwellings they vacated. In 1925, the *Irish Times* pointed out this theory at work in Marino where the tenants 'are among the aristocracy of labour … the housing problem is being solved – how slowly!

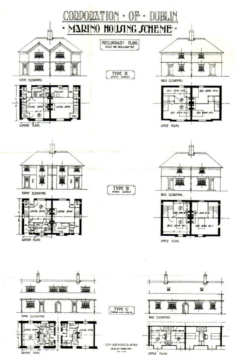

Figure 167 (above) Raymond Unwin, Perspective drawing for Marino, 1914.
Figure 168 (left) Preliminary plans for the Marino housing scheme, March 1919.

Figure 169 Campaign poster from 1932 general election. The incumbent Cumann na nGaedheal party sought to portray their opponents in Fianna Fáil as radical socialists.

– by a process of moving up'.[11] While such criticism was valid, it should not entirely distract from the important new tracts of working-class housing being built in the 1920s. There were significant projects at Drumcondra, Donnycarney, Cabra and Emmett Road in Inchicore, all built between 1928 and 1931. Such new construction helped make home-ownership an achievable aspiration for a growing segment of the population. Yet for those workers who were not part of the 'aristocracy of labour', conditions for those trapped in the congested inner city were actually worsening. What was needed was not just suburban houses, but also affordable, centrally located apartments.

By the end of the 1920s, change was in the air. Dublin Corporation had been suspended in 1924 by the Free State government, fearful that it might provide a platform for anti-Treaty politicians. For the next six years (1924–30) the city was instead governed by three 'commissioners' appointed by the government. However, in 1931, local government was restored, in a move that also expanded Dublin's boundaries: finally, after forty years of resistance, Rathmines and Pembroke townships were fully absorbed into the city. Yet an even greater change was to come with the 1932 general election.

This election, in which de Valera's Fianna Fáil party replaced their former Civil War opponents in government, was a watershed in more than just political terms. Fianna Fáil had fought the election on social issues as much as political ones. One Cumann na nGaedheal candidate, addressing a crowd in Dublin's Smithfield, warned of a Fianna Fáil victory, asking whether electors were prepared to see 'the red flag flying in Dublin'.[12] As history would show, such critics need not have worried about de Valera being a secret communist (to put it mildly). However, the Fianna Fáil government of the 1930s certainly did embark on an impressive project to provide

EPILOGUE: DUBLIN OF THE FUTURE?

Figure 170 Chancery House apartments, designed by Herbert Simms and constructed 1934–5.

badly needed accommodation in the inner city, as well as some remarkable suburban schemes. This housing drive commenced with the 1932 Housing Act, in which the state provided additional funds to local authorities, offsetting the loan costs of rehousing those relocated from slum housing. This provision allowed the authorities to set rents at lower than the economic cost, providing lower-income families access to new housing. This was a crucial difference to the approach of the 1920s, in which schemes like Marino were aimed at the more prosperous working class and the lower-middle class. In addition to targeting all sections of the working class, the 1930s housing drive also differed in its sheer scale.[13] Some of the statistics from these years are astounding. For instance, in the forty-four years between 1887 and 1931, Dublin Corporation built 7,246 dwellings. In the eight years that followed (1931–9) the Corporation built more than this number of homes again.[14]

The Corporation also oversaw twenty-one schemes within the city core, comprising 1,002 inner-city flats that were completed between 1932 and 1939. Many of these blocks were of a remarkably high quality, with an international influence apparent, particularly that of Dutch Expressionist design. A good number of these apartments were designed by Herbert Simms, who had been appointed the housing architect of Dublin Corporation in 1932. Simms' career has undergone something of a reappraisal in recent years, with a growing appreciation of his skill and relentless work ethic. Simms once declared how they 'were now trying to do in one generation what should have been done by the last four or five generations'. He oversaw the construction of over 17,000 dwelling units in the inner city at places like Marrowbone Lane, Chancery

Figure 171 The flats at Greek Street under construction, with St Michan's visible in the background, 1935.

Place and the Greek Street scheme. He tragically committed suicide as a result of overwork in 1948.¹⁵

A great example of these Corporation-built flats was Henrietta House, constructed between 1936–9. The complex consisted of two blocks, containing forty-eight units, with galleries and stairwells facing an inner courtyard, including one-, two- and three-bedroom flats. Each flat contained a WC, sitting room, hallway and scullery, with the scullery housing a bath with a hinged wooden table-top for when not in use, a gas stove, and a sink, with hot water provided by a back-boiler. The courtyard of these flats included sheds for bicycles and prams, as well as communal laundry drying areas and a garden. The scheme was built on the site of what had been Henrietta Place, a location that in 1913 had been one of the most miserable locations in the city, featuring in the shocking photographs by John Cooke. For those residents who had been relocated from former tenement buildings, the features provided by Henrietta House constituted a dramatic improvement in living conditions.

While the provision of inner-city apartments was important, the big story was the construction of 5,000 new houses in schemes in the suburbs, the biggest of which was at Crumlin. Commencing in 1932 with the compulsory purchase of 250 acres, this development saw the construction of over 3,200 houses between 1934 and 1939. Many of these homes were semi-detached, most with three to five rooms and a garden. However, the high standard of layout and multiple designs that characterized Marino

EPILOGUE: DUBLIN OF THE FUTURE?   211

Figure 172 Henrietta House, at the rear of 14 Henrietta Street, completed in 1937.

were not carried over. There was an emphasis on economies of scale and hence the reuse of designs, with the result that the new tracts of housing could seem like a maze. Both Brendan Behan and his brother Dominic, whose family had been relocated to Crumlin from Russell Street, described the new suburb as a disorientating and sometimes alienating experience, 'like moving to Siberia'.[16] While the sheer scale of Crumlin was impressive, there were some worrying signs for similar projects in the future. The initial failure to provide social amenities and infrastructure caused significant problems. For instance, the demographic profile of those who moved to the development tended to be young families, creating a huge demand for schools that were not completed when the first residents moved in. A lack of parks, playing fields and shops represented similar problems early on. While some of these bottlenecks were overcome, they should have been a cautionary tale to planners about the need to pay attention to the 'after-treatment' of those who were being rehoused.[17]

The developers of these estates had not considered the social and psychological aspects of moving out of the tenements. In 1938, the Citizen's Housing Council, a group composed of social workers, clergymen and Labour Party activists, noted that in estates in Crumlin and Cabra 'there is a sameness, amounting in large schemes to dullness, if not actual dreariness'.[18] Yes, there was a material improvement in living conditions that could not be denied. Almost anything would have been an

Figure 173 Alexander Campbell Morgan, Aerial view of the estates in Crumlin, 1950s.

improvement over the dreadful situation of overcrowded tenements, many of which were unfit for habitation. However, a move to the new suburbs was frequently accompanied by a deterioration in the social structure of friends and extended family. The fact that the expense of bus fares between the suburbs and the city was a recurring political issue in the 1940s and 1950s indicates the desire of those rehoused to keep in contact with the city and the networks they had there. In this sense, the blocks of flats that had been constructed within the city were highly desired. In the 1940s the newspapers often contained notices from those rehoused in the Corporation's suburban houses looking to swap homes with those who lived in Corporation dwellings in the inner city.[19]

The activity of Fianna Fáil during the 1930s in building houses was an impressive achievement, particularly when one considers that it took place during the Great Depression, and at a time when Ireland was engaged in an economic war with its largest trading partner. Fianna Fáil reaped the rewards, establishing an electoral dominance in Dublin (and other cities) that would last into the twenty-first century. De Valera may have talked about rural simplicity and 'maidens at the crossroads', but his party's representatives in the cities knew how to secure an urban following: provide houses. By 1939, Dublin Corporation had provided 7,650 dwellings under the 1932 Housing Act. Significantly for the future, two-thirds of the houses built with State aid in these years were in private ownership, with a growing contrast between

(Clockwise from top left) **Figure 174** The Housing Department Estate Offices, Kimmage. **Figure 175** The Hill of Howth Tramway, which ceased running in 1959. Following the closure of the city's tramlines in the 1940s and '50s, they were replaced with a bus network which many in the suburbs felt was inadequate. **Figure 176** Ballyfermot's library van, 1950s. The use of mobile library vans was an important service for those in large or remote suburbs which did not yet have adequate libraries.

the predominantly middle-class suburbs (occupied mainly by home-owners) and the working-class suburbs (where most tenants rented from the local authority). Despite the undoubted achievements in construction, the number of houses built still fell short of the estimated 19,000 new dwellings that were required.[20] In 1936, the Fianna Fáil-aligned *Irish Press* had run a series of articles that described the conditions in Dublin's tenements, using language and imagery that would have been very familiar to Victorian reformers. Significantly, the paper considered these slums a legacy of British rule, rather than interrogating the very domestic origins of such conditions.[21]

Figure 177 (right) An image for the 'slum crusade' of the *Irish Press*, 1 October 1936.
Figure 178 (below) A rent book from the 1930s for No. 2 Bishop Lane, a residence that was located in the stable yard behind 15 Henrietta Street.

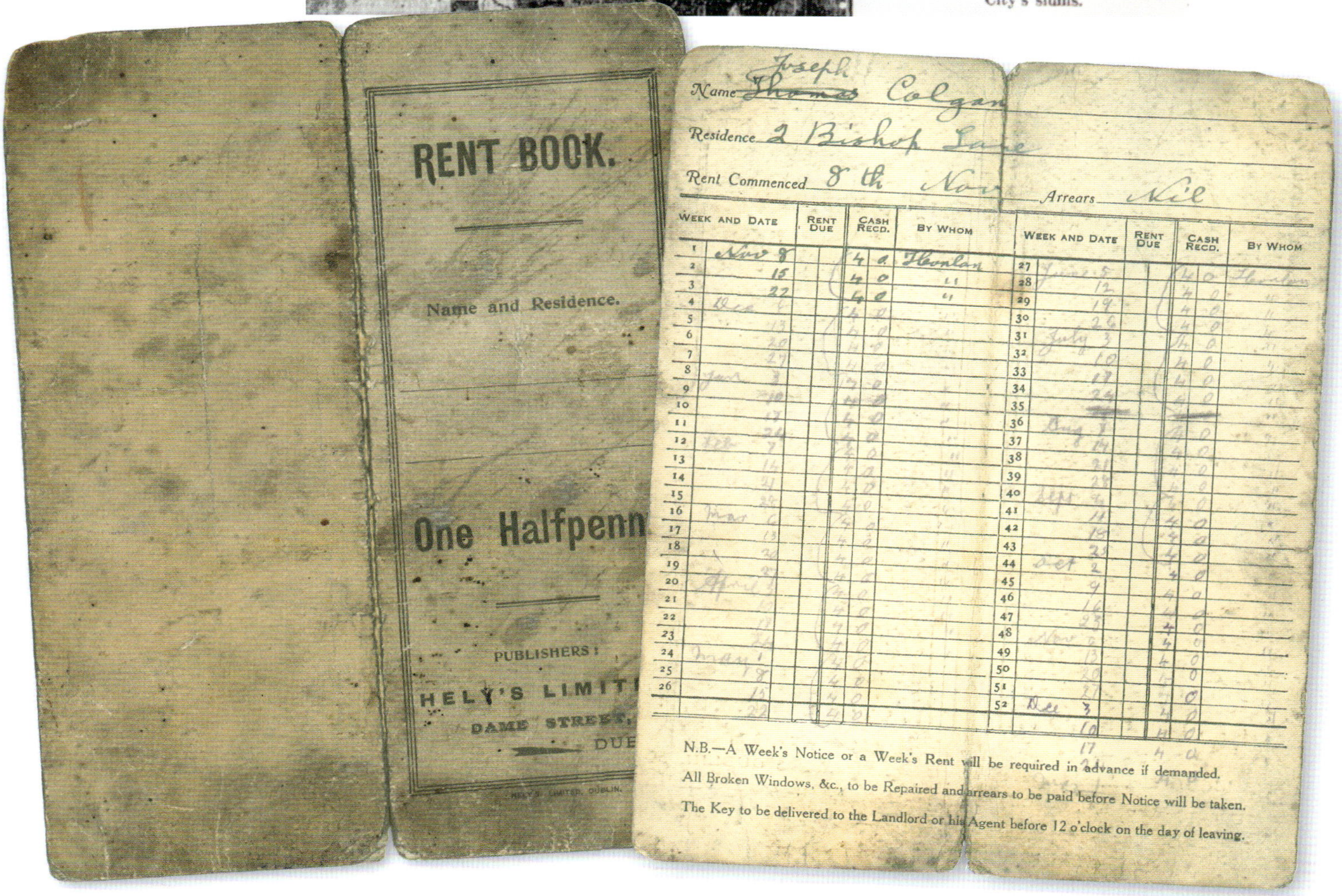

Figure 179 The houses destroyed by German bombing on the North Strand, 1941.

The Emergency

At the end of the 1930s, there was clearly still a need for a strong programme of house construction. Yet, with the outbreak of the Second World War in 1939, housing supply began to contract due to fiscal constraints, inflation, and the disruption to supplies of building materials. While Ireland remained neutral in the conflict, Dublin did experience aerial bombardment, with German bombs falling on parts of the city in the first half of 1941, destroying more than 300 homes and swelling the number of Dublin's homeless. The Emergency (as the war was called in Ireland) also saw the publication of yet another inquiry into Dublin's housing, the devastating *Report of inquiry into the housing of the working classes of the city of Dublin* (1943). This inquiry revealed that over 22,000 families in the city still lived in overcrowded tenements, a number that was comparable to the situation in 1914. Once again, it was accompanied by a far-reaching plan for the remaking of the city. In fact, it was written by the same man, Patrick Abercrombie, who produced the *Sketch development plan for Dublin* (1939).

The *Report of inquiry* seemed to suggest the insolubleness of Dublin's housing problem, a fact confirmed by the 1946 Census, which revealed that 23,000 Dubliners still lived in single-room dwellings. As the 1940s ended, the proposed answer to this seemingly insolvable problem was a 'thinning out' of the city centre. Essentially, this meant the expansion and acceleration of moving the poor of the inner city outwards into the suburbs, with a 1948 Housing Act providing increased government subsidies for house-building. There were massive extensions of the suburbs that had been commenced in the 1930s, such as Crumlin and Cabra. However, the 1950s were defined by new suburbs on the city's peripheries, like Walkinstown, Finglas, Donnycarney, and Ballyfermot. In the 1920s and 1930s, suburban schemes had been designed to *augment* the inner city. Now, the suburbs were intended to *supplant* the city centre, with the spread of suburbs to the west and north transforming the city as a whole. As Donal Fallon and others have described, some of the same sort of alienation that occurred with the move to areas like Crumlin was replicated, with Ballyfermot popularly known as 'Bally-far-out'.[22]

For those who remained in the city centre, conditions in the tenements remained poor. In 1947, the writer Frank O'Connor described walking down Henrietta Street in terms eerily similar to those Joyce had used a generation before, describing its 'funereal air':

> tall houses, tall flights of steps, leading to tall narrow doorways ... One slum house attracted us because a first-floor window had been lifted out body and bones, and through it you could see the staircase ceiling, heavy circles and strapwork which suggest a Jacobean hang-over. The poor people sunning themselves on the steps drew aside to let us pass. The staircase had been many times coated with salmon-colour wash which half obscured the rich plaster panelling, but a ray of light through a ruined window-frame lit a beautiful stair carved treads and delicate Restoration newel posts. It would have been alright but for the smell.[23]

Like Joyce before him, O'Connor appreciated how the faded elegance of Henrietta Street was a metaphor for the city as a whole. The street's 'funereal air', its 'spectral mansions', were the ghosts of a lost past that now haunted an impoverished population living in their ruins – a brutal contrast between eighteenth-century splendour and modern-day destitution. For O'Connor, and others, the decaying buildings of the Gardiner Estate were potent symbols for the failings of independence, both economic and cultural.

1960s and beyond

For those still living in the tenements, history was still alive and could repeat itself in disastrous ways. In 1963, half a century after the tragic collapse of tenements in Church Street, there were two tenement collapses in Bolton Street and Fenian Street, killing four people. Elsewhere on the north side, there was evidence of structural problems

Figure 180 Aerial view of the Ballymun tower development, 1960s.

in other tenement buildings, as in No. 3 Henrietta Street, where rubble fell into the living space of the sixteen families who called the building home. The resulting panic, known as the 'dangerous buildings scare' of 1963–4, saw the evacuation of people out of 367 buildings across the city. There were multiple reactions to this disaster, some very far-reaching. Among officials in Dublin Corporation and within the government, the dangers posed by the unsafe buildings further solidified the drive to relocate the working class from the city centre to the outer suburbs. Several years later, in 1967, a British town planner named Myles Wright was commissioned by the government to produce a development plan for the Dublin region. This landmark report proposed a significant relocation of the inner-city population to several 'new towns' running in an arch to the west: Tallaght, Clondalkin, Lucan and Blanchardstown.[24] Positioning the city within the concept of the greater 'Dublin region' for the first time, Wright's strategy was largely adopted by city and county planning authorities who incorporated it into their development plans over the following two decades, with a massive growth of the western new towns like Tallaght, and significant new estates also built in the northeast of the city, in Kilbarrack and Coolock. It could be argued that, by 1980, this development had transformed Dublin from a compact and high-density city into a sprawling, decentralized metropolis, with a declining inner city. Yet the 1970s also saw the high-point of housing output in Ireland, albeit with a shift from state-sponsored

Figure 181 Demolition of one of the towers in Ballymun.

to private development. The decade of the 1970s saw 176,230 private homes built across the country, with just under 62,000 social homes also constructed. Crucially, this same decade saw over 60,000 local authority houses sold via tenant purchase, further entrenching a preference for ownership over rental from a local authority.[25]

While low-density suburbs were one reaction to the housing crisis of the early 1960s, they were not the only measure taken. The construction of the Ballymun Housing Scheme on the city's northern outskirts was another response to the urgency of rehousing the city's working class. Ireland's first experiment with residential tower-blocks, Ballymun was the product of Dublin Corporation officials having visited cities like Stockholm and Copenhagen, where high-rise housing was common. Opened to residents in 1966, the year that was the demi-centenary of the Easter Rising, the seven towers were named after executed leaders of the Rising, consisting of eight- and fifteen-storey blocks of flats. Ballymun was initially planned as an entire new community, with integrated shops, parks, schools and amenities. Unfortunately, it seems that no lessons had been learned from earlier such developments and that important social infrastructure was not provided. Located at some distance from the city centre, the resources that were required for a new community to thrive (schools, shops, necessary maintenance to the towers) were not adequately provided for, gravely damaging the neighbourhood.[26] As Diarmaid Ferriter has commented: 'In retrospect, it seems blindingly obvious why the original project was doomed. Creating large-scale housing schemes that were physically and socially excluded from normal city economic and social activity was a recipe for malaise'.[27] The towers in Ballymun would eventually be demolished between 2004 and 2015.

While suburbanization may have been the big development in these decades, there were also significant changes occurring within the old city core. One of the first and most dramatic responses to the 1963 tenement collapses was the passage of a Sanitary Services Act (1964), an attempt to speed up the removal of dangerous buildings. It enabled landlords to remove long-standing tenants, as well as removing planning permission requirements for demolition. Consequently, something in the region of 1,200 Georgian terrace houses and mews were destroyed within two years. For decades, the priority among Dublin housing reformers had been simply to get people out of insanitary tenements and into safer housing. Now questions were increasingly asked about what the policy of 'slum clearance' was doing to the city and to the working-class communities who were being relocated. There were also some serious questions about the nature of property development now taking place in the inner city and its larger effects on public life. The 1960s was a period of increasing land values, with a boom in the construction of office blocks. Approximately eighty such blocks were constructed within the twelve square miles of the inner city during this decade.[28] Speculative developers made huge profits by replacing Georgian terraces with office blocks, often of an uninspiring architectural quality.

In response to the astonishing wave of demolition and office construction, several groups sprang up in opposition. The disappearance of many of the city's Georgian buildings elicited a response from the Irish Georgian Society (IGS), a society promoting the conservation of the country's eighteenth-century architectural heritage. The Society fought plans to demolish Georgian houses in Fitzwilliam Street, Hume Street and Mountjoy Square. Much was made of the social composition of the IGS, which included several notable Anglo-Irish aristocrats. Hostile observers described them as 'a group of dilettantes', a 'consortium of belted earls and their ladies', and (perhaps more believably), 'the remnants of the ascendancy seeking to preserve what was widely seen as the heritage of the ascendancy'.[29] In fact, some people questioned whether Dublin's Georgian architecture could even be described as *Irish* heritage. Several politicians (including at least one minister for local government) argued that Dublin's eighteenth-century buildings were simply a legacy of its colonial past, testaments to Ireland's subjugation to Britain, built by a 'foreign' elite and now best forgotten. While this mindset may have found support in some quarters, it is important to note that the IGS were only one of a number of groups who opposed the demolition of these buildings. The closure of so many tenements had exacerbated housing shortages in the inner-city, inspiring the establishment of the Dublin Housing Action Committee (DHAC) in 1967. The creation of left-wing republicans, the DHAC organized tenants to resist evictions, as well as agitating for the better provision of working-class housing in the inner city. While the DHAC could occasionally find itself on the same side as the IGS, there were also significant differences. For instance, in Mountjoy Square, the DHAC gathered signatures for a petition demanding that the square be rebuilt as working-class housing, in contrast to the IGS who hoped to return the Georgian buildings

Figure 182
Uinseann MacEoin.

to being owner-occupied private residences. Was the emphasis to be on preserving the eighteenth-century buildings? Or preserving the working-class communities that called them home?[30]

These two options were not necessarily mutually exclusive, as demonstrated by one activist with close links to Henrietta Street: Uinseann MacEoin. A trained architect and town planner, MacEoin was also a dedicated republican, in addition to being a tireless advocate of preserving Dublin's historic buildings. However, unlike many of his fellow IGS members, MacEoin brought a socially conscious approach to the preservation of Dublin's Gardiner Estate. Crucially, he linked the preservation of Georgian architecture with broader social issues. In journals like *Build* and *Plan*, MacEoin decried the Corporation's abandonment of its responsibility towards its citizens, allowing private interests to shape the city. In one issue of *Plan*, MacEoin proclaimed that 'if the present policy is pursued to its logical conclusion, Dublin will become a Great Dead City'.[31] This was a call for the city to serve the social and cultural needs of its citizens, rather than the desires of developers, and has been an argument that has found resonance among subsequent generations of Dublin activists. Moreover, during the 1960s and 70s, MacEoin put his ideas into practice, showing how Georgian buildings could be saved while still contributing to the broader community. Along with his wife, MacEoin established Luke Gardiner Ltd, a company that purchased and leased houses in the north-side Gardiner Estate and which was appropriately named after the estate's creator. Among the properties that MacEoin purchased were three houses in Henrietta Street. The first of these properties was No. 5 Henrietta Street, which, when the MacEoins first visited it in 1966, was still home to seventy-four people, twelve of whom shared a single front-room apartment. Having purchased the house for a small sum, MacEoin converted the house into artists' workshops, enabling a community that over several decades included some of the leading lights of the Irish arts scene. The MacEoins later purchased the adjoining Nos. 6 and 7 Henrietta Street, seeking to make these houses financially viable by letting out some sections as work space or artists' studios, while retaining the upper floors as affordable accommodation. The list of artists who would go on to maintain a studio in Henrietta Street included five members of Aosdána: Fergus Martin, Mick O'Dea, Mick Cullen, Gwen O'Dowd and Charlie Cullen.[32]

The houses that MacEoin had purchased had originally been built for some of the wealthiest and most powerful men of the eighteenth century: Nos. 5 and 6 had originally been one house, constructed in 1739 for Henry O'Brien, earl of Thomond, while No. 7 had been built the year before for Nathaniel Clements, the protégé of Luke Gardiner and one of the men responsible for Henrietta Street's very existence. Yet, for MacEoin, preserving these buildings was now part of a critique of the modern Irish state. This was something he made explicit with the plaques he put on the exteriors of the houses in Henrietta Street. For instance, MacEoin rechristened No. 5 as James Bryson House, naming it after a young member of the Provisional IRA who was shot by British troops in 1973. As Erika Hanna has argued, MacEoin was using the building 'to recall not so much a side-lined past as an alternative present ... His Georgian houses became symbols of an alternative secular, socialist, thirty-two county republic dreamed of at independence'. As the 1960s drew to a close, Dublin seemed to offer proof that some of MacEoin's arguments were correct; namely that the ideals of the nation's founders had been abandoned, with the corruption of the political class by developers, with endemic housing shortages and a brutal system of town planning (or lack of it) which had created dehumanizing environments.[33]

Yet the future was not all doom and gloom. Slowly, but surely, there emerged a greater public commitment to preserving Dublin's architectural heritage, including that of Henrietta Street. The year 1975 was declared the European Architectural Year by the European Union, adopting a charter which aimed to develop a common European policy for protecting architectural heritage. In time, the effects of this charter would be felt in Dublin. 1980 saw a Dublin City Development plan which listed 613 houses

Figure 183 View of Henrietta Street, 1981.

Figure 184 The interior of a room in No. 14 Henrietta Street in 1981. This photo shows the apartment that was located in what is today the first-floor stair hall. Note that the partitions from the tenement period have already been removed, while the layers of wallpaper have been stripped back to show the original Georgian features.

for preservation, although initially only 23 of these were on the northside of the city. This list was then extended with further classifications in subsequent development plans.[34]

In Henrietta Street, the 1970s and 1980s witnessed several people and groups following in Uinseann MacEoin's footsteps, repopulating once-dilapidated houses and demonstrating the continuing potential of the street. For instance, in 1973, the Casey family (with the aid of a loan from the IGS) reoccupied No. 13 as a single-family unit. During the 1980s, the trade unionist Sé Geraghty (like MacEoin, a left-wing republican and a patron of the arts) purchased No. 4 Henrietta Street with his partner, the artist Alice Hanratty. The same decade also saw Ian Lumley move into No. 12, and Na Píobairí Uilleann (a non-profit organization dedicated to the promotion of the Irish Uilleann pipes) take on a 99-year lease on No. 15. The 1970s saw the end of No. 14's use as a tenement, with the last families moving out of the house in 1979. Crucially, the reoccupation of some of these buildings by private individuals was done compassionately, allowing previous tenants the time to find new accommodation. At the same time, the reoccupation of these buildings began a process of 're-Georgianization', by which traces of a house's tenement past were removed in favour of original eighteenth-century features.

By demonstrating the potential of these houses, these new residents proved themselves more than just 'neo-Georgians'. They likely saved Henrietta Street from dereliction or destruction, an outcome that had been a very real threat, as several studies carried out in the 1980s and 1990s had warned.[35] In 2004, the heritage office of Dublin City Council commissioned a Conservation Plan for Henrietta Street. This document, produced by Shaffrey Associates, was crucial in establishing and promoting the cultural and historical significance of the street, as well as identifying threats to its future.[36] As a result, several ambitious policies were put forward to safeguard the street, the most urgent of which was to address the precarious condition of Nos. 3 and 14, which had both suffered from periods of vacancy and neglect. The Council commenced emergency stabilization works on both houses in 2008. In the case of No. 14, the year 2011 saw the beginning of extensive repair work to stabilize the building. In 2013, as part of the Decade of Centenaries, No. 14 played host to the innovative *Living the Lockout*, an interactive dramatic performance, presented by ANU productions with the support of Dublin City Council and the Irish Congress of Trade Unions. The decision was also taken to develop the property as the current museum, which opened in 2018.

The construction of the museum at No. 14 Henrietta Street involved more than just the physical stabilization or refurbishment of the house. While the building itself is the primary 'artifact' which the museum is based around, its development included an oral history project, devised and undertaken by the National Folklore Foundation based in University College Dublin on behalf of Dublin City Council. Following the opening of the museum, a programme of community engagement has continued, with *Your Tenement Memories*, an oral history project that has continued to visit community centres and libraries in order to gather memories about life in Dublin's tenements. The hope is that the current museum will act as a lightning rod, capturing the vital first-hand accounts of former residents, as well as those of Dubliners who lived in houses like those in Henrietta Street. By recording these experiences, 14 Henrietta Street may hopefully capture the historical complexity of the building's story. Much like the multiple layers of wallpaper that once covered its walls, the current museum is attempting to peel back the various stages of the house's history, revealing its many incarnations, from Georgian heyday through Victorian tenement to twentieth-century apartments. While the present book has attempted to explore the story of Henrietta Street during the nineteenth and early-twentieth century, it has only hinted at its twentieth-century working-class heritage. This epilogue has briefly sketched the twentieth-century responses to Dublin's tenement houses at the municipal and government level. What still remains to be told is the personal stories of families from the decades after the 1920s; the experience of life in a tenement that can still be captured and reconstructed with oral histories of former residents. It is these experiences that the new museum hopes to collect and archive, in order to provide a richer understanding of Dublin's tenement history. Undoubtedly, much remains to be told of Henrietta Street's story.

Abbreviations

BL	British Library
DADC	Dublin Artisans' Dwellings Company
DMP	Dublin Metropolitan Police
IGS	Irish Georgian Society
IPP	Irish Parliamentary Party
ITGWU	Irish Transport and General Workers Union
MS	manuscript
NAI	National Archives of Ireland
NGI	National Gallery of Ireland
NLI	National Library of Ireland
NUI	National University of Ireland
PP	Parliamentary Papers, Britain
PRONI	Public Records Office of Northern Ireland
RSAI	Royal Society of Antiquaries of Ireland
TCD	Trinity College Dublin
UCD	University College Dublin

Illustrations

1 Photograph of the door of No. 14 Henrietta Street. © The Royal Society of Antiquaries of Ireland.
2 'A tenement nocturne', *The Capuchin Annual*, 1940, p. 94. © Irish Capuchin Archives.
3 Joseph Tudor, *Prospect of the Parliament House in College Green*, 1753. National Library of Ireland.
4 John Rocque, *An exact survey of the city and suburbs of Dublin*, 1756, detail showing north city centre. © Royal Irish Academy.
5 'The doors of Dublin', Aer Lingus postcard showing colourful 'Georgian' doors. Scala Archives.
6 John Brooks after Charles Jervas, *Luke Gardiner, MP (d.1755)*, mezzotint, 29.2cm x 24.5cm, NGI.10242, National Gallery of Ireland Collection. Photo © National Gallery of Ireland.
7 John Rocque, *An exact survey of the city and suburbs of Dublin*, 1756, detail showing Henrietta Street and environs. © Royal Irish Academy.
8 John Brooks after Francis Bindon, *His Grace Doctor Hugh Boulter*, 1742. Mezzotint. © National Library of Ireland.
9 Allan Ramsay (attrib.), *George Stone, archbishop of Armagh (1708-64)*, c.1750s. Oil on canvas. By permission of the Governing Body of Christ Church, Oxford.
10 Stephen Slaughter, *The Rt. Hon. Henry Boyle*, 1733. Oil on canvas. Reproduced by kind permission of the governor and company of Bank of Ireland.
11 John Opie, *Mary Wollstonecraft*, 1797. Oil on canvas. © Bridgeman Images.
12 Mary Wollstonecraft, *Original stories from real life*, 1788. Washington University Digital Gateway.
13 *Margaret King, Lady Mount Cashell in profile*, 1801. Etching. New York Public Library Digital Collection.
14 Joseph Tudor, *Sackville Street and Gardiner's Mall*, c.1750. © National Gallery of Ireland.
15 James Malton, *Charlemont House, Dublin*, 1793. © National Library of Ireland.
16 James Malton, *Tholsel, Dublin*, 1793, detail showing sedan chair-man talking to women. © National Library of Ireland.
17 James Malton, *View from Capel Street, looking over Essex Bridge*, 1793, detail showing beggar and tradesmen in distance. © National Library of Ireland.
18 Hugh Douglas Hamilton, *A crippled beggar*, 1760, pen and ink. Private collection.
19 Hugh Douglas Hamilton, *Rags and old clothes*, 1760, pen and ink. Private collection.
20 Hugh Douglas Hamilton, *A rambling cobbler and his boy*, 1760, pen and ink. Private collection.
21 Hugh Douglas Hamilton, *Rare news in the Evening Post*, 1760, pen and ink. Private collection.
22 John Nixon, *The surroundings of St Patrick's Cathedral, Dublin*, c.1790. Private collection.
23 Sir Joshua Reynolds, *Richard Boyle, 2nd earl of Shannon*, 1759. Oil on canvas. Private collection.

24　Sir Joshua Reynolds, *Luke Gardiner, Viscount Mountjoy*, 1773. Oil on canvas. Private collection.
25　Street elevation of Nos. 13–15 Henrietta Street, c.1756.
26　Francis Wheatley, *The Irish House of Commons*, 1780.
27　*The Patriot Almanack: containing, a list of the members of the Hon. House of Commons of Ireland, who voted for and against the altered money-bill* (London, 1754). © National Library of Ireland.
28　*The United Irish Patriots of 1798* (Dublin, 1848). Lithograph. Wikicommons.
29　James Gillray, *United Irishmen upon duty*, June 1798. Hand-coloured aquatint. National Army Museum, London.
30　'College Green before the Union', 1812, published by J.J. Stockdale, London. Etching, 19cm x 25cm. © National Library of Ireland.
31　'College Green after the Union', 1812, published by J.J. Stockdale, London. Etching, 19cm x 25cm. © National Library of Ireland.
32　Thomas Kelly (attrib.), *Union Street, or ease and plenty*, 1800. © National Library of Ireland.
33　William Brocas, *Moira House, Dublin*, 1811. Etching, 9.1cm x 13.9cm. © National Library of Ireland.
34　James Holmes, *Charles Gardiner, 1st Earl Blessington*, 1812. Oil on canvas. © National Portrait Gallery.
35　William Hincks *A view of the Linenhall in Dublin*, 1791. Engraving. © Library of Congress, Washington DC.
36　'Panorama of the City of Dublin', published in *The Illustrated London News*, June 1846. Detail showing St Michan's Parish. Wood engraving, 44cm x 127cm. © National Library of Ireland.
37　Ordnance Survey of Ireland, map of Dublin, 1847. Detail showing part of St Michan's.
38　Drawing of Jameson's Bow Street distillery, published as part of Alfred Barnard, *The whiskey distilleries of the United Kingdom* (1887).
39　Daniel Heffernan, *Dublin in 1861*, plan of central Dublin with elevations of important architectural sites. Steel engraving, 63.5 cm x 92cm. Leslie Brown Collection.
40　George Petrie, *The King's Inns and Royal Canal Harbour*, from G.N. Wright, *An historical guide to ancient and modern Dublin*, 1821. © National Library of Ireland.
41　Henry Adlard, *Terminus of the Midland Great Western Railway*. Line engraving, 24cm x 33cm. © National Library of Ireland
42　William Brocas, *Dublin's King's Inns*, 1814–68. Pencil and ink drawing, 9.2cm x 13cm. © National Library of Ireland.
43　Photo of the gate between Henrietta Street and King's Inns. © Stephen Farrell Photography. Courtesy Dublin City Council.
44　Drawing of King's Inns with proposed additional buildings and map of planned circle of 'chambers' in front of existing structure. Private collection. Image courtesy the Irish Architectural Archive.
45　Illustration showing Blessington House, labelled 'Mountjoy House, Henrietta Street', *Dublin Penny Journal*, 13 February 1836. © National Library of Ireland.
46　Henry MacManus, *Tristram Kennedy*, 1877. Courtesy of Helen Stack and Colum Kenny.
47　*A view of the Four Courts*, published by J. Sidebotham, Dublin, 1809–20. Hand-coloured etching, image 22 cm x 31.5 cm. © National Library of Ireland.
48　*Ordnance Survey map of Dublin*, 1847, detail showing the north-west of the city. Courtesy of Dublin City Council.

49 Thomas Willis, *Facts connected with the social and sanitary condition of the working classes in the city of Dublin* (Dublin, 1845).

50 Portrait of Thomas Willis. Photograph, late nineteenth century. © Royal College of Physicians of Ireland.

51 James Mahony (1816–59), *Dublin from the spire of Saint George's Church, Hardwicke Place*, 1854, ink and watercolour on paper, 105cm x 164.7cm, NGI.2450, National Gallery of Ireland Collection. Photo © National Gallery of Ireland.

52 John Leech, 'A court for King Cholera', *Punch* (London, 1852).

53 'Heroism of an Irish landlord: the Irish tax-gatherer', *The Illustrated London News* (London, 1845).

54 Advertisement for sale of lands in Tipperary by Incumbered Estates Court, 1857. Tipperary County Council Library Service.

55 'South view of Henrietta Street', advertisement for General Engineering, Geological Survey and Valuation Office, Henrietta Street; John Irwine Whitty, 1860. © National Library of Ireland.

56 Portrait of John McAuliffe, sergeant quarter master at No. 14 Henrietta Street, 1862–75. Private collection.

57 *Land use map of Dublin north city*, Dublin Corporation, 1918. Detail showing north inner-city. Published as 'Survey of the north side of the city of Dublin', *Reports and printed documents of the Corporation of Dublin*, No. 13 (1918). © Dublin City Library and Archive.

58 Detail of land use map, showing area surrounding Henrietta Street. 'Survey of the north side of the city of Dublin', *Reports and printed documents of the Corporation of Dublin*, No. 13 (1918). © Dublin City Library and Archive.

59 Detail showing colour code for land use map of Dublin. 'Survey of the north side of the city of Dublin', *Reports and printed documents of the Corporation of Dublin*, No. 13 (1918). © Dublin City Library and Archive.

60 Robert French, Cattle Market, Dublin. Photograph, 1900. © National Library of Ireland.

61 'James' Gate Brewery'. Engraving, published in *The official illustrated guide to the Midland Great Western; (via London and North-Western,) Great Southern & Western, and Dublin and Drogheda Railways* (London, 1866).

62 Andrew Nicholl, *Dublin and Kingstown Railway, from the Martello Tower Bridge at Seapoint, looking towards Kingstown*, 1834. Aquatint, 20.3 cm x 25.3 cm. © National Library of Ireland.

63 Map of Dublin city and surrounding townships, Municipal boundaries commission (Ireland), 1880. © Leslie Brown Collection.

64 Postcard of Rathmines, Dublin, showing Rathmines Road Lower, *c.*1900. © Dublin City Library and Archive.

65 Daniel O'Connell in robes of lord mayor, late nineteenth-century etching. National Library of Ireland.

66 John Cooke, Stable Lane at rear of 20 South Cumberland Street, 1913. © The Royal Society of Antiquaries of Ireland.

67 John Cooke, Henrietta Place, 1913. ©The Royal Society of Antiquaries of Ireland.

68 'Attic occupied by a family of ten persons', *The Illustrated London News*, 1863. Wellcome Collection, Public Domain Mark.

69 John Cooke, photograph of Dublin tenement, unknown location, 1913. © The Royal Society of Antiquaries of Ireland.

70   William Mooney, No. 46 Wolfe Tone Street, tenement, 1960. © Dublin City Library and Archive.

71   John Cooke, photograph of the exterior of Grenville Street, 1913. © The Royal Society of Antiquaries of Ireland.

72   *Exterior of the model lodging houses for families, Chapel Lane, Bridge St., Cook St., Dublin: the property of Thomas Vance, Esqr. Erected 1854.* Late nineteenth century. Lithograph, 16 cm x 23 cm. © National Library of Ireland.

73   Aerial view of Vance's buildings, 'Oblique aerial photograph taken facing North, Dublin, 1934.' Britain from above collection. © Historic England.

74   Exteriors of Nos. 3–10 Henrietta Street, shown in *The Georgian Society records of eighteenth-century domestic architecture and decoration in Dublin* (Dublin, 1911). Image courtesy of the Royal Society of Antiquaries of Ireland.

75   Photograph of Joseph Meade, *Dublin main drainage scheme: souvenir handbook; published by the authority of the Municipal Council to mark the inauguration of the Dublin main drainage*, 1906. © Dublin City Library and Archive.

76   Photograph of rear of No. 7 Henrietta Street, showing toilet block addition, David Davison, 1981. © Irish Architectural Archive.

77   Cartoon of a Dublin slum owner, *The Lepracaun Cartoon Monthly*, November 1907. © Dublin City Library and Archive.

78   'Dublin illustrated' from *The Graphic*, 17 August 1878.

79   John Cooke, Chancery Lane, off Bride Street, 1913. © The Royal Society of Antiquaries of Ireland.

80   Conjectural re-construction of 14 Henrietta Street, *c.*1880. Drawings by Philip Marron.

81   John Cooke, Interior of Newmarket tenement, 1913. © The Royal Society of Antiquaries of Ireland.

82   John Cooke, Interior of tenement, the Coombe, 1913. © The Royal Society of Antiquaries of Ireland.

83   John Cooke, Engine Alley, Meath Street, 1913. © The Royal Society of Antiquaries of Ireland.

84   John Cooke, A view of Church Street, 1913. © The Royal Society of Antiquaries of Ireland.

85   John Cooke, Faithful Place on Lower Tyrone Street, 1913. © The Royal Society of Antiquaries of Ireland.

86   John Cooke, Waste ground and ruins near Chancery Street, 1913. © The Royal Society of Antiquaries of Ireland.

87   John Cooke, Faddle's Alley, off Dowker's Lane, 1913. © The Royal Society of Antiquaries of Ireland.

88   John Cooke, Interior of tenement at 8 Waterford Street, 1913. © The Royal Society of Antiquaries of Ireland.

89   John Cooke, Interior of tenement at 8 Waterford Street, 1913. © The Royal Society of Antiquaries of Ireland.

90   Census enumerator's form for the Dorgan family in No. 14 Henrietta Street, taken from 1911 Census. © National Archive of Ireland.

91   Children at play on Henrietta Street, *c.*1924, photograph. © Independent Newspapers.

92   Bill Doyle, Children playing on Henrietta Street, 1960s, photograph. Taken from Bill

	Doyle, *Images of Dublin: a time remembered* (Lilliput Press, 2001). Image is courtesy of the Lilliput Press and the estate of Bill Doyle.
93	Ephraim McDowell Cosgrave, 'Street arabs', 1900. © The Royal Society of Antiquaries of Ireland
94	Aerial photograph of Grangegorman complex of institutions, twentieth century. Image courtesy of Grangegorman Development Agency.
95	A workhouse scene, with children, Dublin, 1895. © National Photographic Archive of Ireland.
96	Drawing of the Sick & Indigent Roomkeepers Society, Castle Lane. Johnny Ryan, © Dublin City Council.
97	Robert French, *Back of the Rotunda Hospital*, 1890s. National Library of Ireland.
98	Street view of No. 9 Henrietta Street, 1909. © The Royal Society of Antiquaries of Ireland
99	Graffiti on landing wall of No. 14 Henrietta Street. Image courtesy of Dublin City Council Culture Company.
100	A member of the Dublin Metropolitan Police patrols on Eden Quay, late-nineteenth century. National Library of Ireland.
101	*Map showing Dublin's greatest evil (public houses)*, 1892. Guinness Archive, Diageo Ireland.
102	Constance Gore-Booth, Countess Markievicz, 'Visit to a Dublin family during the tuberculosis epidemic', 1924. © National Library of Ireland.
103	John Cooke, Tenement interior, Francis Street, The Coombe, 1913. © The Royal Society of Antiquaries of Ireland.
104	Disinfectors spraying infected premises with disinfectants, 1911. 'Dirt and Disease Collection, Public Health in Dublin 1903–17', © Dublin City Library and Archive.
105	'The fly peril', pamphlet issued by Dublin Corporation, 1914. 'Dirt and Disease Collection, Public Health in Dublin 1903–17', © Dublin City Library and Archive.
106	Udo Keppler 'The tenement: a menace to all', *Puck* magazine, March 1901. © Library of Congress, Washington, DC.
107	The Sanitary Sub-Officers of the Corporation of Dublin, 1909. 'Dirt and Disease Collection, Public Health in Dublin 1903–17', © Dublin City Library and Archive.
108	'Dear, dirty Dublin', *The Lepracaun Cartoon Monthly*, December 1908. © Dublin City Library and Archive.
109	'Doomed at last', *The Lepracaun Cartoon Monthly*, January 1913. © Dublin City Library and Archive.
110	David Jazay, Ellis Court, Benburb Street, 1992. © David Jazay.
111	Newspaper image of Foley Street flats, *Evening Herald*, 24 June 1977. RTÉ Archives.
112	Plan for the Dublin Artisans' Dwelling Company buildings at Echlin Street. Courtesy Irish Architectural Archive.
113	Photograph , 'Part of a housing scheme of 700 houses for the Dublin Artisans' Dwelling Company', 1903-06. Courtesy of Joseph Brady and UCD Digital Library.
114	Dublin Artisans' Dwellings Company, Blueprints for Type 'E' Cottage for Rialto Scheme Extension, 1895. © Irish Architectural Archive.
115	'Town planning (latest scheme)', *The Lepracaun Cartoon Monthly*, July 1914. © Dublin City Library and Archives.
116	Masthead of *The Irish Worker*. © National Library of Ireland.

117 'Dublin's insanitary monster', *The Lepracaun Cartoon Monthly*, August 1908. © Dublin City Library and Archive.
118 Front page of *The Daily Sketch*, 5 September 1913. © Irish Capuchin Archives.
119 Front cover, *Report of the Departmental committee appointed by the Local Government Board for Ireland to enquire into the housing conditions of the working classes in the city of Dublin*, 1914.
120 Cartoon of Sir Charles Cameron, *The Lepracaun Cartoon Monthly*, September 1906. © Dublin City Library and Archive.
121 'Tumbling tenements or, shelling the slums', *The Lepracaun Cartoon Monthly*, March 1914. © Dublin City Library and Archive.
122 Photograph of boys holding up *Daily Herald* sheets reading 'Murphy Must Go', in front of a large crowd, *Irish Life*, October 1913. © National Library of Ireland.
123 RTÉ Cashman Collection, Baton charge of the Dublin Metropolitan Police during the Dublin Lockout, 1913. © RTÉ archive.
124 Ernest Kavanagh, 'Dublin labour war', 1914. © Dublin City Library and Archive.
125 'La misère à Dublin', *Le Miroir*, 23 November 1913. © National Library of Ireland.
126 Alex Ehrenzweig, photographic portrait of James Joyce, 1915. Wikicommons.
127 Lilian Davidson, Poster for the Civic Exhibition, 1914. © National Library of Ireland.
128 'Who fears to speak of Easter Week?', poster, 1916. © National Library of Ireland.
129 'If the Kaiser came to Dublin', *The Lepracaun Cartoon Monthly*, February 1915. © Dublin City Library and Archive.
130 Cartoon, 'Employers and recruiting', *The Leader*, 26 September 1914. Image courtesy of the Board of Trinity College Dublin.
131 The Dublin Parkgate Street munition factory, *c.*1915–17. © Imperial War Museum.
132 Schedule of separation allowance for wives of soldiers, 1915. © Library of Congress, Washington DC.
133 'College Green, Dublin', *The Lady of the House*, Christmas Annual, 1915. © Dublin City Library and Archive.
134 Photograph of John Brogan. Courtesy of Geraldine Deacon.
135 Photograph of Anthony Morrell. Courtesy of the Morrell family.
136 Photographs of William Dyer and Thomas Dyer reproduced in *Saturday Herald*, 26 October and 16 November 1918.
137 Sackville Street in flames: a photograph taken by a *Daily Sketch* photographer under fire, postcard, May 1916. UCD Library Special Collections. © Unknown.
138 Linenhall Barracks, Dublin, shelled, 1916. Keogh Photographic Collection © National Library of Ireland.
139 The wreck they made of Church Street, Dublin, postcard, 1916. © National Library of Ireland.
140 Members of the Irish Women Workers' Union on the steps of Liberty Hall, with banner 'Freedom's Martyr's members of the Irish Women Workers' Union who suffered terms of imprisonment in the cause of Labour'. © National Library of Ireland.
141 Photo of an older Rosie Hackett, reproduced in *Fifty years of Liberty Hall*, (Dublin, 1959).
142 Nekane Orkaizagirre/Stoneybatter & Smithfield People's History Project. Poster commemorating the 100th anniversary of the North King Street massacre, 2016.
143 Girls gathering firewood after the Rising, *Dublin after the six days' insurrection: thirty-one pictures from the camera of Mr T.W. Murphy*, Digital Library @ Villanova University.

144 Business as usual: a newsvendor resumes business amongst the ruins, 1916. *Dublin after the six days' insurrection: thirty-one pictures from the camera of Mr T.W. Murphy,* Digital Library @ Villanova University.

145 East side of Sackville Street from O'Connell Bridge, 1916. *Dublin after the six days' insurrection: thirty-one pictures from the camera of Mr T.W. Murphy,* Digital Library @ Villanova University.

146 The front page of the *Sunday Independent,* 30 April – 7 May 1916 edition.

147 View of the ruins north of Sackville Street, 1916. *The Manchester Guardian history of the war 1914–18* (Manchester, 1919).

148 'Church St housing scheme bird's eye view', P.C. Cowan, *Report on Dublin housing* (1918).

149 Victory parade going down Westmoreland Street, 19 July 1919. © RTÉ Archives.

150 Thomas Bryan in his Volunteers uniform, 1917–20. Image courtesy of Kilmainham Gaol Museum/Office of Public Works.

151 'Thomas Bryan, died for Ireland March 14th 1921', James Kirwan Collection. © National Library of Ireland.

152 Dublin's latest terror, *Daily Sketch,* 5 April 1920. Image courtesy of Bureau of Military History.

153 The Four Courts during the battle of Dublin, June 1922. © National Library of Ireland.

154 Map showing area of Upper Sackville Street damaged in the Civil War, *The Irish Builder,* 1923. Courtesy Irish Architectural Archive.

155 Cartoon of 'slum landlord', *The Capuchin Annual,* 1940. © Irish Capuchin Archives.

156 Map of proposed road works, Patrick Abercrombie, Sydney Kelly & Arthur Kelly, *Dublin of the future: the new town plan,* 1922. © National Library of Ireland.

157 Sketch showing suggested cathedral site at the head of Capel Street, Abercrombie, Kelly & Kelly, *Dublin of the future: the new town plan, 1922.* © National Library of Ireland.

158 Harry Clarke, 'The last hour of the night', *Dublin of the future: the new town plan,* 1922. © National Library of Ireland.

159 'Bird's-eye view of the Greater Dublin reconstruction proposals', *Organising Committee of the Greater Dublin Reconstruction Movement,* December 1922. Image courtesy of the Irish Architectural Archive.

160 Back stairs in 14 Henrietta Street, 1981. David Davison, Courtesy Irish Architectural Archive.

161 *The civic survey of Dublin and environs,* 1925. © UCD Digital Library.

162 Detail showing Henrietta Street and surroundings, *The civic survey of Dublin and environs,* 1925. © UCD Digital Library.

163 Index to map of central city area, *The civic survey of Dublin and environs,* 1925. © UCD Digital Library

164 A.P. Wilson, *Victims,* published in *The Irish Worker,* 21 December 1912. Reproduced in Irish Labour History Society, *Saothar Studies,* 3 (Christmas 2012).

165 Scene from production of Robert Collis' *Marrowbone Lane* directed by Hilton Edwards at the Gate Theatre Dublin, 1939. In the collections of the Charles Deering McCormick Library of Special Collections and University Archives, Northwestern University.

166 Still from the television adaptation of *Strumpet City,* 1980. © RTÉ Archives.

167 Raymond Unwin, Perspective drawing for Marino, 1914. © Dublin City Library and Archive.

168   Preliminary plans for the Marino housing scheme, March 1919. © Dublin City Library and Archive.
169   Cumann na nGaedheal campaign poster from 1932 general election. © National Library of Ireland.
170   Flats at Chancery Place for the Dublin Corporation, 1935. Courtesy of G. & T. Crampton and UCD Digital Library.
171   The flats at Greek Street under construction, with St Michan's visible in the background, 1935. © Dublin City Library and Archive.
172   Henrietta House, designed by Herbert Simms, at the rear of 14 Henrietta Street. Courtesy of Dublin City Library and Archives.
173   Aerial view of the estates in Crumlin, 1950s. Morgan Aerial Photographic Collection. © National Library of Ireland.
174   The Housing Department Estate Offices, Kimmage. Courtesy of Dublin City Library and Archive.
175   The Hill of Howth Tramway. Courtesy of Fáilte Ireland.
176   Ballyfermot's library van, 1950s. Courtesy of Dublin City Library and Archive.
177   *Irish Press*, 1 October 1936.
178   Rent book for Bishop Lane, 1930s, Dublin City Council Muniment Records. Courtesy of Dublin City Council.
179   The houses destroyed by German bombing on the North Strand, 1941. Courtesy of Dublin City Library and Archive.
180   Aerial view of the Ballymun tower development, 1960s. Courtesy of Dublin City Library and Archive.
181   Photograph of the demolition of one of the towers in Ballymun. Photograph by Darren Hall, Dublin City Library and Archive.
182   Photograph of Uinseann MacEoin in St Catherine's Church, Thomas Street. Image courtesy of the MacEoin family.
183   View of Henrietta Street, 1981. Courtesy of Dublin City Library and Archive.
184   The first-floor stair hall in 14 Henrietta Street, 1981, David Davison. © Irish Architectural Archive.

Notes

Introduction

1 James Joyce, 'A little cloud', *Dubliners* (London, 1914).
2 Paula Meehan, 'Step we gaily, on we go' in Paula Meehan and Dragana Jurišić, *MUSEUM* (Dublin, 2019).
3 Murray Fraser, *John Bull's other homes: state housing and British policy in Ireland, 1883–1922* (Liverpool, 1996), pp 66–8.
4 Valentine Baron Cloncurry, *Personal recollections of the life and times: with extracts from the correspondence of Valentine Lord Cloncurry* (London, 1849), p. 216.
5 John Gamble, *Sketches of history, politics and manners: taken in Dublin, and the north of Ireland, in the autumn of 1810* (London, 1811), p. 55.
6 [Hugh Boulter], *Letters written by His Excellency Hugh Boulter* (Oxford. 1770), vol. ii, p. 223. While there is no academic biography of Luke Gardiner, see David Dickson, 'Large-scale developers and the growth of eighteenth-century Irish cities' in P. Butel and L. Cullen (eds), *Cities and merchants: French and Irish perspectives on urban development* (Dublin, 1986).
7 For the succinct overview of the street's construction and Gardiner's own home, see Melanie Hayes, *14 Henrietta Street: Georgian beginnings, 1750–1800* (Dublin, 2021), pp 12–22.
8 A.P.W. Malcomson, *Nathaniel Clements, 1705–77: politics, fashion and architecture in mid-eighteenth-century Ireland* (Dublin, 2015).
9 Melanie Hayes, *The best address in town: Henrietta Street, Dublin and its first residents, 1730–80* (Dublin, 2020).
10 Ibid., p. 150.
11 Richard Cumberland, *Memoirs of Richard Cumberland, written by himself: containing an account of his life and writings* (London, 1806), pp 172–3; 'My expedition to Ireland' written by George Montagu, cousin to the earl of Halifax, lord lieutenant, *Dublin University Magazine*, September 1854. Caesar Litton Falkiner, *Essays relating to Ireland: biographical, historical and topographical* (London, 1909); Georgian Society of Ireland, *Records of eighteenth-century domestic architecture and decoration in Dublin*. 5 vols (Dublin, 1969), vol. 2, p. 12; A.P.W. Malcomson, *Nathaniel Clements: politics, fashion and architecture* (Dublin, 2015), p. 215.
12 Jacqueline Hill, 'Allegories, fictions and feigned representations: decoding the Money Bill dispute, 1752–6', *Eighteenth Century Ireland,* 21 (2006), pp 66–88.
13 The estimate of ten to fifteen domestics was put forward by Constantia Maxwell, *Dublin under the Georges* (London, 1936), p. 85. Alternatively, the 1798 survey of William Whitelaw estimated that households in fashionable districts had an average of three servants per house. Revd William Whitelaw, *An essay on the population of Dublin* (Dublin, 1805), p. 5.
14 Hayes, *Best Address,* pp 166–9; Patricia McCarthy, 'The planning and use of space in Irish houses, 1730–1830' (PhD, TCD, 2009), pp 222–34.
15 Janet Todd, *Daughters of Ireland: the rebellious Kingsborough sisters and the making of a modern nation* (New York, 2003); Edward C. McAleer, *The sensitive plant: a life of Lady Mount Cashell* (Chapel Hill, 1958).
16 Nicola Pierce, *O'Connell Street: the history and life of Dublin's iconic street* (Dublin, 2021).
17 Edward McParland, 'Strategy in the planning of Dublin, 1750–1800' in Butel and Cullen (eds), *Cities and merchants,* pp 97–108.

18 For a recent analysis of Malton's images, see the essays by Graham Hickey, David Dickson, Merlo Kelly, Katheryn Milligan and Diarmuid Ó Grada in Trevor White and Djinn von Noorden (eds), *Malton's view of Dublin: the story of a Georgian city* (Dublin, 2021).
19 For a comprehensive introduction to Hamilton's drawings, see the essays contained in William Laffan (ed.), *The cries of Dublin from the life by Hugh Douglas Hamilton, 1760* (Dublin, 2003).
20 Mark Hallet, *Hogarth: the artist and the city* (London, 2006); Kate Heard, *High spirits: the comic art of Thomas Rowlandson* (London, 2013).
21 Richard Lewis, *The Dublin guide: or, a description of the city of Dublin* (Dublin, 1787), p. 51.
22 Denis Taaffee's 1796 polemic *Ireland's mirror: exhibiting a picture of her present state* (Dublin, 1795), pp 13-14.
23 Chevalier de la Tocnaye, *A Frenchman's walk through Ireland, 1796-7*, translated by John Stevenson (Belfast, 1984), pp 18-19.
24 For the best analysis of these developments, see Diarmuid Ó Gráda, *Georgian Dublin: the forces that shaped the city* (Cork, 2015), passim.
25 Revd James Whitelaw, *An essay on the population of Dublin* (Dublin, 1805), p. 50.
26 Thomas Bartlett, 'Opposition in late eighteenth-century Ireland: the case of the Townshend viceroyalty', *Irish Historical Studies,* 22 (1980-1), pp 313-30.
27 Declan O'Donovan, 'The Money Bill dispute of 1753' in Thomas Bartlett and David Hayton (eds), *Penal era and golden age: essays in Irish history, 1690-1800* (Belfast, 1979), pp 74-8; Jim Smyth, *The men of no property: Irish radicals and popular politics in the late eighteenth century* (Basingstoke, 1992), pp 125-7.
28 Patrick Fagan, 'The population of Dublin in the eighteenth century', *Eighteenth Century Ireland*, 6 (1991), pp 121-56; David Dickson, '"Centres of motion": Irish cities and the origins of popular politics' in Bergeron and Cullen (eds), *Culture et pratiques politiques*, pp 106-7.
29 For rumour of servants planning to poison their masters, see [Anon.], 'A dark page in the history of the rebellion of 1798' (TCD MS 2575). See also, Thomas Graham, 'Dublin in 1798: the key to the planned insurrection' in Nicholas Furlong and Dáire Keogh (eds), *The mighty wave: the 1798 rebellion in Wexford* (Dublin, 1996), pp 65-78.
30 Sir Richard Musgrave, *Memoirs of the different rebellions in Ireland* (Dublin, 1805); A.T.Q. Stewart, *The summer soldiers: Antrim and Down in 1798* (Belfast, 1995), pp 111-16; Charles Dickson, *Revolt in the North: Antrim and Down in 1798* (Dublin, 1960); Beresford to Lord Auckland, 8 June 1798, BL Add. MS 34,454 f. 324 reproduced in *The '98 Rebellion*, Public Record Office of Northern Ireland, Educational Facsimiles series, no. 83 (Belfast, 1971).
31 Pitt to Camden, 28 May 1798, in Arthur Aspinall (ed.), *The later correspondence of George III* (Cambridge, 1967), iii, pp 68-78.

1. Dublin after the Union, 1800-41

1 Notably, provincial towns like Cork did not share Dublin's opposition, some predicting that the Union would humble the overmighty Irish capital which had monopolized trade and offices. Daniel Mansergh, ' "As much support as it needs": social class and regional attitudes to the Union', *Eighteenth Century Ireland,* 15 (2000), pp 77-97.
2 W.J. McCormack, *The pamphlet debate on the Union between Great Britain and Ireland, 1797-1800* (Dublin, 1996), pp 7-11; *Freemans Journal*, 12 Jan. 1799.
3 PRONI Foster Papers D207/10/9; *Freeman's Journal*, 24 Jan. 1817.
4 Richard Jebb, *A reply to a pamphlet entitled, arguments for and against a union* (London, 1799), p. 46.
5 Cooke to Castlereagh, 2 January 1801, Charles Vane (ed.), *Memoirs and correspondence of Viscount Castlereagh*, 12 vols (London, 1848-53), iv, pp 13-14; 'The mob were delighted with the new flag'; Cornwallis to Portland, 24 December 1798, Charles Ross (ed.), *Correspondence of Charles, First Marquis Cornwallis*, 3 vols (London, 1859), iii, pp 21-2.

6   William Reid, *The remains of William Reid including rambles in Ireland* (London, 1815), p. 45; Walter Scott to Maria Edgeworth 18 July 1825, quoted in Constantia Maxwell, *The stranger in Ireland* (Dublin, 1954), p. 253; Charles Robert Maturin, *Women; or Pour et Contre* (Edinburgh, 1818), quoted in Gillian O'Brien '"What can possess you to go to Ireland?": visitors' perceptions of Dublin, 1800–30' in Gillian O'Brien and Finola O'Kane (eds), *Georgian Dublin* (Dublin, 2008), pp 21–9.

7   Evidence of Michael Malley in PP, *Two reports from the select committee on the local taxation of the city of Dublin*, 2, HC 1823 (549), vi, p. 140; PRONI Foster Papers D207/10/9.

8   John James McGregor, *New picture of Dublin* (Dublin, 1821), p. 312.

9   David Dickson, *Dublin: the making of a capital city* (Dublin, 2014), pp 278, 315.

10   One later commentary on Ireland described how Dublin's 'old mansions are occupied by public functionaries, or affluent professional men, or merchants … occupied as seminaries, club-houses or hotels'. William Stanley, *Commentaries on Ireland* (Dublin, 1833), pp 72–3; *Treble Almanack* (Dublin, 1804); McGregor, *New picture of Dublin*; Elizabeth Bowen, *The Shelbourne* (Dublin, 1951); R.B. McDowell, *Land and learning: two Irish clubs* (Dublin, 1993), p. 46.

11   'Dublin in 1822', *The New Monthly Magazine and Literary Journal*, 4 (London, 1822), p. 508.

12   Anthony Malcomson, *The pursuit of an heiress: aristocratic marriage in Ireland, 1740–1840* (Belfast, 1982), p. 178.

13   The earliest and most vivid account of their lives can be found in R.R. Madden, *The literary life and correspondence of the countess of Blessington* (London, 1855). For more recent evaluation of Blessington and his poor estate management, see Sean J. Murphy, 'The Gardiner family, Dublin and Mountjoy, County Tyrone', *Studies in Irish Genealogy and Heraldry* (2010), pp 28–35. See also, Malcomson, *Pursuit of an heiress*, pp 178–86.

14   Nathaniel Jeffreys, *An Englishman's descriptive acount of Dublin* (Dublin, 1810), p. 85.

15   *The Irish Georgian Society records of eighteenth-century domestic architecture and decoration in Dublin* (reprinted 1969), vol. II, pp 25, 28; [Anon.], *The picture of Dublin, being a description of the city, and a correct guide to all the public establishments* (Dublin, 1810), p. 198; McGregor, *New picture of Dublin*, p. 305. The attribution of Lady Daly's pictures is suspect, they may well have been copies or works done 'in the school of' these notable artists.

16   The homes previously owned by Shannon had been split back into two separate houses after Shannon's death. Bryan is listed on the street by 1815, although it is unclear at which point between 1807 and 1815 he moved there, particularly as Shannon's son (Lord Boyle) is listed on the street until 1810. *Treble Almanack* (Dublin, 1810 and 1815).

17   John Brennan, 'Jenkinstown, Co. Kilkenny and its associations', *Old Kilkenny Review*, 2:3 (1981), pp 213–25; Frank McEvoy, 'The Slane peerage claim', *Old Kilkenny Review*, 2:4 (1982), pp 352–62.

18   C.M. O'Keeffe, *The life and times of Daniel O'Connell* (Dublin, 1863–4), ii, pp 19–36.

19   *Freeman's Journal*, 16 May 1826.

20   The account book contains significant gaps and does not always clearly discern between outgoings at his household in Jenkinstown and in Henrietta Street, making analysis of his spending in Dublin problematic. NLI MS 32,489, 'Account Book of Augusta Bryan', entries for January and May 1826.

21   *The Irish Magazine*, November 1807.

22   Viator, *Letters to the Right Honourable Robert Peel, chief secretary to the lord lieutenant of Ireland* (Dublin, 1816).

23   PP, *Poor inquiry (Ireland), appendix (C) – part II. Report on the city of Dublin, and supplement containing answers to queries; with addenda to appendix (A), and communications* [C 43], HC 1836, xxx, 35, evidence of Francis Diggens, esq. and D.G. Luge, esq. Master Braziers: 'In 1812, I had a large stock of goods in hand, and had great custom with the nobility and gentry. From 1815, when the war terminated, till 1820 in consequence of the absence of the nobility and gentry who went to the Continent, I was reduced from keeping 12 journeymen to a single apprentice, and afterwards was obliged to give up the business entirely'.

24   For instance, the value of cloth produced in Dublin fell by more than half between 1822 and 1837. PP, *Report from select committee on the present state of the silk trade with the minutes of evidence, an appendix, and index*, HC

1831–2, (678), xix; pp 836–8, 930; *Report of the commissioners appointed to take the census for Ireland, for the year 1841* [504], HC 1843, xxxiv, p. 22, table VI; Jacqueline Hill, *From patriots to unionists: Dublin civic politics and Irish Protestant patriotism, 1660–1840* (Oxford, 1997), pp 284–6; David O'Toole, 'The employment crisis of 1826' in David Dickson (ed.), *The gorgeous mask: Dublin, 1700–1850* (Dublin, 1987), pp 157–71.

25 Hill, *Patriots to unionists*, p. 285; Constantia Maxwell, *Dublin under the Georges, 1714–1830* (London, 1956), p. 257.

26 Hill, *Patriots to unionists*, p. 285; Maxwell, *Dublin under the Georges*, p. 257; Frank Cullen, *Dublin 1847: city of the Ordnance Survey* (Dublin, 2015), p. 29. In 1842, a visitor to the city described the Linenhall as a 'huge, useless, lonely, decayed place'. See, W.M. Thackeray, *The Irish sketch book* (London, 1843), p. 179.

27 Patrick Lynch and John Vaizy, *Guinness's Brewery in the Irish economy, 1759–1876* (Cambridge, 1960), pp 120–2; Mary Pollard, *A dictionary of members of the Dublin book trade, 1550–1800* (Dublin, 2000), pp 379–84, 648–9.

28 *Observations on the House of Industry Dublin and on the plans for the Association for suppressing mendacity in that city* (1818), pp 23–4.

29 There was a series of regional famines in 1817–19, 1822, and 1831. David Dickson, 'The gap in famines: a useful myth?' in E.M. Crawford (ed.), *Famine: the Irish experience, 900–1900* (Edinburgh, 1989), pp 107–8; J. Mokyr and C. Ó Gráda, 'Poor and getting poorer? Living standards in Ireland before the Famine', *Economic History Review*, 41:2 (1988), pp 209–35.

30 Francis White, *Report and observations on the state of the poor in Dublin* (Dublin, 1833), p. 27.

31 Ibid., p. 30. For a similar report, see *Report of the Association for the Suppression of Mendicity in Dublin for the year 1818* (Dublin, 1819).

32 Revd G.N. Wright, *An historical guide to ancient and modern Dublin* (London, 1821), p. 228.

33 Hugh Campbell, 'Contested territory, common ground: architecture and politics in nineteenth-century Dublin' (PhD, UCD, 1998), p. 39.

34 Mountjoy to Andrew Caldwell, 24 Mar. 1798, quoted in Patricia McCarthy, *'A favourite study': building the King's Inns* (Dublin, 2006), pp 30–1. The location of the passage from the King's Inns to Henrietta Street might also have been due to some legal right-of-way issue from the fields the site was built on. Edward McParland, *James Gandon: vitruvius hibernicus* (London, 1985), pp 167–8, 174.

35 McCarthy, *Building the King's Inns*, p. 75.

36 The primate's house was in use as the offices of this court for the first two decades of the nineteenth century. The court fell under the remit of the archbishop (hence the link to the primate's house). The jurisdiction of this court was eventually transferred to the probate court after a series of reforms in 1857. Samuel Lewis, *A topographical dictionary of Ireland* (London, 1837); John Warburton, James Whitelaw and Robert Walsh, *History of the city of Dublin, from the earliest accounts to the present time* (London, 1818), vol. ii, p. 1022.

37 *Wilson's Dublin Directory* (1810); *The Gentleman and Citizen's Almanack for Dublin* (1815); *The Treble Almanack* (1822); *Pettigrew and Oulton's Dublin Directory* (1834).

38 Bartholomew Duhigg, *History of the King's Inns, or, An account of the legal body in Ireland, from its connexion with England* (Dublin, 1806), p. 512; Colum Kenny, *Tristram Kennedy and the revival of Irish legal training, 1835–1885* (Dublin, 1996), pp 220–3; McCarthy, *Building the King's Inns*, p. 36; Kings Inns Manuscripts, MS H2/1–2.

39 *The Dublin Magazine*, 2 (June–Dec. 1840), p. 431.

40 *Evening Packet*, 11 Feb. 1840, quoted in Kenny, *Tristram Kennedy*, pp 228–9. While the King's Inns did not rename themselves as the 'Queen's Inns' during the long reign of Victoria, the Queen was popular among liberals like Kennedy and he chose to honour her in naming his new school.

41 *Irish Times*, 7 Aug. 1884.

42 Kenny, *Tristram Kennedy*, pp 228–35; Tristram Kennedy, *The state and the benchers* (Dublin, 1875), p. 14. This suggestion had actually been floated as early as 1806 by Bartholomew Duhigg, *History of the King's Inns*, p. 538.

43 Gamble, *Sketches of history*, pp 28-9. Less flatteringly, a character in Maria Edgeworth's 1812 novel, *The absentee* (London, 1812), described how after the Union 'immediately in Dublin commerce rose into vacated seats of rank; wealth into place of birth', p. 91.

44 *Irish Times*, 20 Jan. 1877.

45 Daire Hogan, *The legal profession in Ireland, 1789-1922* (Dublin, 1986), pp 158-63; The number of surgeons in 1830 was almost four times what it had been fifty years earlier. For comparison, see numbers listed in *Wilson's Dublin Directory* (1788) and *Dublin Almanack* (1836).

46 PP, *Two reports from the select committee on the local taxation of the city of Dublin*, II, HC 1823 (549), vi; *Summary and the documents therein referred to relative to the new valuation of the city of Dublin being the report of the commissioners appointed under the act 5 Geo. IV. c.118: 1830* (Dublin, 1833).

47 Maurice Craig, *Dublin, 1660-1860: the shaping of a city* (Dublin, 1952, reprinted 2006), pp 307-9.

48 Francis White, *State of the poor in Dublin*, p. 27.

49 These are the applotment books for St Michan's 1835, which have been analysed by Priska Jones in an exemplary study of St Michan's. In Pill Lane, directly behind the Four Courts, there were thirteen houses recorded as 'down' by 1835. See P. Jones, 'St Michan's Parish in 1845' in David Dickson (ed.), *The hidden Dublin* (Dublin, 2002), pp 4-11.

50 Thomas Willis, *Facts connected with the social and sanitary condition of the working classes in the city of Dublin* (Dublin, 1845), p. 45.

51 Francis White, *State of the poor in Dublin*, p. 27; John Norwood, *A summary of transactions relative to the proposed formation of a new and wide street, form the terminus of the Midland Great Western Railway and the King's Inns to the Richmond Bridge and the Four Courts* (Dublin, 1853), p. 4.

52 Tomas Willis, *Facts connected with the social and sanitary condition*, pp 44-5.

2. Famine and decline, 1845-90

1 Asenath Nicholson, *Lights and shades of Ireland in three parts* (London, 1850), pp 224, 234.

2 Conversely, many smaller towns and villages were abandoned. At least 165 towns disappeared between 1841 and 1851. See Kevin Hourihan, 'The cities and towns of Ireland, 1841-1851' in John Crowley, William J. Smith and Mike Murphy (eds), *The atlas of the Great Irish Famine* (Cork, 2012), pp 228-39.

3 Minutes of the North Dublin Union, 5 May 1847, quoted in Jacinta Prunty, *Dublin slums, 1800-1925: a study in urban geography* (Dublin, 1998), p. 290. Timothy W. Guinnane and Cormac Ó Gráda, 'Mortality in the North Dublin Union during the Great Famine', *Economic History Review*, 55:3 (2002), pp 487-506.

4 *Freeman's Journal*, 4 Jan. 1847.

5 Kevin Hourihan, 'The cities and towns of Ireland 1841-1851', pp 228-39; Cormac Ó Gráda, 'Famine in Dublin city' in his *Black '47 and beyond: the Great Irish Famine in history, economy and memory* (Princeton, 2000), pp 157-93.

6 J.A. Dowling, 'The landed estates court, Ireland', *Journal of Legal History*, 26:2 (August 2005), pp 143-76. The best analysis of the Encumbered Estates Court can be found in Jacqueline Crowley, ' "This five year experiment": the Encumbered Estates Court, 1849-54' (PhD, NUI Maynooth, 2017).

7 Encumbered Estates Court (Ireland), *Copy of official statement &c relating to the removal of the offices of the Encumbered Estates Court from Henrietta Street to the Four Courts* (Dublin, 1854).

8 Richard Denny Urlin, 'The history and statistics of the Irish Encumbered Estates court', *Journal of the Statistical Society of London*, 44:2 (June 1881), pp 203-34.

9 *Chamber's Journal of Popular Literature*, 16 Oct. 1858.

10 Letter of 23 May 1856, Richard Dixon (ed.), *Karl Marx and Friedrich Engels on Ireland and the Irish question* (London, 1971).

11 A.M. Sullivan, *New Ireland: political sketches and personal reminiscences of thirty years of Irish public life* (London, 1877).

12 *The Times*, 22 June 1850; J.A. Dowling, 'The Landed Estates Court, Ireland', pp 170-3.

13 PP, *Encumbered Estates Court (Ireland), Copy of official statement &c relating to the removal of the offices of the Encumbered Estates Court from Henrietta Street to the Four Courts*, HC 1854 (184), lviii, 377.

14 Richard Denny Urlin, 'The history and statistics of the Irish Encumbered Estates court', *Journal of the Statistical Society of London*, 44:2 (June 1881), p. 211; PP, *Report from the select committee on court of chancery (Ireland) bill, together with the … minutes of evidence*, HC 1856 (311) x, pp 1476-86.

15 The sale of the Gardiner Estate raised £344,000, it originated in disputes over earl of Blessington's will. Residue of estate was sold to Charles Spencer Cooper, the second husband of countess of Blessington, Harriet Gardiner. A.P.W. Malcomson, *The pursuit of the heiress: aristocratic marriage in Ireland, 1750-1820* (Belfast, 1982), p. 183. For adverts for sale of Gardiner Estate in 1846, see *Dublin Evening Mail*, 14 Aug., 2 and 7 Dec. 1846.

16 For growth of tenement numbers, see the table in Joseph O'Brien, *Dear, dirty Dublin: a city in distress, 1899-1916* (Berkeley, 1982), p. 24.

17 *Irish Times*, 20 Mar. 1865.

18 PP, *Municipal boundaries commission (Ireland) Part I. Evidence with appendices. Dublin, Rathmines, Pembroke, Kilmainham, Drumcondra, Clontarf, and also Kingstown, Blackrock, and Dalkey* [C 2725], HC 1880, xxx, 327, pp 52-4.

19 *Thom's Dublin Directory* (1855, 1860).

20 *Irish Builder*, 1 Aug. 1893.

21 Many thanks to Aileen Woods, the great, great grand-daughter of John McAuliffe for providing this information.

22 The 1873 petition is reproduced in Tristram Kennedy, *The state and the benchers* (Dublin, 1878), pp 16-17; Charles Meldon QC speaking in Westminster on 28 May, 1875 quoted in Colum Kenny, *Tristram Kennedy and the revival of Irish legal training, 1835-1885* (Dublin, 1996), pp 103-14; *Irish Times*, 24 Sept. 1874.

23 Kenneth Ferguson, 'The campaign for the removal of the Dublin militia depots from Henrietta Street', *Irish Sword*, 28:111 (2011), pp 101-5; *Irish Times*, 19 Feb. 1876.

24 *Irish Builder*, 1 Aug. 1893. No. 12 was still listed as a militia depot in 1877, despite being vacated the year before.

25 The result was that the overall valuation of the street dropped from £2,280 in 1854, to a mere £542 in 1879.

26 PP, *Third report of her majesty's commissioner's for inquiring into the housing of the working classes (Ireland)* [C 4547], HC 1884-5, xxxi, appendix 22.

27 Prunty, *Dublin slums*, p. 274.

28 'Report of the housing committee, being a survey of the north side of the city of Dublin,' *Reports and printed documents of the Corporation of Dublin*, 1:13 (1918), appendix 2.

29 PP, *Report from the select committee on Dublin hospitals*, HC 1854 (338), xii.

30 For the role of cattle in Dublin's late Victorian development, see Juliana Adelman, *Civilized by beasts: animals and urban change in nineteenth-century Dublin* (Manchester, 2020), pp 91-126.

31 For an overview of Dublin's nineteenth-century economy, see Daly, *Dublin: the deposed capital*, chapters 1 and 2.

32 David Dickson, *Dublin: the making of a capital city* (London, 2014), pp 344-5.

33 PP, *Return of the number of manufacturing establishments in which the hours of work are regulated by any act of parliament* [105], HC 1871, lxii, 440; *Report from the select committee on the present state of the silk trade with the minutes of evidence, an appendix, and index*, HC 1831-2 (678) xix, pp 936-9, 930.

34 Census Office (Ireland), *Census of Ireland, 1911: general report, with tables and appendix* (Dublin, 1913), Table 'City of Dublin, occupations of people'.

35 *Freeman's Journal*, 26 July 1900, quoted in Séamas Ó Maitiú, *Dublin's suburban towns, 1834-1930* (Dublin, 2003), p. 23.

36 The most important of these suburbs were the two townships of Rathmines and Pembroke, with over half of Dublin suburbanites living in one of these two area. Sources for census, see Daly, *Dublin, the*

37 PP, *Municipal boundaries commission (Ireland), Part II, Report. Dublin, Rathmines, Pembroke, Kilmainham, Drumcondra, Clontarf, and also Kingstown, Blackrock, and Dalkey* [C.2827], HC 1881, L, 21, p. 19.

38 PP, *Municipal boundaries commission (Ireland) Part I. Evidence with appendices. Dublin, Rathmines, Pembroke, Kilmainham, Drumcondra, Clontarf, and also Kingstown, Blackrock, and Dalkey* [C 2725], HC 1880, xxx, 327, pp 22, 42.

39 Ibid., p. 41.

40 Jacqueline Hill, *From patriots to unionists: Dublin civic politics and Irish Protestant patriotism, 1660–1840* (Oxford, 1997), pp 362–83; Daly, *Dublin: the deposed capital*, pp 203–6; Mary E. Clark, 'Daniel O'Connell and Dublin's quest for a new mayoral image, 1841–71' in Ruth McManus and Lisa-Marie Griffith (eds), *Leaders of the city: Dublin's first citizens, 1500–1950* (Dublin, 2013), pp 107–19.

41 Despite Dublin being an overwhelmingly Catholic city by the mid-nineteenth century, in 1871 Catholics constituted only 48 per cent of the population of Rathmines. Daly, *Dublin: the deposed capital*, p. 159.

42 Prunty, *Dublin slums*, p. 14.

43 PP, *Municipal boundaries commission (Ireland) Part I. Evidence with appendices. Dublin, Rathmines, Pembroke, Kilmainham, Drumcondra, Clontarf, and also Kingstown, Blackrock, and Dalkey* [C 2725], HC 1880, xxx, 327, p. 3.

44 O'Brien, *Dear, dirty Dublin*, p. 14. For city-suburban relations in the nineteenth century see, Daly, *Dublin, the deposed capital*, pp 226–39.

45 PP, *Report of the departmental committee appointed … to inquire into the housing conditions of the working classes in the city of Dublin* [C 7273], HC 1914, xix, p. 3.

46 PP, *Third report of her majesty's commissioner's for inquiring into the housing of the working classes (Ireland)* [C 4547], HC 1884–5, xxxi, p. 13; Niall McCullough, *Dublin: an urban history* (Dublin, 1989), p. 91. Note: the *proportion* of families living in one-room dwellings had peaked at 49 per cent in 1851, almost certainly the result of the Famine.

47 PP, *Third report of her majesty's commissioner's for inquiring into the housing of the working classes (Ireland)* [C 4547], HC 1884–5, xxxi p. 13

48 *Thom's Dublin Directory* (1850).

49 PP, *Third report of her majesty's commissioner's for inquiring into the housing of the working classes (Ireland)* [C 4547], HC 1884–5, xxxi, appendix A, evidence of Dr Cameron, p. 103.

50 Bureau of Military History, Witness Statement 1770, Statement of Kevin O'Sheil, part 2, p. 215.

51 PP, *Third report of her majesty's commissioner's for inquiring into the housing of the working classes (Ireland)* [C 4547] HC 1884–5, xxxi, pp 14, 18–22, 25–6. For details on legal challenges to ownership and relevant bye-laws, see Prunty, *Dublin slums*, pp 83–4.

52 *Freeman's Journal*, 22 Feb. 1900.

53 Tony Farmar, 'The building society that refused Patrick Pearse (and his mother)', *Dublin Historical Record*, 55: 1 (Spring, 2002), pp 64–77.

54 Daly, *Dublin: the deposed capital*, p. 284.

55 F.R. Falkiner, 'Report on the homes of the poor', *Journal of the Statistical and Social Inquiry Society of Ireland*, 8:59 (1881/2), pp 261–70.

56 PP, *Third report of her majesty's commissioner's for inquiring into the housing of the working classes (Ireland)*, [C 4547] HC 1884–5, xxxi, p. 304.

57 C. Tweedy, 'Housing of the poor in Dublin', *Dublin Journal of Medical Science,* 105:3 (1898), p. 291.

58 *Reports and printed documents of the Corporation of Dublin*, iii (1879), app. v, pp 789–90, 'Statement read before the Royal Commission at the close of the inquiry, on 16 October 1879 by the secretary of the public health committee'.

59 PP, *Third report of her majesty's commissioner's for inquiring into the housing of the working classes (Ireland)* [C 4547] HC 1884–5, xxxi, appendix to evidence of Dr Cameron, p. 102.

60 *Belfast Newsletter*, 10 Oct. 1889.

61 *Freeman's Journal*, 17 Mar. 1865.

62 *Freeman's Journal*, 31 Mar. 1890.

63 R. Denny Urlin, 'On the dwellings of working men in cities', *Journal of the Statistical and Social Inquiry Society of Ireland*, 4 (1865), pp 158–64; Fraser, *John Bull's other homes*, p. 69; *Reports on the Paris Universal Exhibition, 1867* (London, 1868), vol. 6, pp 201–11.

64 PP, *Report of the royal commission on sewerage and drainage of the city of Dublin* [C 2605] HC 1880, xxx, p. 163.

65 *Irish Times*, 20 May 1878. See also advert in *Irish Times*, 22 Aug. 1887.

66 *Freeman's Journal*, 8 Apr. 1898; 11 Jan. 1900.

67 *Freeman's Journal*, 31 May 1881.

68 *Freeman's Journal*, 8 Apr., 15 July 1898; 11 Jan. 1900.

69 *Freeman's Journal*, 8 July 1890.

70 *Irish Builder*, 1 Aug. 1893; PP, *Report of the departmental committee appointed … to inquire into the housing conditions of the working classes in the city of Dublin* [C 7273] HC 1914, xix, p. 130. No. 12 and 13 Henrietta Street are listed as 'vacant' up until 1891. See *Thom's Dublin Directory* (1891).

71 Registry of Deeds, memorial books (1887) Book 12, entries 122 and 123; Registry of Deeds, memorial books (1894) Book 36, entry 89; *Thom's Dublin Directory* 1898. This purchase on Henrietta Street was part of a larger purchase by Meade of a portfolio of Kennedy's property, including various townlands in Kildare, as well as property in Upper Dominick Street. The amount Meade paid for this entire portfolio was £4000. In 1898, there were still legal offices in No. 11, a real estate agent in No. 9 and the Property Defense Association in No. 4.

72 PP, *Report of the departmental committee appointed … to inquire into the housing conditions of the working classes in the city of Dublin* [C 7273] HC 1914, xix, p. 35.

73 PP, *Third report of her majesty's commissioner's for inquiring into the housing of the working classes (Ireland)*, [C 4547] HC 1884–5, xxxi, pp 25–6. The street directory lists eight tenement houses and one vacant property in 1885. The tenements include Nos. 2 and 18 (now demolished) and Nos. 5, 6, 7, 14, 15 and 16. Number 12 had been vacant since 1879. By 1887, the number of tenements had increased to nine, including No. 17. This is derived from how the houses are listed in *Thom's Dublin Directory*, for the years 1879–87. Of the eight houses Meade purchased in 1892, three were already in use as tenements (Nos. 3, 5 and 6).

74 PP, *Report of the departmental committee appointed … to inquire into the housing conditions of the working classes in the city of Dublin* [C 7273] HC 1914, xix, pp 130, 205–11.

75 I am grateful to Dr Susan Galavan for pointing this out. Her excellent book, *Dublin's bourgeois homes: building the Victorian suburbs, 1850–1901* (Abingdon, 2017), contains an in-depth study of Meade and his milieu.

76 PP, *Report of the departmental committee appointed … to inquire into the housing conditions of the working classes in the city of Dublin* [C 7273] HC 1914, xix, pp 117, 350; *Report of the departmental committee appointed by the Local Government Board for Ireland to inquire into the public health of the city of Dublin* [C 243 & C 244] HC 1900, xxxix, p. 21; O'Brien, *Dear, dirty Dublin*, p. 135.

77 *Freeman's Journal*, 6 Nov. 1893; 8 Jan. 1894; 30 Jan. 1895; C. Eason, 'The tenement houses of Dublin', *Journal of the Statistical and Social Inquiry Society of Ireland*, 10:79 (Dublin, 1899), p. 397.

78 *Freeman's Journal*, 22 Feb. 1900.

79 Fraser, *John Bull's other homes*, p. 71; Galavan, *Dublin's bourgeois homes*, pp 123–5.

80 *Irish Times*, 2 Jan. 1891; *Freeman's Journal*, 6 July 1892; Fionnuala Waldron, 'Statesmen of the street corners: labour and the Parnell split, 1890–92', *Studia Hibernica*, 34 (2006–7), pp 153–74.

81 Lydia Carroll, *In the fever king's preserves, Sir Charles Cameron and the Dublin slums* (Dublin, 2011), p. 161.

82 PP, *Third report of her majesty's commissioner's for inquiring into the housing of the working classes (Ireland)* [C 4547] HC 1884–5, xxxi, pp 25–6.

83 Ibid., p. 14

84 *Irish Times*, 24 Feb. 1906

85   Charles Dawson, esq., 'The Dublin housing question – sanitary and insanitary', *Journal of Social and Statistical Society of Ireland*, 13:93 (1912/13), pp 90–5.

86   *Irish Times*, 14 Nov. 1900. For an estimate of Meade's *net* profit on two of these tenements, see Daly, *Dublin: the deposed capital*, p. 287.

87   *Freeman's Journal*, 11 Jan. 1900.

88   PP, *Report of the departmental committee appointed … to inquire into the housing conditions of the working classes in the city of Dublin* [C 7273] HC 1914, xix, pp 130, 211.

89   Ibid., p. 298.

90   This information on the valuation of the street's buildings in 1912 kindly provided by the Valuations Office Ireland.

91   Registry of Deeds, memorial books (1909) Book 47, entry 228; (1910) Book 19 entry 21.

92   *Freeman's Journal*, 31 Mar. 1890. The evidence of a continued supervision by the Vance Trust can be discerned from an existing lease agreement between two men listed as trustees of the Vance Estate (Benjamin Beamish and John Mitchell) and a Christopher O'Brien for a mews house at the rear of No. 14 Henriette Street. This mews house was the subject of a compulsory purchase order by Dublin Corporation in 1938. A copy of this lease was provided by Charles Duggan, Heritage Officer for Dublin City Council.

93   *The Daily Nation*, 9 Sept. 1898.

94   Ibid.

95   PP, *Third report of her majesty's commissioner's for inquiring into the housing of the working classes (Ireland)* [C 4547] HC 1884-5, xxxi; F.H.A. Aalen, 'Health and housing in Dublin *c.*1850–1921' in F.H.A. Aalen and Kevin Whelan (eds), *Dublin city & county: from prehistory to present* (Dublin, 1992), p. 281.

96   *The Daily Nation*, 9 Sept. 1898.

97   Sir John Carr, *The stranger in Ireland* (London, 1806), p. 45. For visitors' impressions at the start of nineteenth century, see Gillian O'Brien, '"What can possess you to go to Ireland?": visitors' perceptions of Dublin, 1800–30' in Gillian O'Brien and Finola O'Kane (eds), *Georgian Dublin* (Dublin, 2008), pp 17–29.

98   Madame de Bovet, *Three months in Ireland* (London, 1891), p. 42.

99   George Moore, *A drama in muslin* (London, 1886).

3.   Life and death in a tenement, 1880–1910

1   *Irish Times,* 24 Feb. 1906.

2   Ibid.

3   Patricia McCarthy, 'The planning and use of space in Irish houses, 1730–1830' (PhD, TCD, 2009).

4   Nugent Robinson, 'The conditions of the dwellings of the poor in Dublin with a glance at the model lodging houses', *Transactions of the National Association for the Promotion of Social Science, 1861* (London, 1862), pp 521–2.

5   This information is courtesy of the Valuations Office Ireland.

6   For commentary on these estimates, see Janet Moody, *The tenement dwellers of Church Street, Dublin, 1911* (Dublin, 2017), pp 46–8.

7   PP, *Appendix to the report of the departmental committee appointed by the Local Government Board for Ireland to inquire into the housing conditions of the working classes in the city of Dublin* [C 7317] 1914, xix, p. 28.

8   Bureau of Military History, Witness Statement No. 1770, Statement of Kevin O'Sheil, pp 216–17.

9   Information taken from the 1901 and 1911 Census.

10   PP, *Appendix to the report of the departmental committee appointed by the Local Government Board for Ireland to inquire into the housing conditions of the working classes in the city of Dublin* [C 7317] 1914, xix, p. 102.

11   Charles Cameron, *How the poor live* (Dublin, 1908); T.J. Stafford and C.D. La Touche, *Note on the social*

    condition of certain working-class families in Dublin (Dublin, 1907), p. 14.

12 Charles A. Cameron, *Reminiscences* (Dublin, 1913), p. 169; PP, *Report of the departmental committee appointed by the Local Government Board for Ireland to inquire into the public health of the city of Dublin* [C 243 & C 244] HC 1900, xxxix, p. 86.

13 Bureau of Military History, Witness Statement No. 1770, Statement of Kevin O'Sheil, pp 215–16.

14 PP, *Report of the departmental committee appointed … to inquire into the housing conditions of the working classes in the city of Dublin* [C 7273] HC 1914, xix, pp 87–93.

15 The original collection of images by Cooke can now be viewed online at the Royal Society of Antiquaries of Ireland's website: www.rsai.ie. In 2010, the Digital Projects Section of Dublin City Public Libraries discovered a further set of previously unidentified photos that were likely to have been taken in 1913. These may also be viewed online as part of Dublin City Libraries Digital Collection 'Derelict Dublin, 1913': http://www.dublincity.ie/derelict-dublin-1913. For a modern printing and commentary on the photos, see Christiaan Corlett, *Darkest Dublin: the story of the Church Street disaster and a pictorial account of the slums of Dublin in 1913* (Dublin, 2008).

16 In 1901, 668 out of 956 occupants give Dublin city as their place of birth. Another 33 were from County Dublin. The proportion of native Dubliners in Henrietta Street in 1901 roughly corresponds to the proportion within the city as a whole. Charles A. Cameron, *A brief history of municipal public health administration in Dublin* (Dublin, 1914), p. 7.

17 The numbers employed in manufacturing had fallen from 33 per cent in 1841, to 20 per cent in 1911. Mary Daly, *Dublin: the deposed capital: a social and economic history, 1860–1914* (Cork, 1988), pp 18–19.

18 Unless explicitly stated, all data relating to workhouse and prison registers has been accessed via the online sources at www.findmypast.ie.

19 Daly, *Dublin: the deposed capital*, pp 78–9.

20 *Irish Times*, 3 Jan. 1906; *Irish Times*, 7 Aug. 1907; PP, *Report of the inter-departmental committee on the employment of children during school-age, especially in street trading in the large centres of population in Ireland*, p. 1 [C 1144] HC 1902, xlix, p. 12.

21 Jacinta Prunty, *Dublin slums, 1800–1925: a study in urban geography* (Dublin, 1998), pp 247–50, 253–5; PP, *Special report of convent schools in connection with the Board of National Education* [C 405] HC 1864, xlvi, pp 63, 73–7.

22 PP, *Report of the inter-departmental committee on the employment of children during school-age, especially in street trading in the large centres of population in Ireland*, p. 1 [C 1144] HC 1902, xlix, appendix 3, pp 62, 143–61, 179.

23 D.A. Chart, 'Unskilled labour in Dublin: its housing and living conditions', *Journal of the Statistical Society of Ireland*, 13 (Dec. 1914), p 172.

24 Cameron, *How the poor live*, p. 3.

25 Admission and Discharge Register for North Dublin Union, June–Dec. 1904.

26 *Church of Ireland Social Services Union, social service handbook* (Dublin, 1901).

27 Admission and Discharge Register for the North Dublin Union, 30 Aug. 1892.

28 Fintan O'Toole, *Irish Times book of the century* (Dublin, 1999), p. 47.

29 Admission and Discharge Registers for the North Dublin Union, 1895, 1900, 1901.

30 Audrey Woods, *Dublin outsiders: a history of the Mendicity Institution, 1818–1998* (Dublin, 1998); Deirdre Lindsay, 'The Sick and Indigent Roomkeepers Society' in David Dickson (ed.), *The gorgeous mask: Dublin, 1700–1850* (Dublin, 1987), pp 132–56.

31 In 1871, 44 per cent of all Protestant occupied males could be classified as working class. By 1911, workers still composed 38 per cent of the city's Protestant population. Martin Maguire, 'A socio-economic analysis of the Dublin Protestant working class, 1870–1926', *Irish Economic and Social History*, 20 (1993), pp 36–61.

32 Jacinta Prunty and Louise Sullivan (eds), *The Daughters of Charity of St Vincent de Paul in Ireland: the early years* (Dublin, 2014). See also, Bill Lawlor and Joe Dalton (eds), *The Society of St Vincent de Paul in Ireland: 170 years of fighting poverty* (Dublin, 2014).

33 Account by Benjamin Higgins quoted in Sir William Wilde, 'Illustrious physicians and surgeons in Ireland: No. 2 Bartholomew Mosse', *Dublin Quarterly Journal of Medical Science* (1846), 2, p. 567. See also, Cormac Ó Gráda, 'The Rotunda and the people of Dublin, 1745–1995: glimpses from the hospital's records' in Alan Browne (ed.), *Masters, midwives and ladies-in-waiting: the Rotunda Hospital, 1745–1995* (Dublin, 1995).

34 Julia Anne Bergin, 'Birth and death in nineteenth-century Dublin's lying-in hospitals' in Elaine Farrell (ed.), *'She said she was in the family way': pregnancy and infancy in modern Ireland* (London, 2012), pp 106–10; Ó Gráda, 'Infant and child mortality in Dublin a century ago', *Working Paper Series, Centre for Economic Research* (UCD, 2002); T.W. Grimshaw, 'Child mortality in Dublin', *Journal of the Statistical and Social Inquiry Society of Ireland*, 9 (1890), appendix, 1–19

35 *Nos. 8–10 Henrietta Street* (Dublin, 2003), pp 14–19.

36 Jacinta Prunty, 'Our Lady's Henrietta Street, Dublin: accommodation for discharged prisoners' in Prunty and Sullivan (eds), *The Daughters of Charity of St Vincent de Paul in Ireland*, pp 181–95.

37 Registry of Deeds, memorial books (1908) Book 98, entry 176 (12 Dec. 1908); Registry of Deeds, memorial books (1910) Book 33, entry 176 (12 Apr. 1910).

38 The income derived from running the laundry as a commercial enterprise accounted for 80 per cent of the home's total income. Without the laundry it is doubtful the home could have continued. Jacinta Prunty, 'Our Lady's Henrietta Street, Dublin', pp 181–95.

39 Ibid., p. 186. The references Prunty specifically points to concerning the benign nature of the Home are: *Annual report of the Dublin Catholic Discharged Female Prisoners' Aid Society*, 26th Report (Henrietta Street) for 1906/7 (Dublin, 1907), pp 8–9; *Annual report of Dublin Catholic Discharged Female Prisoners' Aid Society*, 33rd Report for 1913 (Dublin, 1914), p. 8.

40 Maria Luddy, *Prostitution and Irish society, 1800–1940* (Cambridge, 2007), pp 113–14, 121–3.

41 Ibid., pp 121–3; Oireachtas Reports: Written answer from Minister for Justice, Equality and Law Reform (Deputy Dermot Ahern) 19 July; National Archives of Ireland. Department of Justice File, Our Lady's Home, Henrietta Street Dublin 16/62A.

42 *Irish Times*, 23 Apr. 1878; *Irish Times*, 11 May 1892; *Dublin Daily Express*, 11 May 1892.

43 This twenty-year period not only provides an interesting cross sample, it was also a period in which Dublin's economy was relatively buoyant. After recovering from a recession in the early 1880s, an upturn commencing after roughly 1887 lasted until the start of a depression in 1905. This means the sample is in some ways a 'best case' scenario. As a control for this, additional samples have been taken for 1911 and 1914. These seem to confirm the results of the 1885–1905 sample, in both the nature and level of crime and convictions.

44 Mountjoy Female Prison Register for the year 1898, and Mountjoy Male Prison Register for the year 1906.

45 *Irish Times*, 28 Nov. 1904.

46 Statistical returns of the Dublin Metropolitan Police, quoted in Joseph O'Brien, *Dear, dirty Dublin: a city in distress, 1899–1916* (Berkeley, 1982), pp 188–9.

47 PP, *Third report of her majesty's commissioner's for inquiring into the housing of the working classes (Ireland)* [C 4547] HC 1884–5, xxxi, p. 54.

48 Mark Finnane, 'A decline in violence in Ireland? Crime, policing and social relations, 1860–1914', *Crime, Histoire & Societes/Crime, History & Societies* (1997), pp 51–70; O'Brien, *Dear, dirty Dublin*, pp 180, 184–6; Anastasia Dukova, 'Crime and policing in Dublin, Brisbane and London, c.1850–1900' (PhD, TCD, 2011), pp 72–3.

49 Luddy, *Prostitution and Irish society, 1800–1940*, p. 34.

50 For example, Dory Ryan, a 33-year-old prostitute living in No. 14 Henrietta Street was imprisoned for drunkenness in 1893. Similarly, two other women described as prostitutes, Mary Wilson and Ellen Kelly, were arrested for being drunk and disorderly in 1889 and 1906, respectively. Another, Mary Louise Exham, living in No. 9 Henrietta Street, was arrested in 1897 for assault. For Dora Ryan, see

Grangegorman Female Prison Register (1893); Mary Wilson – Grangegorman Female Prison Register (1889); Ellen Kelly – Mountoy Female Prison Register (1906); Mary Louise Exham – Grangegorman Female Prison Register (1887).

51   Mountjoy Female Prison Records, entries for 31 Jan., 25 Apr., 15 June and 1 Aug. 1914.

52   Oliver St Gogarty, *It isn't this time of year at all!* (Dublin, 1983 edition), pp 236–7.

53   Kevin Kearns, *Dublin tenement life* (Dublin, 2006), pp 54–5.

54   D.A. Chart, 'Unskilled labour in Dublin: its housing and living conditions', *Journal of the Statistical Society of Ireland*, 13 (Dec. 1914), pp 160–75.

55   All of the examples in this paragraph are from a transcription of the 1916 Ledgers of the Dublin Metropolitan Police, kindly shared by Padraig Yeates.

56   Mary Rafferty and Eoin O'Sullivan, *Suffer the little children: the inside story of Ireland's industrial schools* (Dublin, 2009), pp 60–9.

57   Transcript of DMP Ledger for the year 1916, courtesy of Padraig Yeates.

58   Carriglea Park is the subject of Chapter 10 of *Report of the Commission to inquire into child abuse* (Dublin, 2009).

59   C.A. Cameron and Edward Mapother, 'Report on the means for the prevention of disease in Dublin' in *Reports and printed documents of the Corporation of Dublin*, 1:63 (1879), p. 344; Lydia Carroll, 'The 1913 Housing Inquiry: Sir Charles Cameron, public health and housing in Dublin' in Francis Devine (ed.), *A capital in conflict: Dublin city and the 1913 Lockout* (Dublin, 2013), pp 57–81.

60   The data here is reproduced with the kind permission of the Glasnevin Trust.

61   The city Registrar-General, T.W. Grimshaw, reported that 24 per cent of deaths of children under 5 in the greater Dublin area in the years 1884–5 were due to 'convulsions'. T.W. Grimshaw, 'Child mortality in Dublin', *Journal of the Statistical and Social Inquiry Society of Ireland*, 9 (1890), appendix, 1–19.

4. The beginnings of reform, 1900–14

1   Ciarán Wallace, '"Fighting for Unionist Home Rule": competing identities in Dublin, 1880–1929', *Journal of Urban History*, 38:5 (2012), pp 932–49

2   The only other ward in the city which saw a greater bump in its electorate was Usher's Quay, which went from 368 to 3367 votes, an increase of 815 per cent. See, Ciarán Wallace, 'Local politics and government in Dublin city and suburbs, 1899–1914' (PhD, TCD, 2010), p. 110.

3   *Irish Times*, 24 Apr. 1895; *Freeman's Journal*, 11 Jan. 1900. Carroll had rented a three-room flat on the second floor (the 'two-pair' apartment), at a rent of 6*s*. a week, a quite high rent at that time. Within a five-month period, he ended up owning Meade £5 19*s*. Carroll's eviction did not take place on 11 January, and we have no further records of him or his family. However, he was not a resident in the building by the following year's census of 1901. I am grateful to Dr Susan Galavan for pointing this out.

4   The infant death rate in Dublin was 153 deaths per 1,000 births. For comparison, the next worst instances in the UK were Liverpool (133 infant deaths per 1,000 births), Glasgow (129 per 1,000) and London (106 per 1,000). Enda Leaney, '"Infernos of degradation": a visual record of tenement life in Dublin' in Francis Devine (ed.), *A capital in conflict: Dublin city and the 1913 Lockout* (Dublin, 2013), pp 156–7.

5   Edgar Flinn, *Report on the sanitary circumstances and administration of the city of Dublin, with reference to the high death rate* (Dublin, 1906); Prunty, *Dublin slums, 1800–1925*, p. 154.

6   *Report of the committee appointed by the Local Government Board for Ireland to inquire into the probable health of the city of Dublin* (1900).

7   Sir Charles Cameron, *How the poor live* (Dublin, 1904); Sir Charles Cameron, *A brief history of municipal public health administration in Dublin* (Dublin, 1914), p. 16.

8   Cameron, *A brief history of municipal public health administration in Dublin*, pp 67–9; PP, *Report of the*

8   *departmental committee appointed by the Local Government Board for Ireland to inquire into the public health of the city of Dublin* [C 243-4] HC 1900, xxxix; F.H.A. Aalen, 'Health and housing in Dublin, c.1850–1921' in Aalen and Whelan (eds), *Dublin city & county: from prehistory to present* (Dublin, 1992), pp 294–7.

9   PP, *Report of the Royal Commissioners appointed to inquire into the public health of the city of Dublin* [C 2605] HC 1880, xxx, p. 1.

10   Murray Fraser, *John Bull's other homes: state housing and British policy in Ireland, 1883–1922* (Liverpool, 1996), p. 66.

11   PP, *Tenements in administrative counties and urban and rural districts (Census Office)* [C 6910] HC 1913, lxxxxvii, Table XIX. See also, Prunty, *Dublin slums, 1800–1925*, pp 171–2.

12   'London and Dublin tenements compared' in *Reports and printed documents of the Corporation of Dublin*, 1:32 (Dublin, 1894).

13   Fraser, *John Bull's other homes*, p. 66.

14   Minutes of the Municipal Council of the City of Dublin, April 1914, quoted in Wallace, 'Local politics and government in Dublin city and suburbs, 1899–1914', pp 233–5.

15   Anthony S. Wohl, *The eternal slum: housing and social policy in Victorian London* (London, 1977), p. 141.

16   Fraser, *John Bull's other homes*, p. 82.

17   The 1900 boundary extension only brought in about £90,000 additional revenue.

18   *The United Service Journal and Naval Military Magazine, Part 1* (London, 1837), pp 125–7; Fraser, *John Bull's other homes*, p. 76; PP, *Report of the departmental committee appointed … to inquire into the housing conditions of the working classes in the city of Dublin* [C 7273] HC 1914, xix, pp 118–35.

19   For an account of the Foley Street development, see Joseph Brady and Ruth McManus, *Dublin Corporation's first housing schemes, 1880–1925* (Dublin, 2021), pp 89–95.

20   The best account of the early Corporation housing schemes can be found in Brady and McManus, *Dublin Corporation's first housing schemes, 1880–1925*, passim.

21   C.H. Ashworth, 'Some aspects of the housing question', *Irish Builder and Engineer*, 49 (1907), pp 198–202; PP, *Report of the departmental committee appointed … to inquire into the housing conditions of the working classes in the city of Dublin* [C 7273] HC 1914, xix, p. 22; F.H.A. Aalen, 'The working-class housing movement in Dublin, 1850–1920' in Michael J. Bannon (ed.), *The emergence of Irish planning, 1880–1920* (Dublin, 1985), p. 140.

22   Aalen, 'The working-class housing movement in Dublin, 1850–1920', pp 152–3, 161.

23   Natalie de Róiste, 'Case study: Dublin Artisans' Dwelling Company Housing Estate, Stoneybatter' in Ellen Rowley (ed.), *More than concrete blocks, vol. 1, 1900–40: Dublin city's twentieth-century buildings and their stories* (Dublin, 2016), pp 90–9.

24   Prunty, *Dublin slums, 1800–1925*, pp 174–7. Only 18 per cent of municipal housing before 1918 were one-room dwellings affordable by the very poor.

25   Fraser, *John Bull's other homes*, p. 36; Ruth McManus, *Dublin 1910–1940: shaping the city & suburbs* (Dublin, 2002), p. 41.

26   PP, *Report of the Belfast Health Commission to the Local Government Board (Ireland)* [C 4128] HC 1908, xxxi, p. 710.

27   Fraser, *John Bull's other homes*, p. 62. *The Irish Builder*, 8 Nov. 1913, p. 711. *Irish Times*, 10 Nov. 1902.

28   C.A. Cameron, *A brief history of municipal public health administration in Dublin* (Dublin, 1914), p. 69

29   *Reports and printed documents of the Corporation of Dublin*, vol. iii, no. 176 (1903), pp 383–96.

30   Aalen, 'The working-class housing movement in Dublin 1850–1920', pp 169–75. See also, Peter Connell, 'From hovels to homes: the provision of public housing in Irish provincial towns, 1890–1945' (PhD, TCD, 2017).

31   It was only the Housing (Ireland) Act of 1919 that provided substantial state subsidies, but obviously the War of Independence precluded Dublin from enjoying these gains.

32   A good example was the election of the former trades-council president, J.P. Nanetti, as lord mayor in

33 Daly, *Dublin the deposed capital*, pp 216–19.
34 A higher figure of 30,000 members is sometimes given, being a year-end figure. Francis Devine, *Organising history: a centenary of SIPTU, 1909–2009* (Dublin, 2009), pp 104–5.
35 *Irish Worker*, 11 Nov. 1911.
36 *Irish Worker*, 13 Jan. 1912; Emmet O'Connor, *James Larkin* (Cork, 2002), pp 80–90.
37 Niamh Puirséil, 'The echo of the battle: Labour politics and the 1913 Lockout' in Francis Devine (ed.), *A capital in conflict: Dublin city and the 1913 Lockout* (Dublin, 2013), pp 215–37.
38 *The Times* (London), 22 Oct. 1913; James Connolly, *Workers republic,* edited by Desmond Ryan (Dublin, 1951), pp 46, 103.
39 *Irish Times,* 11 Oct. 1902; Daly, *Dublin the deposed capital*, p. 289.
40 Minutes of the Municipal Council of the City of Dublin, April 1914, quoted in Ciarán Wallace, 'Local politics and government in Dublin city and suburbs 1899–1914', pp 233–4.
41 *Irish Times,* 12 Apr. and 22 May, 1911.
42 PP, *Report of the departmental committee appointed … to inquire into the housing conditions of the working classes in the city of Dublin* [C 7273] HC 1914, xix, appendix, p. 118.
43 The best overview and analysis of Cameron's career is Lydia Carroll *In the fever king's preserves: Sir Charles Cameron and the Dublin slums* (Dublin, 2011).
44 PP, *Report of the departmental committee appointed … to inquire into the housing conditions of the working classes in the city of Dublin* [C 7273] HC 1914, xix, appendix, pp 52, 85, 97,176, 245, 249, 344.
45 Ibid., pp 279–94.
46 Padraig Yeates, *A city in wartime: Dublin, 1914–18* (Dublin, 2011), p. 11.
47 Minutes of the Municipal Council of the City of Dublin, 20 April 1914, Item 311, quoted in Wallace, 'Local politics and government in Dublin city and suburbs, 1899–1914', p. 235.
48 Mary Daly, *Dublin the deposed capital,* pp 317–18; *Irish Times,* 14 Jan. 1914.
49 *Freeman's Journal,* 3 Sept. 1913.
50 Arnold Wright, *Disturbed Dublin: the story of the great strike of 1913–14, with a description of the industries of the Irish capital* (London, 1914), p. 151.
51 *Irish Worker,* 3 Jan. 1914.
52 *Irish Builder,* 25 Oct. 1913.
53 *Irish Independent,* 4 Sept. 1913; *Irish Worker,* 16 May 1914. See also other editorials in the *Irish Independent* on 8 and 11 Nov. 1913.
54 Fraser, *John Bull's other homes,* p. 107.
55 PP, *Appendix to report of the Dublin disturbances commission* [7272] HC 1914, xviii, pp 30, 177, 441.
56 Aalen, 'The working-class housing movement in Dublin, 1850–1920', pp 175–80; Fraser, *John Bull's other homes,* p. 134.
57 Unpublished paper by Philip Crowe, UCD School of Architecture, 'Patrick Geddes in Dublin: civic engagement and vacant sites'.
58 Yeates, *A city in wartime,* p. 31; Seán O'Leary, *Sense of place: a history of Irish planning* (Dublin, 2014), pp 45–7.

5. Henrietta Street and the Irish Revolution, 1914–23

1 Diarmaid Ferriter, *A nation and not a rabble: the Irish Revolution, 1913–1923* (London, 2015), p. 82.
2 Richard Grayson, *Dublin's great wars: the First World War, the Easter Rising and the Irish Revolution* (Cambridge, 2018), pp 37–43.
3 Quoted in Niamh Puirséil, 'War, work and labour' in John Horne (ed.), *Our war: Ireland and the Great War* (Dublin, 2008), p. 186.

4   Ibid., p. 185.
5   Padraig Yeates, *A city in wartime: Dublin, 1914–1918* (Dublin, 2011), p. 217.
6   David Fitzpatrick, 'Ireland and the Great War' in Thomas Bartlett (ed.), *The Cambridge history of Ireland Volume 4: 1880 to the present* (Cambridge, 2018), pp 246–9.
7   1901 Census date for Henrietta Street, accessed via www.census.nationalarchives.ie; Gertie Keane, 'The census, mobility and Henrietta Street', blogpost on dublintenementexpereince.wordpress.com, 4 Aug. 2013.
8   Grayson, *Dublin's great wars*, pp 37–9.
9   *Evening Herald*, 28 Dec. 1922; for the death of his wife in 1921 see *Evening Herald*, 9 Sept. 1922.
10 The author is grateful for the information and images concerning Thomas Anthony Morrell (1899–1947) provided by his great-granddaughter Siobhan Morrell.
11 Conor Dodd, 'Henrietta Street men in WWI', blogpost on dublintenementexpereince.wordpress.com, 23 Aug. 2013.
12 Cissie was born Ellen May Dorgan in March 1895. The 1911 Census shows her living with her parents and five siblings in No. 14 Henrietta Street, although the family moved at some point in 1913–14. The above information of Cissie and Jack is courtesy of Paul Appleby, who very kindly gave the author access to his research on his relation Jack Appleby.
13 There are at least five more entries from Henrietta Street within Ireland's First World War 'Honour Roll': Michael Cullen, Christopher Hanlon, Christopher O'Brien, Christopher Russell, Gordon Stewart Veitch. There are, however, several more names, not all of which could be included here. Thanks to popular history groups such as the online 'Dublin and the Great War 1914–1918' several more instances of servicemen from Henrietta Street and neighbouring addresses have been collected.
14 'In search of the Linen Hall Barracks', https://thearchaeologyof1916.wordpress.com; Charles Townshend, *Easter 1916: the Irish Rebellion* (London, 2015), pp 205–7.
15 James Curry, 'The little rose of the ITGWU' in *Crossing the Liffey in style: the Rosie Hackett Bridge* (Dublin, 2014); Bureau of Military History, Witness Statement No. 546, Statement of Miss Rosie Hackett.
16 Quoted in Padraig Yeates, *Rioters, looters, lady patrols & mutineers: some reflections on lesser visited aspects of the Irish Revolution in Dublin* (Dublin, 2017), p. 31.
17 UCD Digital Library, Dublin Metropolitan Police general register. https://digital.ucd.ie/view/ucdlib:53467.
18 PP, *Royal commission on the rebellion in Ireland, report of the commission, minutes of evidence* [C 8279] HC 1916, xi, p. 7; Murray Fraser, *John Bull's other homes: state housing and British policy in Ireland, 1883–1922* (Liverpool, 1996), pp 154–5.
19 Quoted in Leon Ó Broin, *Dublin Castle and the 1916 Rising* (New York, 1971). p. 166.
20 Ruth McManus, *Dublin, 1910–1940: shaping the city and suburbs* (Dublin, 2002), pp 42–6; Fraser, *John Bull's other homes*, pp 157–69.
21 P.C. Cowan, *Report on Dublin housing* (Dublin, 1918). See also, Lambert McKenna, 'The housing problem in Dublin', *Studies: An Irish Quarterly Review*, 8:308 (June 1919).
22 Not all of the Irish veterans of the First World War returned to Ireland. Some re-enlisted, some stayed in Britain after demobilization, emigrated elsewhere or had been invalided out of the forces before November 1918. Jane Leonard, 'Survivors' in John Horne (ed.), *Our war: Ireland and the Great War* (Dublin, 2008), pp 211–14.
23 Curiously, it is only recently that historians in Ireland have begun to direct their attention to this pandemic, most notably in the work of Ida Milne. See her *Stacking the coffins: influenza, war and revolution in Ireland, 1918–19* (Manchester, 2018), esp., pp 60–81.
24 For the debate on the experience of ex-servicemen see Grayson, *Dublin's great wars*, pp 324–5; Paul Taylor, *Heroes or traitors?: experiences of southern Irish soldiers returning from the Great War, 1919–39* (Liverpool, 2015), pp 243–50.

25 Fraser, *John Bull's other homes*, pp 186–91.
26 Taylor, *Heroes or traitors?*, pp 141–2.
27 McManus, *Dublin, 1910-40*, p. 47.
28 Eunan O'Halpin, 'Counting terror: Bloody Sunday and the dead of the Irish Revolution' in David Fitzpatrick (ed.), *Terror in Ireland, 1916-1923* (Dublin, 2012), pp 141–57.
29 Bureau of Military History, Witness Statement No. 206, Statement of Jerry Golden; Witness Statement No. 755, Statement of Sean Prendergast. See also report in *Skibbereen Eagle,* 5 June 1920.
30 Thomas Bryan to Bridget, 11 Mar. 1921; Thomas Bryan to Dick Glynn, 25 Feb. 1921, both quoted in Tim Carey, *Hanged for Ireland: the forgotten ten* (Dublin, 2001), pp 109, 117.
31 Bureau of Military History, Military Service Pensions Collection, Disability Pensions, DP869 – 'Letter sent to Minister for Defence on 12/06/34 by Miss Kathleen Lynn'.
32 *Freeman's Journal,* 2 Dec. 1920. Interestingly, one of the men, Michael McGrath, was described as an ex-soldier.
33 *Evening Herald,* 19 Oct. 1922.
34 *Freeman's Journal,* 31 Mar. 1921.
35 The exception was the constituency of 'Mid Dublin', where independent nationalists outpolled both sides. Michael Gallagher, 'The pact general election of 1922', *Irish Historical Studies,* 22:84 (1979), pp 404–21.

Epilogue: Dublin of the future?

1 In Dublin this was initially a new force known as 'Políní Átha Cliath' (Police of Dublin), replacing the DMP. It was in turn absorbed into An Garda Síochána in 1925.
2 P.C. Cowan, *Report on Dublin housing* (Dublin, 1918), p. 41; Prunty, *Dublin slums, 1800-1925*, p. 171.
3 Padraig Yeates, *A city in turmoil: Dublin, 1919-1921* (Dublin, 2012), pp 281–2; Yvonne Whelan, *Reinventing modern Dublin: streetscape, iconography, and the politics of identity* (Dublin , 2002), pp 214–32.
4 David Dickson, *Dublin: the making of a capital city* (London, 2014), p. 477.
5 Oliver St John Gogarty, *It isn't this time of year at all!* (Dublin, 1983 edition), pp 203–4.
6 H.T. O'Rourke and the Dublin Civic Survey Committee, *The Dublin Civic Survey report* (Dublin, 1925), p. 58.
7 During the early years of the Abbey, cynics used to speculate that the theatre tested every play for its 'PQ' (its 'peasant quality'). For a discussion of the Abbey's 'tenement' plays, see Elizabeth Manion, *Beyond O'Casey: the urban plays of the early Abbey Theatre* (Syracuse, 2014).
8 *Irish Builder and Engineer,* 8 Mar. 1924, quoted in Ruth McManus, *Dublin 1910-40: shaping the city and suburbs* (Dublin, 2002), p. 80.
9 Murray Fraser, *John Bull's other homes*, pp 284–5; McManus *Dublin, 1910-1940*, pp 104–5, 182–94.
10 Joseph Brady and Ruth McManus, *Building healthy homes: Dublin Corporation's first housing schemes 1880-1925* (Dublin, 2021), pp 255–7.
11 Fraser, *John Bull's other homes*, pp 288–90.
12 Donal Fallon, 'War on the slums? A look at housing in 1930s Dublin', blog entry November 29, 2016 at https://comeheretome.com. See also, Fallon's excellent *14 Henrietta Street: from tenement to suburbia, 1922-1979* (Dublin, 2021).
13 Cathal O'Connell, *The state and housing in Ireland: ideology, policy and practice* (New York, 2007), p. 29; Michelle Norris, *Financing the golden age of Irish social housing, 1932-1956* (Dublin, 2018).
14 McManus, *Dublin, 1910-40*, pp 98–9.
15 Fallon, 'War on the slums? A look at housing in 1930s Dublin'; 'Herbert Simms' entry in the *Dictionary of Irish architecture*. Simms' career was the subject of a conference in Dublin's Civic Offices: 'Simms 120 Conference, 21 October 2018). For the best recent analysis of Simms' role, see the introduction of Ellen Rowley's, *Housing, architecture and the edge condition: Dublin is building, 1935-1975* (Abingdon, 2019).

16   Brendan once joked that the family's options had been 'To Hell or to Kimmage'. Michael O'Sullivan, *Brendan Behan: a life* (Portlaoise, 2000), pp 31–2, 165.

17   For an analysis of Crumlin, see Rowley's *Housing, architecture and the edge condition: Dublin is building*.

18   McManus, *Dublin 1910–40*, p. 211.

19   Ibid., p. 160.

20   O'Connell, *The state and housing in Ireland*, pp 24–9

21   An interesting commentary on this campaign by Donal Fallon can be found on the blog *Come Here To Me* (https://comeheretome.com/2013/10/29/images-from-the-irish-press-slum-campaign-1936). See also the comments by Jacinta Prunty, 'The town house as tenement in nineteenth- and early twentieth-century Dublin' in Casey (ed.), *The eighteenth-century Dublin town house: form, function and finance* (Dublin, 2010).

22   Donal Fallon, *14 Henrietta Street: from tenement to suburbia 1922–1979* (Dublin, 2021), pp 41–6.

23   Frank O'Connor, *Irish miles* (New York, 1947), pp 12–13.

24   *Advisory regional plan and final report part I: the Dublin region* (Dublin, 1966) and *The Dublin region: advisory regional plan and final report part II* (Dublin, 1967).

25   Ellen Rowley, 'Housing in Ireland, 1740–2016' in E. Biagini and M. Daly (eds), *The Cambridge social history of modern Ireland* (Cambridge, 2017), pp 226–9.

26   Mary Daly, *Sixties Ireland: reshaping the economy, state and society, 1957–1973* (Cambridge, 2016), pp 112–13; Rowley, *Housing, architecture and the edge condition*, Chapter 6 passim.

27   Diarmaid Ferriter, *Ambiguous Republic: Ireland in the 1970s* (London, 2012).

28   Erika Hanna, 'Dublin's north inner city, preservationism and Irish modernity', *The Historical Journal*, 53:4 (2010), p. 1029. See also, Frank McDonald, *The destruction of Dublin* (Dublin, 1985) and *Saving the city: how to halt the destruction of Dublin* (Dublin, 1989).

29   The famous description of preservationists as 'belted earls' was by the Minister for Local Government Kevin Boland in 1970. For other descriptions of IGS see, Rosita Sweetman, *On our knees: Ireland 1972* (Dublin, 1972), p. 78; McDonald, *The destruction of Dublin*, pp 12, 78–9.

30   For the best discussion of these conflicts, see Erika Hanna, *Modern Dublin: urban change and the Irish past, 1957–1973* (Oxford, 2013).

31   Donal Fallon, 'A rebel preservationist', *Dublin Inquirer*, 14 June 2017.

32   Hanna, *Modern Dublin*, pp 15–160. For MacEoin's obituary, *Irish Times*, 29 Dec. 2007. For artists presence, *Henrietta Street conservation plan: an action of the Dublin city heritage plan* (Dublin, 2005).

33   Hanna, *Modern Dublin*, pp 160, 192–3.

34   Elene Negussie, 'Dublin, Ireland' in Robert Pickard (ed.), *Management of historic centres* (Abingdon, 2013), pp 138–50.

35   Photographic inventories of houses on the street were carried out by the Irish Architectural Archive (on behalf of Dublin City Council) in 1980 and 1985. In 1986, a survey and report on the street was carried out by student from DIT Bolton Street. The following year, Cathal Crimins produced 'Henrietta Street: a conservation study' (M.Arch.Sc., UCD, 1987). In 1997, the Dublin Civic Trust carried out an intensive inventory of houses on the street, again on behalf of Dublin City Council.

36   This was carried out as part of the Dublin City Heritage Plan. *Henrietta Street conservation plan: an action of the Dublin City Heritage Plan* (Dublin, 2005).

Bibliography

Newspapers and periodicals
Belfast Newsletter
Chamber's Journal of Popular Literature
Daily Nation
Dublin Builder
Dublin Daily Express
Dublin Evening Mail
Dublin Journal
Dublin Journal of Medical Science
Dublin Magazine
Dublin Quarterly Journal of Medical Science
Evening Herald
Freeman's Journal
Irish Builder
Irish Builder and Engineer
Irish Independent
Irish Magazine
Irish Quarterly Review
Irish Sword
Irish Times
Irish Worker
Journal of Legal History
Journal of Statistical and Social Inquiry Society of Ireland.
Journal of the Statistical Society of London
New Monthly Magazine and Literary Journal
Old Kilkenny Review
United Service Journal and Naval Military Magazine

Almanacs and directories
Gentleman's and Citizen's Almanack for Dublin
Pettigrew and Oulton's Dublin Directory and General Register of Ireland
Thom's Dublin Directory
Treble Almanack & Dublin Directory
Wilson's Dublin Directory

Official records
British Parliamentary Papers

Report of the select committee on the local taxation of the city of Dublin, HC 1822 (394), vii.

Second report of the select committee on the local taxation of the city of Dublin, HC 1823 (549), vi.

Report from the select committee on the silk trade, HC 1831–2 (678), xix.

Summary and the documents therein referred to relative to the new valuation of the city of Dublin [1828], HC 1833 (5), xxxv.

Poor inquiry (Ireland), appendix C, parts I and II: part I: reports on the state of the poor, and on the charitable institutions in some of the principal towns; with supplement containing answers to queries; part II: report on the city of Dublin, and supplement containing answers to queries; with addenda to appendix A, and communications [C 35], HC 1836 (35), xxx.

Report from the select committee on Dublin hospitals, HC 1854 (338), xii.

Encumbered Estates Court (Ireland), Copy of official statement &c relating to the removal of the offices of the Incumbered Estates Court from Henrietta Street to the Four Courts, HC 1854 (184), lviii, 377.

Report from the select committee on the chancery (Ireland) bills, Report from the select committee on court of chancery (Ireland) bill, together with the ... minutes of evidence, HC 1856 (311), x.

Report of the commissioners appointed to inquire into the working of the Factory and Workshops Act, HC 1871 (440), lxii.

Report of the royal commission appointed to inquire into the sewerage and drainage of the city of Dublin and other matters connected therewith, evidence, appendix [C 2605], HC 1880, xxx.

Report of the royal commission appointed to inquire into the boundaries and municipal areas of cities and towns in Ireland, 1 [C 2725], HC 1880, xxx.

Report of the royal commission appointed to inquire into boundaries and ... and municipal areas of cities and towns in Ireland, 2 [C 2827], HC 1881, l.

Minutes of evidence, etc ... of the 3rd report of her majesty's commissioners for inquiring into the housing of the working classes (Ireland) [Cd 4547-1], HC 1884–5, xxxi.

Report of the departmental committee appointed by the Local Government Board to inquire into the public health of the city of Dublin [Cd 243-4], HC 1900, xxxix.

Report of the inter-departmental committee on the employment of children during school-age, especially in street trading in the large centres of population in Ireland, p. 1 [C 1144], HC 1902, xlix.

Belfast Health Commission: report to the Local Government Board of Ireland [Cd 4128], HC 1908, xxxi.

Report of the departmental committee appointed ... to inquire into the housing conditions of the working classes in the city of Dublin , [C 7273], HC 1914, xix; *Appendix to the report of the departmental committee appointed by the Local Government Board for Ireland to inquire into the housing conditions of the working classes in the city of Dublin*, [C 7317] 1914, xix.

Report of the Dublin disturbances commission [Cd 7269], HC 1914, viii; *Evidence and appendices, report of the Dublin disturbances commission* [Cd 7272], HC 1914, xviii.

Royal commission on the rebellion in Ireland, report of the commission, minutes of evidence [C 8279], HC 1916, xi.

Census of Population (Ireland)
City of Dublin, 1841, 1851, 1861, 1871, 1881, 1891, 1901, 1911

Dáil Éireann
Report of inquiry into the housing of the working classes of the city of Dublin (Dublin, 1943).

Dublin Corporation
Minutes of the Municipal Council
Reports and Printed Documents of the Corporation of Dublin

Irish Military Archive
Bureau of Military History, Witness Statements, 1913–21
Military Service Pensions Collection, 1916–23

National Library of Ireland
Account book of Augusta Bryan re: management of households of Major George Bryan of Henrietta Street, Dublin and Jenkinstown, Co. Kilkenny, sometimes M.P. for Co. Kilkenny, 1819–33 (MS 32,489)
King's Inns Manuscripts (MS H2/1-2)

Registry of Deeds
Memorials Transcription Books

Secondary works

Aalen, F.H.A., 'Health and housing in Dublin *c*.1850–1921' in F.H.A. Aalen and Kevin Whelan (eds), *Dublin city and county from prehistory to present* (Dublin, 1992).
Aalen, F.H.A., 'The working-class housing movement in Dublin 1850–1920' in Michael J. Bannon (ed.), *The emergence of Irish planning, 1880–1920* (Dublin, 1985).
Adelman, Juliana, *Civilised by beasts: animals and urban change in nineteenth-century Dublin* (Manchester, 2020).
Anonymous, 'Dublin in 1822', *New Monthly Magazine and Literary Journal*, 4 (London, 1822).
Anonymous, *The picture of Dublin, being a description of the city, and a correct guide to all the public establishments* (Dublin, 1810).
Anonymous, *Observations on the House of Industry, Dublin and on the plans for the association for suppressing mendicity in that city* (Dublin, 1818).
Ashworth, C.H., 'Some aspects of the housing question', *Irish Builder and Engineer*, 49 (1907).
Association for the Suppression of Mendicity, *Report of the Association for the Suppression of Mendicity in Dublin for the year 1818* (Dublin, 1819).
Bartlett, Thomas (ed.), *Revolutionary Dublin: the letters of Francis Higgins to Dublin Castle, 1795–1801* (Dublin, 2003).
Bergin, Julia Anne, 'Birth and death in nineteenth-century Dublin's lying-in hospitals' in Elaine Farrell (ed.), *'She said she was in the family way': pregnancy and infancy in modern Ireland* (London, 2012).
Boulter, Hugh, *Letters written by His Excellency Hugh Boulter …* (Oxford, 1770).
Bowen, Elizabeth, *The Shelbourne* (Dublin, 1951).
Brady, Joseph, and Ruth McManus, *Building healthy homes: Dublin Corporation's first housing schemes, 1880–1925* (Dublin, 2021).
Brennan, John, 'Jenkinstown, Co. Killenny and its associations', *Old Kilkenny Review*, 2:3 (1981).
Cameron, Charles A., *Homes of the working classes* (Dublin, 1885).

Cameron, Charles, *How the poor live* (Dublin, 1904).

Cameron, Charles A., *Reminiscences* (Dublin, 1913).

Cameron, Charles, *A brief history of municipal public health administration in Dublin* (Dublin, 1914).

Cameron, Charles A., and Edward Mapother, 'Report on the means for the prevention of disease in Dublin', *Reports and Printed Documents of the Corporation of Dublin*, 1:63 (1879).

Campbell, Hugh, 'Contested territory, common ground: architecture and politics in nineteenth-century Dublin' (PhD, UCD, 1998).

Carr, Sir John, *The stranger in Ireland* (London, 1806).

Carroll, Lydia, *In the fever king's preserves: Sir Charles Cameron and the Dublin slums* (Dublin, 2011).

Carroll, Lydia, 'The 1913 Housing Inquiry: Sir Charles Cameron, public health and housing in Dublin' in Francis Devine (ed.), *A capital in conflict: Dublin city and the 1913 Lockout* (Dublin, 2013).

Carlyle, Thomas, *Reminiscences of my Irish journey in 1849* (London, 1882).

Casey, Christine (ed.), *The eighteenth-century Dublin town house: form, function, and finance* (Dublin, 2010).

Chart, David Alfred, 'Unskilled labour in Dublin: its housing and living conditions', *Journal of the Statistical and Social Inquiry Society of Ireland*, 13:94 (1914).

Church of Ireland Social Services Union, *Social service handboook* (Dublin, 1901).

Clark, Mary E., 'Daniel O'Connell and Dublin's quest for a new mayoral image, 1841–71' in Ruth McManus and Lisa-Marie Griffith (eds), *Leaders of the city: Dublin's first citizens, 1500–1950* (Dublin, 2013).

Cloncurry, Valentine, *Personal recollections of the life and times of Valentine, Lord Cloncurry* (London, 1849).

Connell, Peter, 'From hovels to homes: the provision of public housing in Irish provincial towns, 1890–1945' (PhD, TCD, 2017).

Connolly, James, *The Workers' Republic*, ed. Desmond Ryan (Dublin, 1951).

Corlett, Christiaan, *Darkest Dublin: the story of the Church Street disaster and a pictorial account of the slums of Dublin in 1913* (Dublin, 2008).

Cowan, P.C., *Report on Dublin housing* (Dublin, 1918).

Craig, Maurice, *Dublin, 1660–1860: the shaping of a city* (Dublin, 1952; repr. 2006).

Crimins, Cathal, 'Henrietta Street: a conservation study' (M.Arch.Sc., UCD, 1987).

Crowley, Jacqueline, ' "This five-year experiment": the Incumbered Estates Court, 1849–54' (PhD, NUI Maynooth, 2017).

Cullen, Frank, *Dublin, 1847: city of the Ordnance Survey* (Dublin, 2015).

Cumberland, Richard, *Memoirs of Richard Cumberland* (London, 1807).

Curry, James, 'The little rose of the ITGWU' in *Crossing the Liffey in style: the Rosie Hackett Bridge* (Dublin, 2014).

Curry, William, *Ancient and modern Dublin* (Dublin, 1820).

Daly, Mary, *Dublin, the deposed capital: a social and economic history, 1860–1914* (Cork, 1988).

Daly, Mary, *Sixties Ireland: reshaping the economy, state and society, 1957–1973* (Cambridge, 2016).

Dawson, Charles, 'The Dublin housing question – sanitary and insanitary', *Journal of the Statistical and Social Inquiry Society of Ireland*, 13:93 (1912/13).

de Bovet, Marie-Anne, *Three months in Ireland* (London, 1891).

de Latocnaye, Chevalier, *A Frenchman's walk through Ireland, 1796–7*, trans. John Stevenson (Belfast, 1984).

Devine, Francis, *Organizing history: a centenary of SIPTU, 1909–2009* (Dublin, 2009).

Dickson, Charles, *Revolt in the north* (Dublin, 1960).

Dickson, David, 'Large-scale developers and the growth of eighteenth-century Irish cities' in P. Butel and L.M. Cullen (eds), *Cities and merchants: French and Irish perspectives on urban development* (Dublin, 1986).

Dickson, David, 'The gap in famines: a useful myth?' in E.M. Crawford (ed.), *Famine: the Irish experience, 900–1900* (Edinburgh, 1989).

Dickson, David, *Dublin: the making of a capital city* (London, 2014).

Dickson, David, 'In search of the old Irish poor law' in Rosalind Mitchison and Peter Roebuck (eds), *Economy and society in Scotland and Ireland, 1500–1939* (Edinburgh, 1988).

Dickson, David (ed.), *The hidden Dublin: the social and sanitary conditions of Dublin's working classes in 1845 described by Thomas Willis* (Dublin, 2000).

Dixon, Richard (ed.), *Karl Marx and Friedrich Engels on Ireland and the Irish question* (London, 1971).

Dodd, Conor, 'Henrietta Street men in WWI', dublintenementexpereince.wordpress.com, 23 Aug. 2013.

Dowling, J.A., 'The Landed Estates Court, Ireland', *Journal of Legal History*, 26:2 (Aug. 2005).

Dublin Civic Trust, *Nos. 8–10 Henrietta Street* (Dublin, 2003).

Dublin Corporation, *County borough of Dublin and neighbourhood town planning report sketch development plan by Professor Patrick Abercrombie, Sydney A. Kelly, Manning Robertson* (Dublin, 1941).

Duhigg, Bartholomew, *History of the King's Inns, or, An account of the legal body in Ireland, from its connexion with England* (Dublin, 1806).

Dukova, Anastasia, 'Crime and policing in Dublin, Brisbane and London *c*.1850–1900' (PhD, TCD, 2011).

Eason, Charles, 'The tenement houses of Dublin', *Journal of the Statistical and Social Inquiry Society of Ireland*, 10:79 (Dublin, 1899).

Edgeworth, Maria, *The absentee* (London, 1812).

Fagan, Patrick, 'The population of Dublin in the eighteenth century', *Eighteenth Century Ireland*, 6 (1991).

Falkiner, Caeser Litton, *Essays relating to Ireland: biographical, historical and topographical* (London, 1909).

Falkiner, F.R., 'Report on the homes of the poor', *Journal of the Statistical and Social Inquiry Society of Ireland*, 8:59 (1881).

Fallon, Donal, *14 Henrietta Street: from tenement to suburbia 1922–1979* (Dublin, 2021).

Fallon, Donal, 'Images from the Irish press slum campaign, 1936', *Come Here To Me!*, 29 Oct. 2013, comeheretome.com/2013/10/29/images-from-the-irish-press-slum-campaign-1936.

Fallon, Donal, 'War on the slums? A look at housing in 1930s Dublin', *Come Here to Me!*, 29 Nov. 2016, https://comeheretome.com/2016/11/29/war-on-the-slums-a-look-at-housing-in-1930s-dublin-part-1.

Farmar, Tony, 'The building society that refused Patrick Pearse (and his mother)', *Dublin Historical Record*, 55:1 (Spring, 2002).

Ferguson, Kenneth, 'The campaign for the removal of the Dublin militia depots from Henrietta Street', *Irish Sword*, 28:111 (2011).

Ferriter, Diarmaid, *A nation and not a rabble: the Irish Revolution, 1913–1923* (London, 2015).

Finnane, Mark, 'A decline in violence in Ireland? Crime, policing and social relations, 1860–1914', *Crime, Histoire & Sociétés/Crime, History & Societies*, 1:1 (1997).

Fitzpatrick, David, 'Ireland and the Great War' in Thomas Bartlett (ed.), *The Cambridge history of Ireland*, iv: *1880 to the present* (Cambridge, 2018).

Flinn, Edgar, *Report on the sanitary circumstances and administration of the city of Dublin, with reference to the high death rate* (Dublin, 1906).

Fraser, Murray, *John Bull's other homes: state housing and British policy in Ireland, 1883-1922* (Liverpool, 1996).

Galavan, Susan, *Dublin's bourgeois homes: building the Victorian suburbs, 1850-1901* (London, 2017).

Gallagher, Michael, 'The pact general election of 1922', *Irish Historical Studies*, 22:84 (1979).

Gamble, John, *Sketches of history, politics and manners in Dublin, and the north of Ireland, in 1810* (Dublin, 1826).

Georgian Society of Ireland, *Records of eighteenth-century domestic architecture and decoration in Dublin*, 5 vols (Dublin, 1969).

Gogarty, Oliver St John, *It isn't this time of year at all!* (Dublin, 1983).

Graham, Thomas, 'Dublin in 1798: the key to the planned insurrection' in Nicholas Furlong and Dáire Keogh (eds), *The mighty wave: aspects of the 1798 Rebellion in Wexford* (Dublin, 1996).

Gray, Peter, *The making of the Irish poor law, 1815-43* (Manchester, 2009).

Grayson, Richard, *Dublin's great wars: the First World War, the Easter Rising and the Irish Revolution* (Cambridge, 2018).

Grimshaw, T.W., 'Child mortality in Dublin', *Journal of the Statistical and Social Inquiry Society of Ireland*, 9 (1890).

Hallet, Mark, *Hogarth: the artist and the city* (London, 2006).

Hanna, Erika, *Modern Dublin: urban change and the Irish past, 1957-1973* (Oxford, 2013).

Hanna, Erika, 'Dublin's north inner-city: preservationism and Irish modernity', *Historical Journal*, 53:4 (2010).

Hayes, Melanie, *The best address in town: Henrietta Street, Dublin and its first residents, 1730-80* (Dublin, 2020).

Heard, Kate, *High spirits: the comic art of Thomas Rowlandson* (London, 2013).

Hill, Jacqueline, 'Allegories, fictions and feigned representations: decoding the Money Bill dispute 1752-6' in *Eighteenth Century Ireland*, 21 (2006).

Hill, Jacqueline, *Patriots to unionists: Dublin civil politics and Irish Protestant patriotism, 1660-1840* (Oxford, 1997).

Hogan, Daire, *The legal profession in Ireland, 1789-1922* (Dublin, 1986).

Hourihan, Kevin, 'The cities and towns of Ireland, 1841-1851' in John Crowley, William J. Smyth and Mike Murphy (eds), *The atlas of the Great Irish Famine* (Cork, 2012).

Jebb, Richard, *A reply to a pamphlet entitled, Arguments for and against a union* (London, 1799).

Jeffreys, Nathaniel, *An Englishman's descriptive account of Dublin* (London, 1810).

Jones, Priska, 'St Michan's Parish in 1845' in David Dickson and Trinity History Workshop (eds), *The hidden Dublin: the social and sanitary conditions of Dublin's working classes in 1845 described by Thomas Willis* (Dublin, 2002).

Joyce, James, 'A little cloud', *Dubliners* (London, 1914).

Keane, Gertie, 'The census, mobility and Henrietta Street', dublintenementexpereince.wordpress.com, 4 Aug. 2013.

Kearns, Kevin, *Dublin tenement life: an oral history* (Dublin, 2006).

Kennedy, Tristram, *The state and the benchers* (Dublin, 1875).

Kenny, Colum, *Tristram Kennedy and the revival of Irish legal training, 1835-1885* (Dublin, 1996).

Lawlor, Bill, and Joe Dalton (eds), *The Society of St Vincent de Paul in Ireland: 170 years of fighting poverty* (Dublin, 2014).

Leaney, Enda, '"Infernos of degradation": a visual record of tenement life in Dublin' in Francis Devine (ed.), *A capital in conflict: Dublin city and the 1913 Lockout* (Dublin, 2013).

Leonard, Jane, 'Survivors' in John Horne (ed.), *Our war: Ireland and the Great War* (Dublin, 2008).

Lewis, Richard, *The Dublin guide: or, a description of the city of Dublin* (Dublin, 1787).

Lewis, Samuel, *A topographical dictionary of Ireland* (London, 1837).

Lindsay, Deirdre, 'The Sick and Indigent Roomkeepers Society' in David Dickson (ed.), *The gorgeous mask: Dublin, 1700–1850* (Dublin, 1987).

Lowe, N.F., 'Mary Wollstonecraft and the Kingsborough scandal', *Eighteenth-Century Ireland*, 9 (1994).

Luddy, Maria, *Prostitution and Irish society, 1800–1940* (Cambridge, 2007).

Lynch, Patrick, and John Vaizy, *Guinness' Brewery in the Irish economy, 1759–1876* (Cambridge, 1960).

Madden, R.R., *The literary life and correspondence of the countess of Blessington* (London, 1855).

Maguire, Martin, 'A socio-economic analysis of the Dublin Protestant working class, 1870–1926', *Irish Economic and Social History*, 20 (1993).

Malcomson, A.P.W., *Nathaniel Clements, 1705–77: politics, fashion and architecture in mid-eighteenth-century Ireland* (Dublin, 2015).

Malcomson, A.P.W., *Pursuit of an heiress: aristocratic marriage in Ireland, 1740–1840* (Belfast, 2006).

Manion, Elizabeth, *Beyond O'Casey: the urban plays of the early Abbey Theatre* (New York, 2014).

Mansergh, Daniel, '"As much support as it needs": social class and regional attitudes to the Union', *Eighteenth-Century Ireland*, 15 (2000).

Maturin, Charles Robert, *Women, or, Pour et contre* (Edinburgh, 1818).

Maxwell, Constantia, *The stranger in Ireland* (London, 1954).

Maxwell, Constantia, *Dublin under the Georges, 1714–1830* (London, 1956).

McAleer, Edward, *The sensitive plant: a life of Lady Mount Cashell* (Chapel Hill, 1958).

McCarthy, Patricia, 'The planning and use of space in Irish houses, 1730–1830' (PhD, TCD, 2009).

McCarthy, Patricia, *'A favourite study': building the King's Inns* (Dublin, 2006).

McCormack, W.J., *The pamphlet debate on the Union between Great Britain and Ireland, 1797–1800* (Dublin, 1996).

McCullough, Niall, *Dublin: an urban history* (Dublin, 1989).

McDonald, Frank *The destruction of Dublin* (Dublin, 1985).

McDonald, Frank, *Saving the city: how to halt the destruction of Dublin* (Dublin, 1989).

McDowell, Robert Brennan, *Land and learning: two Irish clubs* (Dublin, 1993).

McEvoy, Frank, 'The Slane peerage claim', *Old Kilkenny Review*, 2:4 (1982).

McKenna, Lambert, 'The housing problem in Dublin', *Studies: An Irish Quarterly Review*, 8:30 (June 1919).

McGregor, John James, *New picture of Dublin* (Dublin, 1821).

McManus, Ruth, *Dublin 1910–40: shaping the city and suburbs* (Dublin, 2002).

McParland, Edward, *James Gandon: vitruvius hibernicus* (London, 1985).

McParland, Edward, 'Strategy in the planning of Dublin 1750–1800' in P. Butel and L.M. Cullen (eds), *Cities and merchants: French and Irish perspectives on urban development* (Dublin, 1986).

Meehan, Paula, and Dragana Jurišić, *MUSEUM* (Dublin, 2019).

Milne, Ida, *Stacking the coffins: influenza, war and revolution in Ireland, 1918–19* (Manchester, 2018).

Mitchel, John, *The last conquest of Ireland* (Dublin, 1861).

Mokyr, Joel, and Cormac Ó Gráda, 'Poor and getting poorer? Living standards in Ireland before the Famine', *Economic History Review*, 41:2 (1988).

Montagu, George, 'My expedition to Ireland', *Dublin University Magazine* (Sept. 1854).

Moody, Janet, *The tenement dwellers of Church Street, Dublin, 1911* (Dublin, 2017).

Mooney, T., and F. White, 'The gentry's winter season' in David Dickson (ed.), *The gorgeous mask: Dublin 1700–1850* (Dublin, 1987).

Moore, George, *A drama in muslin* (London, 1886).

Murphy, Sean J., 'The Gardiner family, Dublin and Mountjoy, County Tyrone', *Studies in Irish Genealogy and Heraldry* (2010).

Musgrave, Sir Richard, *Memoirs of the different rebellions in Ireland* (Dublin, 1805).

Negussie, Elene, 'Dublin, Ireland' in Robert Pickard (ed.), *Management of historic centre* (Abingdon, 2013).

Nicholson, Asenath, *Lights and shades of Ireland in three parts* (London, 1850).

Norwood, John, *A summary of transactions relative to the proposed formation of a new and wide street, from the terminus of the Midland Great Western Railway and the King's Inns to the Richmond Bridge and the Four Courts* (Dublin, 1853).

O'Brien, Gillian '"What can possess you to go to Ireland?": visitors' perceptions of Dublin, 1800–30' in Gillian O'Brien and Finola O'Kane (eds), *Georgian Dublin* (Dublin, 2008).

O'Brien, Joseph, *Dear, dirty Dublin: a city in distress, 1899–1916* (Berkeley, CA, 1982).

Ó Broin, Eoin, *Home: why public housing is the answer* (Dublin, 2019).

Ó Broin, Leon, *Dublin Castle and the 1916 Rising* (New York, 1971).

O'Connell, Cathal, *The state and housing in Ireland: ideology, policy and practice* (New York, 2007).

O'Connor, Emmet, *James Larkin* (Cork, 2002).

O'Connor, Frank, *Irish miles* (Dublin, 1947).

O'Donovan, Declan, 'The Money Bill dispute of 1753' in Thomas Barlett and David Hayton (eds), *Penal era and golden age* (Belfast, 1979).

Ó Gráda, Cormac, *Black '47 and beyond: the Great Irish Famine in history, economy and memory* (Princeton, NJ, 2000).

Ó Gráda, Cormac, 'The Rotunda and the people of Dublin, 1745–1995: glimpses from the hospital's records' in Alan Browne (ed.), *Masters, midwives and ladies-in-waiting: the Rotunda Hospital, 1745–1995* (Dublin, 1995).

Ó Gráda, Cormac, 'Infant and child mortality in Dublin a century ago', Working Paper Series, UCD Centre for Economic Research (Dublin, 2002).

Ó Gráda, Cormac, *Jewish Ireland in the age of Joyce: a socio-economic history* (Princeton, NJ, 2006).

Ó Gráda, Diarmuid, *Georgian Dublin: the forces that shaped the city* (Cork, 2015).

O'Halpin, Eunan, 'Counting terror: Bloody Sunday and the dead of the Irish Revolution' in David Fitzpatrick (ed.), *Terror in Ireland, 1916–1923* (Dublin, 2012).

O'Keeffe, C.M., *The life and times of Daniel O'Connell* (Dublin, 1863-4).

O'Leary, Sean, *Sense of place: a history of Irish planning* (Dublin, 2014).

O' Mahony, Eoin, 'Some Henrietta Street residents, 1730–1849', *Quarterly Bulletin of the Irish Georgian Society*, 2:2 (April-June 1959).

Ó Maitiú, Séamas, *Dublin's suburban towns, 1834–1930* (Dublin, 2003).

O'Rourke, H.T., and the Dublin Civic Survey Committee, *The Dublin Civic Survey report* (Dublin, 1925).

O'Sullivan, Michael, *Brendan Behan: a life* (Portlaoise, 2000).

O'Toole, David, 'The employment crisis of 1826' in David Dickson (ed.), *The gorgeous mask: Dublin, 1700–1850* (Dublin, 1987).

O'Toole, Fintan, *Irish Times book of the century* (Dublin, 1999).

Pašeta, Senia, 'Nationalist responses to two royal visits to Ireland, 1900 and 1903', *Irish Historical Studies*, 31:124 (Nov. 1999).

Pickard, Robert (ed.), *Management of historic centre* (London, 2013).

Pollard, Mary, *A dictionary of members of the Dublin book trade, 1550–1800* (Dublin, 2000).

Prunty, Jacinta, *Dublin slums, 1800–1925: a study in urban geography* (Dublin, 1998).

Prunty, Jacinta, 'The town house as tenement in nineteenth- and early twentieth-century Dublin' in Christine Casey (ed.), *The eighteenth-century Dublin town house: form, function and finance* (Dublin, 2010).

Prunty, Jacinta, 'Our Lady's Henrietta Street, Dublin: accommodation for discharged prisoners' in Jacinta Prunty and Louise Sullivan (eds), *The Daughters of Charity of St Vincent de Paul in Ireland: the early years* (Dublin, 2014).

Puirséil, Niamh, 'The echo of the battle: labour politics and the 1913 Lockout' in Francis Devine (ed.), *A capital in conflict: Dublin city and the 1913 Lockout* (Dublin, 2013).

Puirséil, Niamh, 'War, work and labour' in John Horne (ed.), *Our war: Ireland and the Great War* (Dublin, 2008).

Rafferty, Mary, and Eoin O'Sullivan, *Suffer the little children: the inside story of Ireland's industrial schools* (London, 2009).

Reid, William, *The remains of William Reid, including rambles in Ireland* (London, 1815).

Robinson, Nugent, 'The conditions of the dwellings of the poor in Dublin with a glance at the model lodging houses' in *Transactions of the National Association for the Promotion of Social Science* (London, 1862).

Rowley, Ellen, *Housing, architecture and the edge condition: Dublin is building, 1935–1975* (Abingdon, 2019).

Rowley, Ellen (ed.), *More than concrete blocks, vol. 1: Dublin's twentieth-century buildings and their stories* (Dublin, 2016).

Shaffrey Associates, *Henrietta Street Conservation Plan: an action of the Dublin City Heritage Plan* (Dublin, 2005).

Smyth, James, *The men of no property: Irish radicals and popular politics in the late eighteenth century* (London, 1992).

Stanley, William, *Commentaries on Ireland* (Dublin, 1833).

Stewart, A.T.Q., *The summer soldiers: Antrim and Down in 1798* (Belfast, 1995).

Sullivan, A.M., *New Ireland: political sketches and personal reminiscences of thirty years of Irish public life* (London, 1877).

Sweetman, Rosita, *On our knees: Ireland 1972* (Dublin, 1972).

Taaffee, Denis, *Ireland's mirror: exhibiting a picture of her present state* (Dublin, 1795).

Taylor, Paul, *Heroes or traitors? Experiences of southern Irish soldiers returning from the Great War, 1919–39* (Liverpool, 2015).

Thackeray, W.M., *Irish sketch book* (London, 1843).

Todd, Janet, *Mary Wollstonecraft: a revolutionary life* (New York, 2000).

Townshend, Charles, *Easter 1916: the Irish Rebellion* (London, 2015).

Tweedy, C., 'Housing of the poor in Dublin', *Dublin Journal of Medical Science*, 105:3 (1898).

Urlin, Richard Denny, 'The history and statistics of the Irish Incumbered Estates Court', *Journal of the Statistical Society of London*, 44:2 (June 1881).

Urlin, Richard Denny, 'On the dwellings of working men in cities', *Journal of the Statistical and Social Inquiry Society of Ireland*, 4:29 (1865).

Vance, Charles, *Memoirs and correspondence of Viscount Castlereagh, second marquess of Londonderry*, 12 vols (London, 1850–3).

Viator, *Letter to the Right Hon. Robert Peel* … (Dublin, 1816).

Waldron, Fionnuala, 'Statesmen of the street corners: Labour and the Parnell split, 1890–92', *Studia Hibernica*, 34 (2006).

Wallace, Ciarán, '"Fighting for Unionist Home Rule": competing identities in Dublin, 1880–1929', *Journal of Urban History*, 38:5 (2012), pp 932–49.

Wallace, Ciarán, 'Joseph P. Nannetti, lord mayor, 1906–8: "a rather mild sort of rebel"' in Ruth McManus and Lisa-Marie Griffith (eds), *Leaders of the city: Dublin's first citizens, 1500–1950* (Dublin, 2013).

Wallace, Ciarán, 'Local politics and government in Dublin city and suburbs, 1899–1914' (PhD, TCD, 2010).

Warburton, John, James Whitelaw and Robert Walsh, *History of the city of Dublin, from the earliest accounts to the present time*, 2 vols (London, 1818).

Whelan, Yvonne, *Reinventing modern Dublin: streetscape, iconography and the politics of identity* (Dublin, 2002).

White, Francis, *Report and observations on the state of the poor in Dublin* (Dublin, 1833).

White, Trevor, and Djinn von Noorden (eds.), *Malton's view of Dublin: the story of a Georgian city* (Dublin, 2021).

Whitelaw, Rev. William, *An essay on the population of Dublin* (Dublin, 1805).

Wilde, Sir William, 'Illustrious physicians and surgeons in Ireland: No. 2 Bartholomew Mosse', *Dublin Quarterly Journal of Medical Science*, 2 (1846).

Willis, Thomas, *Facts connected with the social and sanitary condition of the working classes in the city of Dublin* (Dublin, 1845).

Wohl, Anthony S., *The eternal slum: housing and social policy in Victorian London* (London, 1977).

Woods, Audrey, *Dublin outsiders: a history of the Mendicity Institution, 1818–1998* (Dublin, 1998).

Wright, Arnold, *Disturbed Dublin: the story of the Great Strike of 1913–14, with a description of the industries of the Irish capital* (London, 1914).

Wright, George Newenham, *An historical guide to ancient and modern Dublin* (London, 1821).

Wright, Myles, *Advisory regional plan and final report, part 1: the Dublin region* (Dublin, 1966).

Wright, Myles, *The Dublin region: advisory regional plan and final report, part II* (Dublin, 1967).

Yeates, Padraig, *A city in wartime: Dublin, 1914–1918* (Dublin, 2011).

Yeates, Padraig, *A city in Turmoil: Dublin, 1919–1921* (Dublin, 2012).

Yeates, Padraig, *Rioters, looters, lady patrols and mutineers: some reflections on lesser visited aspects of the Irish Revolution in Dublin* (Dublin, 2017).

Yeates, Padraig, 'Dublin in the War of Independence' in John Crowley, Donal Ó Drisceoil, Mike Murphy and John Borgonovo (eds), *Atlas of the Irish Revolution* (Cork, 2017).

Young, Arthur, *A tour in Ireland* (London, 1780).

Young, Arthur, *Autobiography of Arthur Young* (London, 1898).

Index

Abercrombie, Patrick, 196, 199, 216-17
Abbey Theatre, 204
Act of Union (1801), 29-33, 35-7
Aldborough House, 33
Aosdána, 221

Ballyfermot, 217
Ballymun, 218-19
Belfast, 79, 146
Benburb Street, 140-1
Boulter, Hugh, archbishop of Armagh, 9
Bowes, John, lord chancellor of Ireland, 10
Boyle, Henry, earl of Shannon, 11-12
Broadstone, 42
Brogan, John, 171
Bryan, Captain George, 34-5
Bryan, Thomas, 187-8

Cameron, Charles, 153-4
Capel Street, 15, 37
Chart, David Alfred, 101
cholera, 50, 128, 136
Church Street, 150-1
Civil War (1922-3), 190-3
Clarke, Harry, 197-8
Clements, Nathaniel, 10-12, 222
Collis, Robert, 205
Cosgrave, William Thomas, 194
Cooke, John, 104-7
Coombe, 103, 129
Connolly, James, 148, 158
Custom House, 15

Daly, Lady Harriet, 34
Daly, Mary (historian), 156
Daughters of Charity, 120-2
de Valera, Éamon, 209

death rate (Dublin), 50, 55, 119, 127, 128, 131, 135-6
diet, 101-2
disease, 97, 127-31, 136, 183-4
distilling, 38, 68
Douglas Hamilton, Hugh, 16-9
Dowling, Elizabeth, 189
Dublin Artisans' Dwellings Company (DADC), 142-6
Dublin Civil Survey (1925), 201-2
Dublin Corporation, 74, 134-5, 139-42, 148-50, 155-6, 183, 195, 209
Dublin, economy of, 6, 35-7, 47-9, 65-70, 110-11, 156-9
Dublin Housing Action Committee, 220-1
Dublin Metropolitan Police, 124, 178, 193
Dublin, municipal boundaries of, 70-1, 74, 209
Dublin of the Future (1922), 196-200

Easter Rising (1916), 173-82
Encumbered Estates Court, 56-60, 76
eviction, 100, 134-5

Fairbrothers Fields, 183, 207
Fallon, Donal (historian) 212, 215, 217
Famine, 53-6
Fenian Street, 217-18
Ferriter, Diarmaid (historian), 166
Fianna Fáil, 210-14
First World War, 167-73
Fitzwilliam Estate, 15, 91-2
Foley Street, 141-2
Four Courts, 15, 191, 200

Gandon, James, 15, 43-4
Garden City ideal, 206-7

Gardiner, Charles, 33-4, 43
Gardiner, Luke, I, 7-9
Gardiner, Luke, II, 21, 27, 33
Gardiner Estate, 7-8, 15, 32-4, 60, 91-2
Glasgow, 79-81, 138
Gogarty, Oliver St John, 201-2
Grangegorman, 40-2, 115-18
Grattan, Henry, 23
Greater Dublin Reconstruction Movement, 200

Hackett, Rosie, 174-7
Hayes, Melanie (historian), 10
Henrietta Place, 76, 215
hospitals, 118-20
hotels, 33
Housing Inquiry (1914), 150-7, 183

infant mortality, 119
Irish Georgian Society, 220-3
Irish Parliamentary Party, 134, 147-9, 185
Irish Transport and General Workers' Union (ITGWU), 148, 156-9, 167
Ivy Trust, 146

Joyce, James, 2, 161-2, 217

Kennedy, Tristram, 44-7, 64
Killester, 185
King Street, 177-8
King, Margaret, 12-14
King's Inns, 43-4, 62-5
King's Inns Library, 44
Kingstown (Dun Laoghaire), 70, 85

Larkin, James, 148-9, 157-9
Leprecaun Cartoon Monthly, 136-7, 149-50
Liberties (Dublin), 64-5, 104-6
Linenhall, 35-7
Local Government Board, 150, 155-6
Lockout (1913), 156-61
lying-in hospital (Rotunda), 118-19

MacEoin, Uinseann, 221-3
Mahony, James, 53-4
Malton, James, 15-16
Marino, 207-8
Martin Murphy, William, 156-9

McAuliffe, John, 62
McManus, Ruth (historian), 210-13,
Meade, Joseph, 85-91
Meehan, Paula, 3
'middlemen', 76-9, 90-1, 138
militia, 62-4
Molesworth Street, 8
Molesworth, Richard, 10
Money Bill dispute, 11-12, 23-4
Mount Brown, 182

Nixon, John (artist), 19-20

O'Brien, Sir Lucius, 22
O'Casey, Sean, 202-4
O'Connell, Daniel, 34, 73-4
O'Connor, Frank, 217
O'Neill, Sir John, Viscount O'Neill, 21

Pembroke (township), 70-5, 140, 209
penal laws, 5, 24-25
Plunkett, Joseph, 205
Poor Law Union, 114-18
poor relief, 50-1, 54-5, 120-2
Primate's Hill, 9, 195
prostitution, 126-7
Prunty, Jacinta (historian), 122
public health, 88, 131, 135-6, 153-6, 183-4

railways, 40, 68
Rathmines (township), 70-5, 119, 140, 209
religion, 25, 74, 106-9
rents, 98-101, 141, 144-5, 208, 219
Royal Canal, 41-2
Rutland Square, 14-16

Sackville Street (O'Connell Street), 15
schools, 112-14
Second World War, 216-17
Separation women, 169, 181
sewage, 49, 84, 88, 131, 136
Shaffrey Associates, 224
silk industry, 36, 68
Simms, Herbert, 210-11
Sinn Féin, 185
Society of St Vincent de Paul, 51, 118
St Michan's (parish), 37-42, 49-51

Stone, George, archbishop of Armagh, 10–12
street cleaning, 136
street names, 7, 36–7, 195
suburban townships, 70–5
Swift, Jonathan, 19–20

Tallaght, 218
tenements:
    changing geography of, 60–2, 75–7
    closure of, 136, 138, 153–4, 220
    depictions of, 202–6
    landlords of, 78, 82–90
    layout of, 96–100
    number of, 49–50, 60, 75, 92, 138, 214, 216
    regulation, 130, 133–4, 153–4
tuberculosis, 131

unemployment, 68, 110
United Irishmen, 25–7

Valuations Office, 98, 100
Vance, Thomas, 82–5, 90

wages, 101–2, 110
Willis, Thomas, 50–1
Wide Streets Commission, 15
Wilson, Andrew Patrick, 204
Wollstonecraft, Mary, 12–14
women:
    employment, 110–11, 168
    politics of, 134, 173–7
    workhouse, 115–17, 120–2